Global Financial Crisis

Volume - I

Edited by

K.R. Gupta

ATLANTIC

PUBLISHERS & DISTRIBUTORS (P) LTD

Published by

ATLANTIC

PUBLISHERS & DISTRIBUTORS (P) LTD

7/22, Ansari Road, Darya Ganj,
New Delhi-110002
Phones : 23273880, 23275880, 23280451
Fax : 91-11-23285873
Web : www.atlanticbooks.com
E-mail : info@atlanticbooks.com

Branch Office
5, Nallathambi Street, Wallajah Road,
Chennai-600002
Phones : +91-44-64611085, 32413319
E-mail : chennai@atlanticbooks.com

ISBN 978-81-269-1215-5 (Vol. I)
ISBN 978-81-269-1218-6 (Set)

Printed in India at Nice Printing Press, A-33/3A, Site-IV,
Industrial Area, Sahibabad, Ghaziabad, U.P.

Preface

Though sharp eyes noticed the global financial crisis much earlier, it became prominently visible to everyone in September 2008 with the failure, merger and conservatorship of several large financial firms of the United States. The crisis was faced by leading United States and European investment banks, insurance firms and mortgage banks as a consequence of subprime mortgage crisis.

The failure of large financial institutions in the United States rapidly evolved into global credit crisis, deflation, sharp reductions in shipping and commerce, leading to failure of several European banks, declines in various stock indexes, substantial reductions in market values of equities and commodities all over the world including centrally-controlled economies, e.g. China and Russia. In America, Section 128 of the Emergency Economic Stabilisation Act of 2008 aggravated the crisis, as it permitted the Federal Reserve Bank to pay interest on excess reserve requirement balances held with it as deposit from banks, removing the long-standing incentive for banks to extend credit instead of keeping hard cash with the Federal Reserve Bank. It led to a liquidity problem and the de-leveraging of financial institutions, particularly in the United States and Europe where the liquidity crisis intensified and decline in international shipping and commerce became sharper. Inspite of coordinated efforts of the governments and finance and central bank directors to mitigate fears, the crisis went on worsening, resulting in currency crisis leading to transfer of vast capital resources by investors in stronger currencies like yen, US dollar and Swiss franc. It compelled many emerging economies to seek aid from the International Monetary Fund.

The crisis originated from widespread subprime mortgage failures and quickly engulfed the entire financial system as well as industry, resulting in widespread layoffs, for example, nearly 70,000 job losses in a single day in leading companies including manufacturer Caterpillar, pharma major Pfizer, telecom firm Sprint Nextel Corporation and home improvement retailer Home Depot.

When the financial crisis erupted in a comprehensive manner on Wall Street, there was some premature triumphism among the Indian policymakers who argued that India would be relatively immune to this crisis because of the strong fundamentals of its economy and a well-regulated banking system even while the other developing countries in Asia clearly showed signs of significant negative impact through domestic credit stringency. However, the crash in the Indian stock market, triggered by a pull-out of Foreign Institutional Investors (FIIs) funds, October 2008 onwards is not only an indicator of the impact of international contagion, but also a sign of the integration of Indian economy with the world economy despite claims of decoupling.

However, the effects of global financial crisis have been most marked among those developing countries where the foreign ownership of banks is already well advanced and where the US-style financial sectors have been created with the merging of banking and investment functions. Even though we are slightly better protected from the financial meltdown, largely because of the major role of the nationalised banks and other controls on domestic finance through the Reserve Bank of India and other regulatory authorities, there is no room for complacency. It is an accepted fact now that the Indian economy is experiencing a downturn, industrial growth is faltering, the current account deficit is widening, foreign exchange reserves are depleting and rupee has depreciated against the dollar. The financial crisis could also affect India through the exposure of foreign banks operating in India due to impaired assets resulting from the subprime crisis. But there are no clear estimates of the extent of that exposure, if any. Another indirect fallout of the global crisis and its ripple effects on India has been in the form of losses sustained by non-bank financial institutions including mutual funds and corporates as a result of their exposure to domestic stock and currency markets. In the current uncertain environment, banks and financial institutions, concerned about their balance sheets, have been cutting back on credit—leading to liquidity crunch and its resultant effects of shelving or delaying of some projects by some large companies, and consequent downsizing of staff.

There is no question that the global financial crisis has crippled economic growth around the world. But the malaise—combined with the significantly reduced inflation that has resulted partly from the downturn and partly from the measures taken by the RBI—has opened up a straightaway into which India can shift its policies and re-accelerate growth.

Apart from various conventional measures such as adjusting CRR, repo rate, reverse repo rate and some unconventional steps like dollar swap facilities for banks, India has introduced a new measure of special purpose vehicle for non-banking finance companies to the tune of Rs. 25,000 crore, which has improved liquidity position.

Global response to the financial crisis has been prompt, and by and large adequate, though it will take some time to have the desired impact. There have been relief plans, bailout packages, etc. in many countries of Europe, Asia and America. China has announced a $556 billion domestic stimulus package. Federal Reserve has reduced its fund rates six times in 2008—from 3.5 per cent to 1.5 per cent. The European Central Bank and the Bank of England have pumped in billions of dollars in the money-market auction. President Barack Obama has brought another relief package to revive the economy, apart from sector-specific measures like housing rescue plan, and buyback plan of banks' toxic assets.

There is a strong consensus among observers that the crisis will get worse in 2009 before it gets better. While the risk of a total systemic financial meltdown has been somewhat reduced by the actions of the G7 and other economies to backstop their financial systems and provide economic stimulus, severe vulnerabilities remain. It is likely that the credit crunch will get worse as de-leveraging by major institutions and the household sector continues. Further declines in trade, flows of foreign direct investment and remittances will affect labour markets and employment. In turn, the sharp increases in unemployment will translate into further decreases in aggregate demand. These are open questions whether the fiscal stimulus provided will be sufficient, and at what point the vicious downward spiral will stop.

The unprecedented economic stimulus packages announced by governments will take time to have an effect on economic growth and employment. The recent turmoil has presented a new set of challenges to most, if not all, regions of the world by rendering the achievement of a path, toward sustainable and socially equitable growth, and decent work for all, increasingly more difficult. According to the International Monetary Fund, the world economy is now entering a major downturn in the face of the most dangerous shock in mature financial markets since the 1930s, and governments have to act accordingly. The most significant measure being taken is the sweeping overhaul of the financial regulation. In America, hedge funds, private equity firms and derivative markets will come under government supervision for the first time. These regulatory changes are necessary to restore confidence in business enterprises, institutions, markets and public at large. The G20 meeting of 2 April 2009, held in London, can be termed as landmark in many ways. The member countries—which are virtually world's main financial powers—pledged more than $1 trillion for emergency loans to reverse the recession. They not only decided to reject protectionism but also to bring tighter financial regulation. Positive results can be expected sooner than later, though much will depend on the extent to which policy interventions, at the national and global levels, are successful.

The book *Global Financial Crisis*, in three volumes, attempts to provide a holistic view of the financial turmoil which, undeniably is the biggest after the Great Depression of 1930s, and which has presented new challenges to the entire world. It thoroughly studies the factors that led to this crisis and its debilitating effects on economic growth, employment, industrial production, stock markets, liquidity, fiscal position, exchange rates, money market, rates of interest and projects of development in private as well as public sectors. It contains articles by leading economists and experts in the field. It also consolidates in one source important documents—speeches, reports, declarations, etc.—relating to the issue.

To complete this monumental task I had to refer to a number of sources like speeches of eminent pesronalities at various international platforms, reports by established institutions, newspaper articles, information portals and websites. I take this opportunity to acknowledge them all.

The book will be useful to the students, teachers and researchers of Economics, parliamentarians, policymakers, economists, and entrepreneurs in India and abroad. Common readers interested in knowing about the present global economic conditions will find it inculcating and informative.

K.R. Gupta

Contributors

D. Subbarao, Governor, Reserve Bank of India.

Rakesh Mohan, Deputy Governor, Reserve Bank of India.

John Tamny is editor of RealClearMarkets, a senior economist with H.C. Wainwright Economics, and a senior economic advisor to Toreador Research and Trading (www.trtadvisors.com). He can be reached at jtamny@realclearmarkets.com

Ravi Batra. Professor, Department of Economics, Southern Methodist University, Dallas, Texas 75275, USA.

Jorge Heine holds the Chair in Global Governance at the Balsillie School of International Affairs and is a Distinguished Fellow at the Centre for International Governance Innovation in Waterloo, Ontario. He serves currently as Vice-President of the International Political Science Association.

Tapomoy Deb holds M.Phil (Management), MBA (HRM), MSW (PM&IR), PGDHRD, DLL and B.Sc (Hons) Physics. He is a merit rank holder and a prolific writer. He has published numerous articles and several books. He is recipient of several medals and prizes in his academic career. Currently he is a Research Scholar (HRM) in Jamia Millia Islamia.

Uma Narula is Ph.D. in Communication from the University of Massachusetts, Amerst, USA. At present she is Director/ Communication Consultant (Research & Training) with Communication Newworks (CNET), New Delhi. She has published eleven books. She has a number of research publications and articles to her credit. She has been associated with a number of national and international research projects, teaching, and training since 1958.

Contents

VOLUME - II

VOLUME - III

Introduction

The world is going through its worst economic slowdown since the Great Depression of 1930s, as a massive financial crisis has slashed global investment, brought sharp drops in commodity prices and severely hurt exports. The World Bank has lowered its estimates of global growth to 0.9 per cent in 2009—well below the 3 per cent rate typically considered the dividing line between growth and contraction.

The current economic slowdown is notable for both its length and breadth across all the regions of the world, leading to a contraction in the most wealthy nations and a sharp downturn in emerging economies, including China, India, Russia and Brazil. The indicators of this slowdown include contraction of world trade volumes for the first time since 1982; nearly 50 per cent fall in investment from the 2007 levels; and an unprecedented liquidity crunch which has affected businesses all over the world.

The Origin of Crisis

Though sharp eyes noticed the global financial crisis much earlier, it became prominently visible to everyone in September 2008 with the failure, merger and conservatorship of several large financial firms of the United States. The crisis was faced by leading United States and European investment banks, insurance firms and mortgage banks as a consequence of subprime mortgage crisis.

The failure of large financial institutions in the United States rapidly evolved into global credit crisis, deflation, sharp reductions in shipping and commerce, leading to failure of several European banks, declines in various stock indexes, substantial reductions in market values of equities and commodities all over the world including in the centrally-controlled economies like China and Russia. The crisis was sharpened by Section 128 of the Emergency Economic Stabilisation Act of 2008 which permitted the Federal Reserve Bank to pay interest on excess reserve requirement balances held on deposits from banks, removing the long standing incentive for banks to extend credit instead of hard cash with America's premier bank which plays a leadership role in monetary policy, financial supervision and the payment system. It led to a liquidity problem and the de-leveraging of financial institutions particularly in the United States and Europe which aggravated liquidity crisis and brought about a decline in international shipping and commerce.

The crisis which originated from widespread subprime mortgage failures quickly engulfed the entire financial system and industry resulting in widespread layoffs, for example, nearly 70,000 job losses in a single day in six companies ranging from manufacturing to telecom across the United States and Europe as a measure of cost cutting to grapple with slump in consumer spending. Construction machinery manufacturer Caterpillar, pharma major Pfizer, telecom firm Sprint Nextel Corporation and home improvement retailer Home Depot were among the top companies adversely affected.

A Chronology of the Crisis

Though the present global crisis can be attributed to several causes, the subprime mortgage crisis is unarguably the major among these. What started it all was the dramatic rise in mortgage delinquencies and foreclosures in the United States, with major adverse consequences for banks and financial markets around the globe. The crisis, which has its roots in the closing years of the 20th century, became apparent in 2007 and has exposed pervasive weaknesses in financial industry regulation and the global financial system.

Many US mortgages issued in recent years were made to subprime borrowers, defined as those with lesser ability to repay the loan based on various criteria. When US house prices began to decline in 2006-07, mortgage delinquencies soared, and securities backed with subprime mortgages, widely held by financial firms, lost most of their value. The result has been a large decline in the capital of many banks and USA government sponsored enterprises (GSEs), tightening credit around the world.

The subprime crisis had begun to show its signs in the early 2007 which reached a critical stage during September 2008. It was characterised by substantial decline in liquidity in the global credit markets and insolvency threats to investment banks and other financial institutions. In February 2008, the US Congress approved a $168 billion economic stimulus package and sent it to the then US President George W. Bush for his approval. In March, the US investment bank Bear Stearns got emergency funding from JPMorgan Chase with the backing of Federal Reserve Bank of New York. During this time JPMorgan Chase announced plans to buy investment bank Bear Stearns for $2 a share following the liquidity problems caused by the crisis. The US Federal Reserve System became lender to various other large investment banks. It cut the federal funds rate by 75 basis points to 2.25 per cent, which was followed by another cut of quarter percentage points to 2 per cent.

In July 2008, the European Central Bank increased interest rates in the Eurozone to 4.25 per cent to tackle inflation. The US Federal Reserve tightened mortgage regulation in an attempt to stamp out the practices that had led to the subprime mortgage crisis. In response to the subprime mortgage crisis, the then US President George W. Bush signed the Housing and Economic Recovery Act in 2008. The unemployment in the United States rose to 5.7 per cent, the highest in more than four years. The New York Attorney General Andrew Cuomo reached a $7 billion settlement with Citigroup to buy back auction rate securities from about 40,000 clients throughout the United States. The UK home repossessions rose by 48 per cent. The Consumer Price Index in the United States rose by nearly one per cent in July 2008, leading to an annual inflation rate of 5.6 per cent, the highest in 17 years.

In the beginning of September 2008, reserve balances from banks in the Federal Reserve System started increasing over required levels of about $10 billion just before the stock market crash. Gradually the signs of recession began to appear in other parts of the country as well. The European Commission predicted the fall of UK, Germany and Spain into recession and further added that the outlook for the rest of the Eurozone was gloomy. The Washington Mutual, the largest savings and loan company in the United States, fired its Chief Executive for heavy losses incurred due to the subprime mortgage crisis. It was this time that the AIG sought an emergency $40 billion loan from the United States Federal Reserve. The AIG, which is not only the largest insurer but also a significant participant in the credit default swaps markets, suffered a liquidity crisis following the downgrade of its credit rating. The Federal Reserve took several measures to expand emergency lending to tackle the crisis. At the request of AIG, it agreed to lend it $85 billion in exchange for a 79.9 per cent equity interest and the right to suspend dividends to previously issued common and preferred stock.

On September 19, Troubled Assets Relief Program (TARP), a plan to combat the subprime mortgage crisis was proposed by the Secretary of the Treasury, which was later incorporated into the Emergency Economic Stabilisation Act. It permitted the United States government to purchase illiquid assets—formally termed toxic assets—from financial institutions. Within a couple of days the then Secretary of the Treasury and President Bush announced a proposal for the federal government to buy up to US$700 billion of illiquid mortgage-backed securities to increase the liquidity of the secondary mortgage markets and reduce potential losses encountered by the financial institutions. This draft proposal of the plan was received favourably by investors in the stock market. US President George W. Bush, addressing the nation on prime time television to discuss the crisis, warned that the United States would face a "long and painful recession" if the package was not passed.

The Russian government lent the country's three biggest banks—Sberbank, VTB Bank and Gazprombank—1.13 trillion roubles ($44 billion) to boost liquidity. Trading remained suspended for three consecutive days, in Russia's two main stock exchanges—the MICEX and the dollar-denominated RTS—amidst fears of financial collapse. Russian President

Dimtry Medvedev ordered ministers to inject another 500 billion roubles (£10.8 billion, US$20 billion) of funds from the state budget to stabilize the markets.

The key risk indicators became highly volatile during September 2008, which led the US government to pass the Emergency Economic Stabilisation Act of 2008. As mentioned earlier, Section 128 of the Emergency Economic Stabilisation Act of 2008 permitted the Federal System to pay interest from October 6 onwards, on the excess balances, causing further pressure on international credit markets. By the end of second week of January 2009, excess on the balances reached $870 billion as against the increase in reserve balances of only $65 billion after September 2001 before declining to normal levels within a month.

Britain also took certain measures to tackle the situation. Britain's Chancellor of Exchequer released details of a rescue package to restore confidence in British banks. As part of the package, the British government announced to provide £50 billion of investment, a further £200 billion in short-term loan and guarantee up to £250 billion of intra-bank loans. The German parliament passed a €500 billion ($673.8 billion) bailout package for banks.

The Australian Prime Minister Kevin Rudd announced to guarantee all deposits in all Australian banks for a period of three years to combat the situation emerging from subprime mortgage crisis. The Reserve Bank of Australia pumped $1.5 billion into the banking system to mitigate the severity of crisis. The amount was nearly three times as much as the market's estimated requirements. New Zealand and United Arab Emirates also announced to guarantee all bank deposits in their banks. Greece, as a part of measure to combat the situation, introduced a €100,000 guarantee for the €230 billion bank deposits in the country for three years, well above the EU-wide Ecofin-mandated minimum of €50,000 for one year. It also assured about the stability of its banking system. The US Federal Reserve Board cut interest rates by half a percentage point to 1.5 per cent as part of a coordinated activity with the European Central Bank and other central banks. It approved the merger of Wells Fargo and Wachovia after Citigroup withdrew the legal case to put on hold a proposed merger. The head of the International Monetary Fund expressed concern over the US financial crises and warned of a global meltdown. It also offered to lend countries, if required.

In *World Economic Outlook* the IMF presented a gloomy projection for the global financial system. The finance ministers of G7, who met with the IMF Chief and World Bank President in Washington, announced a plan to combat the crisis with the help of "all available tools" to support key institutions. The then US President George W. Bush committed to a collaborative action with G7 finance ministers. He announced new measures to attack the current economic crisis including plans for the US government to buy stakes in major banks. The heads of 45 countries from Asia and Europe met in Beijing to discuss the situation emerging from the financial meltdown.

For most of the last decade America was a nation of borrowers and spenders, not savers. The personal savings rate dropped from 9 per cent in the 1980s to 5 per cent in the 1990s, to just 0.6 per cent from 2005 to 2007, and household debt grew much faster than personal income. According to Paul Krugman, it should not have expected its net worth to go up.

Yet until very recently Americans believed they were getting richer, because they received statements saying that their houses and stock portfolios were appreciating in value faster than their debts were increasing. The belief of many Americans that they could count on capital gains forever sounds naive, but it is worth remembering that many influential voices promoted that belief, and ridiculed those who worried about low savings and high levels of debt. When the reality struck, it turned out that those who worried had been right all along. Those who lived in false optimism proved wrong. The surge in asset values had been an illusion—but the surge in debt had been all too real.

And as the great American economist Irving Fisher pointed out in the 1930s, the things people and companies do when they realise they have too much debt tend to be self-defeating when everyone tries to do them at the same time. Attempts to sell assets and pay off debt deepen the plunge in asset prices, further reducing net worth. Attempts to save more translate into a collapse of consumer demand, further deepening the economic slump.

Impact on Various Economies

As the current economic slowdown is a global phenomenon, let us have a look how it has impacted various other economies.

China

International financial crisis has inflicted rather big impact on Chinese real economy. During 2007-08 its growth rate was nine per cent, but economy grew at 6.8 per cent in the fourth quarter of 2008-09. "Under these circumstances we have set the target of the growth rate of eight per cent for 2009," Chinese Premier Wen Jiabao said at the World Economic Forum meeting held in January 2009 in Davos. Calling the achievement of eight per cent growth rate a tall order, Wen said this is a necessary and attainable target through hard work. "I still hold the conviction that with hard work we will be able to attain this goal," he said. The Chinese Premier said his country's economy is facing severe challenges, including notably shrinking external demand, overcapacity in some sectors, difficult business conditions for enterprises, rising unemployment in urban areas and greater downward pressure on economic growth.

In January 2009, China's crude oil imports fell to their lowest level for 15 months—down 8 per cent year-on-year. The country shipped in 12.82 million tonnes of crude oil, nearly 11 per cent lower than in December 2008.

The World Bank cut its forecast of China's 2009 growth from 7.5 per cent to 6.5 per cent due to plunging exports but expressed confidence in Beijing's ability to keep the world's third-largest economy expanding amid global turmoil. The drop in trade will hurt investment and job creation, the bank said in a quarterly report released in March 2009. But it said China still should grow faster than other major countries due to its huge stimulus package and strong banks, which were unhurt by the global crisis.

Japan

Strangled by the collapse in global export demand, Japan's economy shrank at its fastest rate in 35 years in the fourth quarter and shows no signs of reversing course anytime soon. Japan's GDP contracted 3.2 per cent from the previous quarter, or an annual pace of 12.1 per cent, in the October-December period, the government said.

Japan is reeling from what can be called the worst recession since World War II, as its main mainstay exports have been hit by a global collapse in demand. Unemployment is at a three-year high of 4.4 per cent, and personal consumption is falling. The government, whose popularity has fallen alongwith the economy, is trying to rally support with another stimulus package of 15.4 trillion yen.

European Countries

European economies contracted in the fourth quarter of 2008 with some countries registering the worst figures in decades, official data showed. The Eurozone economy shrank by 1.5 per cent in the previous quarter and 1.2 per cent on the year, Eurostat said. Germany's economy shrank by 2.1 per cent compared with the previous quarter, which is its worst quarterly performance since 1990. Germany is being punished for its heavy dependence on exports. France shrank by 1.2 per cent, initial data showed, while Italy registered a drop of 1.8 per cent, the steepest drop since 1980.

The slowdown has been the most dramatic in Germany, which registered the biggest fall since German reunification in 1990. The 2.1 per cent contraction was the third consecutive quarterly drop in Europe's biggest economy, according to the initial data from the Federal Statistics Office, worse than the 1.8 per cent anticipated by analysts. Year-on-year, the German economy shrank by 1.6 per cent, after growing by 1.4 per cent in the third quarter. Many are now gloomy about the prospects for 2009. "This shows things went downhill sharply at the end of the year," said Juergen Michels, an economist at Citigroup, "We'll likely head down again the first and second quarter." "This number makes it plain that we are in a very serious recession—the most serious since World War II. It is no surprise that exports and investment have tumbled," said Dirk Schumacher at Goldman Sachs, adding that the rise in inventories did not bode well for the first quarter.

The slowdown in the French economy was slightly worse than the analysts' expectations of a 1.1 per cent drop. The French economy expanded slightly in the third quarter of 2008, by 0.1 per cent, which means that France has not officially entered a recession—which is defined as two consecutive quarters of contraction.

Gulf

It is not quite the end of the petro-dollar dream yet, but hundreds of Indians employed in the Gulf were forced to return home in the fourth quarter of 2008 as the global recession hit the region. If the steady trickle of Gulf returnees turns into a tide, India could face a major crisis. Authorities say the situation at the moment is not alarming, though reports of wage cuts and spiked jobs have been pouring in from the region hit hard by sinking oil prices and tottering construction, real estate and tourism sectors.

South Africa

South Africa's economy has shrunk for the first time in 10 years, official figures have shown. Gross Domestic Product (GDP) fell by 1.8 per cent in the last three months of 2008 from the previous quarter. Lonmin, the world's third-biggest platinum producer, said it was cutting up to 5,500 jobs at two South African mines. A worldwide commodities slump has seen dramatic falls in demand and prices of metals and other mined products. UK-listed Lonmin said a deal to cut 4,000 jobs at the Marikana mine in North-West province and 1,500 in Limpopo province had been agreed with unions. It has been hit by tumbling demand from the car sector which uses platinum to manufacture catalytic converters. "With the current backdrop of challenging economic conditions, these agreements are an important milestone in our objective of restructuring the company," said Lonmin chief executive Ian Farmer.

Forecast on Recession in US

US Federal Reserve chief Ben Bernanke has warned Congress that without the right policies from the government, the US recession could last into 2010. But he said if the Obama administration and the central bank can restore some measure of financial stability, 2010 could be a year of recovery. Mr Bernanke made the comments to the Senate Banking Committee. He also warned that the global nature of the downturn was a threat because exports would be hit.

In its attempts to revive the economy, the Federal Reserve has cut its key interest rate to nearly zero, while the Obama administration has recently brought a $787 billion (£546 billion) economic stimulus package. Mr Bernanke said that the potential economic turnaround would hinge on the success of such measures in getting credit and financial markets to operate more normally again.

The Indian Scenario

The IMF advised India to initiate more monetary steps to battle the country's slowing economic growth, which the international multilateral agency expects to moderate to 6.25 per cent in 2008-09 and fall further by one percentage point in 2009-10.

The Times of India had first reported in its February 28 edition that government's estimate of 7.1 per cent GDP growth for 2008-09 may not be achieved after Q3 (October-December) figure revealed that growth had dipped to 5.3 per cent.

India is staring at deflation, or negative inflation, with the official inflation rate falling to 0.44 per cent in the first week of April 2009—the lowest since 1977. Food prices, however, continued to be high, with food grains roughly 9 per cent costlier than a year ago, reinforcing a cruel paradox for consumers that they hear about zero inflation but face high prices when they buy their groceries. With the wholesale price index (WPI) falling by one point to 226.7 for the week ending March 7, 2009—the same level at which the index was on March 29, 2008—it now means the year-on-year inflation rate may become zero in the first quarter of 2009-10 even if the index for the current year falls no further.

High interest cost, fall in domestic demand and decline in exports have led to a contraction in the corporate profitability of the 110 companies in the list of BSE 500 companies that had declared their third quarter results for 2008-09 till the third week of January 2009. While margins contracted and profits dipped by 10 per cent over the same quarter previous year, revenues witnessed a growth of 18 per cent, indicating the bad state of the economy and bleeding corporate profitability. The aggregate profits of the 110 companies in the list came down from Rs. 18,017 crore to Rs. 16,377 crore. "I expect the pressure on profits not only in this quarter but also in the next quarter," said Pankaj Pandey, head of research, ICICI Direct.

Except for banks that managed to show good revenue and profit growth because of high treasury income, companies from across sectors and sizes remained under pressure. "Banks have benefited from the fall in bond yields that have come down by 400 basis points, leading to a gain in their treasury incomes," said Pandey. "However, they are witnessing pressure from the non-performing assets," he added.

Impact Across Sectors

Automobile Industry

Revenue of the auto industry has slipped 7 per cent to Rs. 1 lakh crore in the April 2008-January 2009 period, from Rs. 1.1 lakh crore in the same period last fiscal, which reflects the effect of slowdown in sales (in units). Though the fall in revenue is almost across the entire spectrum of the automotive industry, commercial vehicle segment has been the worst-hit.

The commercial vehicle industry—which even saw temporary production closures by companies like Tata Motors and Ashok Leyland due to shrinkage in demand—registered a turnover of Rs. 24,724 crore in the first ten months of the financial year 2008-09, showing a 22 per cent fall against Rs. 31,843 crore in the same period last year. This comes on the back of a 20 per cent fall in sales to 3.11 lakh units in April-January, from 3.88 lakh units in the same period last year.

Airways

The economic slowdown has adversely impacted airlines all over the world. The passenger travel in Indian airlines like Spicejet, Kingfisher, Indigo and International airlines like British Airways, Japan Airlines, among other, has fallen to several years' low.

The Indian government forced airlines to drop fares in January 2009 as jet fuel prices fell dramatically. But even low fares failed to win back passengers in January 2009 in this economic slowdown. In December 2008, when fares were at their peak, 33.73 lakh people flew within the country. In January 2009, when fares were almost halved, this figure was just 33.76 lakh, showing a 14.2 per cent fall from last January's figure of 39.34 lakh.

Airlines now fear that the low travel season with high fares could worsen the passenger load factors. "We had lowered fares in January 2009 in the hope of getting people to fly again and attaining breakeven revenue with volumes. But in the current economic turmoil, both personal and corporate travel is down due to uncertainty over jobs and focus on cost-cutting. Obviously we can't have low fares and low load factors," said an airline CEO.

Banks

Global economic slowdown has hit banks across the globe. Actually it was crisis in two large global financial services firms that triggered the meltdown. It has been widely accepted that the collapse of Lehman Brothers was symbol of the global financial crisis. The announcement on 14 September 2008 that Lehman Brothers would file for bankruptcy after the Federal Reserve Bank declined to participate in a financial support facility for the global financial services firm played a pivotal role in the unfolding of subsequent events.

Immediately following the bankruptcy, JPMorgan Chase provided the broker deal unit of Lehman Brothers with $138 billion to settle securities transactions with latter's customers and clearance parties. The same day, the sale of Merrill Lynch—another global financial services firm to Bank of America—was announced. These two developments heralded a severe global economic slowdown. The banks and financial companies in US and Europe disclosed sharp downturn in their balance sheets as defaults in subprime mortgage loans started eroding their capital and bringing them into losses with the accumulation of toxic assets.

Rising NPAs are yet another proof of banks facing worsening bad loans situation. The addition to bad loans is now higher than recoveries made from defaulted loans—a reversal of the trend of previous few years when bad loan recoveries exceeded fresh slippages. In 2007-08, fresh bad loans constituted 61 per cent of total NPAs, up from 37 per cent in 2003-04, 34 per cent in 2004-05, 41 per cent in 2005-06 and 52 per cent in 2006-07, according to a report by Dun & Bradstreet titled "India's Top Banks 2009". "The movement of NPAs prior to 2006-07 was favourable as the ratio of addition to NPAs was lower than their recovery. Both these ratios were almost the same in financial year 2007," said the report.

Defaults Hit SBI Cards

SBI Cards, the nation's second largest credit card issuer, 60 per cent owned by State Bank of India (SBI), is likely to report a loss for the second consecutive year as defaults mount. ICICI Bank, the top player, has faced similar defaults as well. Both have tightened salary and other norms for the issue of credit cards. CRISIL Ltd., the Indian arm of the global rating agency Standard & Poor's, said in a recent report that SBI Cards & Payment Services Ltd. was expected to report more losses in 2008-09 on high credit costs and lower fee income. In the quarter ended December 31, 2008, ICICI bank, relatively better off but still weak, saw a pre-tax profit of Rs. 85.7 crore in retail banking on business worth Rs. 5,683 crore, as defaults and receivables in loans hit home. Sachin Khandelwal, Head of Credit Cards, ICICI Bank, said, "In 2007-08 the credit cards business grew by 20 to 25 per cent. We had done 1.5 million cards in 2007-08 which has been reduced by 60 per cent in...2008-09. The credit losses have increased by more than 1 percentage point (of the spread between lending rates and cost)."

Retail

Retail malls are facing financial problems as a result of high rentals and decline in demand. Large retailers like the Future Group, Reliance Retail, and Aditya Birla Retail are renegotiating to bring rentals down as their businesses have suffered a blow due to sharp decline in demand for a variety of goods. Reliance Retail spokesperson stated: "We are actively renegotiating rentals across formats and hope that, on an average, this would bring down costs by 20 per cent to 30 per cent."

Real Estate

A correction in the real estate industry has been long overdue, and taking advantage of the situation, modern retailers have called a war on costs to tide over the slowdown. Most of the modern retailers either purchased or rented properties at the peak of the real estate market. This has seriously dented their ability to make profits from the retail business, especially at the time of an economic slowdown. According to Pranay Vakil, chairman of of real estate services company Knight Frank: "The headroom for reducing rentals could be anywhere between 10-35 per cent. In exceptional cases, it could even go up to 40 per cent. The exact amount would depend on the location."

The National Association of Realtors reports that home prices dropped a record 12.4 per cent in the final quarter of 2008—the biggest decline in 30 years. Home prices fell 12.4 per cent during the fourth quarter of 2008, the largest year-on-year decline since the National Association of Realtors began keeping comprehensive records in 1979. The share prices of realtors like DLF and Unitech have plummeted because of a sharp decline in their business.

Job Cuts and Rising Unemployment

Global economic slowdown has led to the shrinking of business, trade, markets, and hence, production. Several companies across various sectors are therefore effecting job cuts in large numbers. The unemployment situation is worsening in all parts of the world.

The US jobless rate jumped in February 2009 to 8.1 per cent, according to official figures from the Labor Department. The number of people out of work rose by 651,000 during the month. Both figures were bigger than expected. The number of job cuts in January 2009 was revised up to 655,000 while December 2008 losses were pushed up to 681,000. The figure for December was the biggest job loss in a single month since October 1949. The unemployment rate was the highest since December 1983. Rising unemployment has meant greater demand for free meals.

President Obama said that the number of jobs lost so far in the recession was "astounding". Speaking in Ohio, he added: "I don't need to tell the people of this state what statistics like this mean," saying that he had signed his economic stimulus package in order to save jobs.

UK unemployment rose to 1.97 million between October and December 2008, the highest level since 1997, figures show. The jobless number climbed 146,000 for the three-month period, data from the Office for National Statistics showed. For January 2009, the number of those getting jobseeker's allowance added 73,800 to reach 1.23 million.

The unemployment rate hit 6.3 per cent, the highest since 1998. The Bank of England had recently warned of a deep recession and rising unemployment in 2009.

The Chinese government has more than trebled its earlier estimates on joblessness caused by the financial crisis. It has now released a fresh survey saying that 20 million migrant workers have lost jobs while revealing that the world's factory is suffering from a much deeper malaise than what was suggested earlier. Government agencies had earlier suggested that the extent of job loss caused by reduction in export orders and production cutbacks was six million. The ministry of agriculture has now released the results of the survey suggesting that 20 million workers have returned to their villages after city-based factories threw them out. The new estimate is based on data collected in a survey covering 50 villages in 15 provinces in the country. It has emerged immediately after the end of the Chinese New Year celebrations when millions of people—who still have jobs—are returning to work after spending a week or more at their rural homes.

As many as 1.5 million people could end up losing their jobs in India, as exports contracted for the third successive month plunging by 1.1 per cent in December 2008 amid the worst slowdown in the world economy in the last 80 years. "If these projections continue...it's quite likely that you can expect another five lakh losses...," commerce secretary G.K. Pillai said. About 1 million jobs have already been lost since August 2008.

The Issue of Wages and Employment

Prof. A.C. Pigou diagnosed the ills of depression mainly due to two causes, viz. (1) an improper allocation of people among jobs and (2) the prevalence of wage-rates above the level warranted by the general demand conditions. He, therefore, advocated a policy of wage cuts to cure unemployment. He held that given flexible wage-rates, the economic system has an automatic tendency towards full employment and the more rigid wages are, the larger would be the fluctuations in employment. He stated:

> With perfectly free competition among work people and labour perfectly mobile, the nature of the relation (i.e., between the real wage-rates for which people stipulate and the demand function for labour) will be very simple. There will always be at work a strong tendency for wage-rates to be so related to demand that everybody is employed. Hence in stable conditions everyone will actually be employed. The implication is that such unemployment as exists at any time is due wholly to the fact that changes in demand conditions are continually taking place and that frictional resistances prevent the appropriate wage adjustments from being made instantaneously.

The process by which the reduction in wage-rates cures unemployment is described by the classical economists as below:

> In a free market economy, a reduction in wage-rates lowers the cost of production and hence prices which lead to an increase in sales. Increase in sales leads to increase in

production which leads to an expansion of employment of the workers. Reduction in costs as a result of lower wages also increases profits of businessmen. Profits increase because it is assumed that the decline in wage-rates is larger than that in prices. The process of declining wages accompanied by rising profits and employment continues till equilibrium is reached at full employment. Thus the classical equilibrium is always at full employment equilibrium.

Keynes' Viewpoint

J.M. Keynes criticized Pigou on the ground that reduction in wages should lead to decline in purchasing power and hence in effective demand. But practical situations have shown that high wage rates increase the cost of production and hence prices, keeping goods beyond the buying capacity of the consumers. This results in decrease in demand leading to unemployment.

There is wide agreement that the world capitalist system is in the midst of its most severe crisis since the Great Depression of 1929. Keynes' *The General Theory of Employment, Interest and Money,* which was published in 1936, recommended massive government investment that would inject purchasing power into the economic system, which would help resuscitate the economy through the multiplier effect.

Keynes' persuasive power was formidable and among the earliest converts to his thinking—other than a close band of students and select professional colleagues—was President Franklin D. Roosevelt. Roosevelt's "New Deal" ushered in a massive public works program as per the Keynesian prescription. The Keynesian idea of having an interventionist state particularly when economic activity was sluggish remained the cornerstone of economic policymaking in the Western capitalist world in the post-World War II era. For more than three decades the capitalist countries in the West recorded uninterrupted economic growth that was without any historical precedence.

In fact, what we require is a combination of reasonable wages, monetary policy (in the form of low interest rates) as well as fiscal policy in the shape of public expenditure on infrastructure, i.e. transportation, education, power supplies, buildings, communication networks, etc.

Impact of Slowdown on Poverty Situation

About 53 million people in developing countries will remain poor because of the world economic slowdown, the World Bank has said. The Bank says the downturn will reverse many of the gains made in reducing poverty in developing countries. It estimates that 40 per cent of the world's 107 developing countries are "highly exposed" to the global crisis. And it calls on the rich countries to devote 0.7 per cent of their bailout packages to help the poor in developing nations.

The global crisis is likely to keep 46 million more people below the absolute poverty line of $1.25 per day, and another seven million under $2 per day, compared with previous World Bank forecasts for 2009. An earlier version had incorrectly stated that 100 million more people would remain poor. "The global crisis threatens to become a human crisis in many developing countries unless they can take targeted measures to protect vulnerable people," said World Bank president Robert Zoellick. "While much of the world is focused on bank rescues and stimulus packages, we should not forget that poor people are much more exposed if their economies falter," he added.

Stimulus Measures

Governments all over the world have taken stimulus measures to mitigate the adverse effects of financial crisis and put their respective economies back on track.

In October 2008, the supplementary demand for grants provided for a gross expenditure amounting to Rs. 2,37,286 crore with net cash outgo of Rs. 1,05,613 crore mainly to finance schemes/plans announced in the Union Budget for 2008-09. However, no provisions were made for the same.

On 7 December 2008, the three major *ad valorem* rates of central excise duty, viz. 14 per cent, 12 per cent and 8 per cent, applicable to non-petroleum products, were reduced by 4 percentage points each.

India's Interim Budget 2009-10

Pranab Mukherjee presented United Progressive Alliance (UPA) government's interim budget 2009-10 on 16 February 2009. Apart from highlighting the initiatives taken by the government and achievements made in agriculture, rural development, education, social sector and public sector enterprises, Mukherjee drew attention to the global financial crisis.

The budget provided 2 per cent cut in excise duty and service tax to give boost to the country's economy. Starting December 2008, this is the third stimulus package announced by the government to counter the crisis faced due to the global economic downturn.

Industry chambers welcomed the move. "It is another stimulus," Pranab Mukherjee told reporters after the passage of the interim budget in the Lok Sabha. The tax concessions would entail a revenue sacrifice of about Rs. 30,000 crore. Mukherjee said, "It will have its desired impact because we have given some concessions to the export sector, particularly those which are employment-generating ones, like gems and jewellery, garments and handicraft." "With the strong export linkages India has with these economies it is unlikely India will not feel the impact. Despite the constitutional constraints, I have some flexibility which I want to use to provide a further stimulus to the economy," he added.

The lack of any populist announcement in the interim union budget has gone down well with both the industry and trade circles. Yet, the same circles also felt cheated that there was no mention of new measures to boost the economy, since they had been expecting some such steps.

America's Stimulus Package—I

In September 2008, the then Secretary of the United States Treasury, Henry Paulson and President George W. Bush proposed legislation for the government to purchase up to US$700 billion of "troubled mortgage-related assets" from financial firms in hopes of improving confidence in the mortgage-backed securities markets and the financial firms participating in it. Discussions, hearings and meetings among legislative leaders were held, and the administration made clear that the proposal would undergo significant change before it could be approved by Congress. On 1 October 2008, a revised compromise version was approved by the Senate with a 74-25 vote. The bill, HR1424 was passed by the House on 3 October 2008 and signed into law. The first half of the bailout money was primarily used to buy preferred stock in banks instead of troubled mortgage assets.

Stimulus Package—II

Members of both houses of Congress reached a deal in February 2009 over US President Barack Obama's economic stimulus plan.

Senate majority leader Harry Reid said the deal "bridged differences" between an $820 billion House version of the bill and a $838 billion Senate version. "The package, now worth $789 billion (£549 billion), includes tax cuts and spending aimed at rescuing the US economy. The middle ground we have reached creates more jobs than the original Senate bill and costs less than the original House bill," said Senate majority leader Harry Reid. He said the stimulus bill should create 3.5 million jobs. He added that more than one-third of it would be dedicated to tax cuts and incentives for middle-class Americans.

The House approved its $825 billion version of the package without any Republican support. The Senate voted 61-37 to approve a different $838 billion version with few Republicans opting to back it. The bill included help for victims of the recession in the form of unemployment benefits, food stamps, health coverage as well as billions for states that face the prospect of making deep cuts in their own public spending.

Obama's Housing Plan

The Obama administration's housing rescue plan commited up to $275 billion in funds to help reduce mortgage payments for up to 9 million families and arrest the devastating fall in US home prices. According to the plan, $50 billion to modify mortgages will come from the $700 billion financial bailout fund approved by Congress in 2008; up to $25 billion in direct costs to finance firms Fannie Mae and Freddie Mac to modify mortgages; up to $200 billion from the US Treasury to increase capital for Fannie and Freddie if necessary, authorized under a housing bill passed in 2008. Fannie and Freddie would increase their mortgage portfolios by $50 billion each.

The plan enables refinancing for 4 million to 5 million "responsible" homeowners who took out conforming 30-year fixed mortgages with a downpayment of 20 per cent or more and are current on payments. The decline in home values means many of these families cannot qualify for conventional refinancing because their loan-to-value ratio now exceeds 80 per cent. The program would allow mortgages owned or guaranteed by Fannie Mae and Freddie Mac to be refinanced through private lenders, reducing monthly payments, as long as the amount owed on a first mortgage does not exceed 105 per cent of the property's current market value. Refinancing rates will be based on market rates in effect at the time of the refinance plus any associated points and fees quoted by the lender. All of the refinanced loans under the plan will be 30-year or 15-year fixed-rate notes. Mortgage lenders started accepting applications after program details were announced on 4 March 2009.

America's Plan to Buy Banks' Toxic Assets

The Obama administration's new plan to liberate the nation's banks from a toxic stew of bad home loans and mortgage-related securities is bigger and more generous to private investors than expected, but it also puts taxpayers at great risk. Taken together, the three programs unveiled on in the third week of March 2009 by the Treasury Secretary, Timothy F. Geithner, could buy up to $2 trillion in real estate assets that have been weighing down banks, paralyzing credit markets and delaying the economic recovery. Investors reacted ecstatically, with all of the major stock indexes soaring as soon as the markets opened. The Dow Jones Industrial Average ended the day up nearly 500 points, or 6.84 per cent, to 7,775.86. The thundering response was in sharp contrast with the bitter disappointment by investors when the plan was first vaguely described on 10 February 2009. "For the first time in seven months, I can say they've done it right," said T. Timothy

Ryan Jr., President of the Securities Industry and Financial Markets Association.

The European Union's current president labelled President Obama's emergency stimulus package "a way to hell" that will "undermine the stability of the global financial market." The blunt comments by the Czech Prime Minister, Mirek Topolanek, whose country holds the rotating presidency of the union, came just a week before a crucial meeting of the Group of 20 that was called to show global solidarity in fighting the recession. The comments were greeted with embarrassment by many Europeans who believe that the Czech leader does not represent a European consensus.

Financial Regulation

The Obama administration has called for a sweeping overhaul of financial regulation. The hedge funds, private equity firms and derivative markets are likely to come under government supervision for the first time. According to Treasury Secretary Timothy Geithner the regulatory changes were essential to restore confidence to the financial markets: "We need much stronger standards for openness, transparency, and plain, common sense language throughout the financial system. And we need strong and uniform supervision for all financial products marketed to consumers and investors, and tough enforcement of the rules to ensure full accountability for those who violate the public trust."

The plan would give the government vast powers over systemically important banks and other financial institutions that are so big that their collapse would jeopardize the economy as a whole. The government will have the power to pear into the inner working of companies that are currently outside the scope of federal supervision. These include insurance companies like the AIG, multi-billion-dollar hedge funds like the Citadel Group, and PE firms like Carlyle Group and Kohlberg, Kravis & Roberts. The big companies would be subjected to much stricter capital requirement. The most striking new proposals that may provoke the most heated opposition would be regarding the regulation of so-called private pools of capital—hedge funds, private equity funds and venture capital funds—and the colossal market in financial derivatives, including instruments-like credit-default swaps, the insurance-like instruments that allow investors to hedge against bond defaults.

It is believed that the ongoing economic crisis was triggered by a dramatic rise in mortgage delinquencies and foreclosures in the US with adverse consequences for banks and financial markets around the world. The crisis "has exposed the pervasive weakness in financial industry regulation and the global financial system." Overhauling of financial regulation is therefore a step in the right direction.

Geithner's Financial Stability Plan

The Financial Stability Plan (FSP), presented by Treasury secretary Timothy Geithner, like the Troubled Assets Relief Program (TARP) before it, is a simple swap of assets and risk between the private and the public sector, albeit on a massive scale. In effect, the federal government is nationalizing the banks' assets, even as it declines to nationalize the banks themselves. Under the FSP, commercial banks, hedge funds and other investors will spring clean their balance sheets by selling the worst assets to the Federal Reserve, or to an off-balance sheet public-private "trust fund" financed with a mixture of public and private capital and a large quantity of cheap loans from the central bank. In return, the Fed will credit their accounts at the central bank with hundreds of billions of dollars of new reserve funds (in essence cash). And the Treasury will issue trillions of dollars of new debt, of which some of the proceeds will be deposited with the Fed to fund its asset purchases and lending activities. Much of this new government debt will be bought by the banks and other investors.

Reduction of Repo and Reverse Repo Rates by RBI

The Reserve Bank of India reduced the repo and reverse repo rates by 50 basis points each, but industry said its effectiveness would depend on how well banks use the cheaper money to provide more credit to an economy rapidly losing steam. While Bank of India said it could take weeks to decide on lowering prime lending rates, UCO Bank announced a reduction in its benchmark by 50 basis points to 12.50 per cent. The money and stock markets had factored in the rate cuts for some time, but they are not expected to sustain a rally. A CII statement said another 50-bps cut would have been more appropriate. Nevertheless, industry captains are hopeful of further rate cuts. Binani Cement MD Vinod Juneja said, "The cut will boost demand for cement as housing loans are now expected to become cheaper and affordable. This will boost housing demand, in turn improve demand for steel and cement."

This is the fifth time that RBI has slashed rates since October 2008, when the global economic crisis broke out. The repo rate—the rate at which banks buy cash from RBI—is now at 5 per cent. To reduce the incentive for banks to park excess cash with RBI, the reverse repo rate has been cut to 3.5 per cent. Governor D. Subbarao said, "It is expected that the reduction in the policy interest rates will further encourage banks to provide credit for productive purposes at viable interest rates. RBI, on its part, would continue to maintain ample liquidity in the system."

The Issue of Protectionism

Barack Obama had declared, long before becoming the American President that he "will stop giving tax breaks to corporations that ship our jobs overseas, and...will start giving them to companies that create good jobs right here in America." If Obama indeed does that, it will adversely affect the massive flow of work to Indian IT and BPO firms. It will also hurt the American economy. Nasscom president Som Mittal points out that "Obama earlier said India and China will help the growth of US. US tech firms have thousands of jobs but not enough talent at home." Mittal added that outsourcing has boosted America's economy by making the US companies competitive. Now if protectionism gets the better of American policymakers, it will serve nobody's cause.

Barack Obama, who started his campaign to become America's 44th President with some protectionist statements, now finds himself in a dilemma after reaching the White House. Backing those statements could start a trade war, but opposing them could mean a backlash from his supporters. The slogan "Buy America or Bye America" has not gone very well with two of the largest US trading partners. Canadian Prime Minister, Stephen Harper, has already expressed concern. The European Union has also warned that it could not "stand idly by" if such measures are taken. Brazilian President, Luiz Inacio Lula da Silva has also responded critically to the protectionist moves coming from America.

India inc has expressed concern over Barack Obama's plans to clamp down on the outsourcing industry. Such a legislation will clearly make outsourcing unattractive to US companies, which is bad news for the Indian tech sector. Reiterating one of his election campaign agenda, in his recent speech, Obama made it clear that there would not be any tax benefits for American companies that outsource jobs to other countries. It would create/save 3.5 million jobs in the country.

The domestic industry in general said such a move will only hurt US as outsourcing makes a lot of economic and logical sense to the country. Reacting to Obama's statement, Kris Gopalakrishnan, CEO, Infosys, said, "Outsourcing has enhanced the competitiveness of US corporations and has created more jobs within US economy. US is an open economy and a strong proponent of free trade globally. We are confident that US will not take any measures which might hurt its own global competitiveness."

After meeting in London, the heads of the Group of 20 nations vowed "to do whatever is necessary to promote global trade and investment and reject protectionism." That pledge is almost identical to one made at a November 15, 2008 summit where they decided to "underscore the critical importance of rejecting protectionism and not turning inward in times of financial uncertainly." Since then, 17 G20 members have implemented 47 trade restrictions, a 1 March 2009 study by the World Bank showed.

Mounting protectionism will lead to a 9 per cent drop in global trade in 2009, its first decline since 1982, according to the World Trade Organization. Led by the US's $17.4 billion bailout of General Motors Corp. and Chrysler LLC, subsidies for the car industry rose to more than $48 billion worldwide, according to the World Bank. While developing countries such as Brazil have been outspoken on the issue, with President Luiz

Inacio Lula da Silva calling it a "drug," there are few signs their warnings are being heard from world's biggest to the smallest nations.

The G20 leaders reaffirmed "the commitment made in Washington to refrain from raising new barriers to investment or to trade in goods and services, imposing new export restrictions or implementing WTO-inconsistent measures to stimulate exports," the G20 statement said, "In addition, we will rectify promptly any such measures. We extend this pledge to the end of 2010." History points to the potentially catastrophic impact of protectionism amid an economic slump. The US Smoot-Hawley Tariff Act of 1930 increased duties on more than 20,000 goods, inviting retaliation by other countries. Within two years of the law's enactment, global trade declined 70 per cent.

Current World Financial Crisis and the Great Depression of 1930s

The current global meltdown cannot be compared to the 1929 crash. Some historians believe that the Great Depression set the stage for the Second World War. But we have compelling reasons to believe that the final denouement of the present crisis will not be as grave as in 1930s.

The roots of the current global crisis lie in the interplay of several developments that have radically changed the finance capitalism which existed in 1929 or as recently as just three decades ago. Traditionally, banks were careful to lend only to trusted clients, and carried the debt on their books. These days there is securitization. Lenders pool the loans and resell them as asset-backed securities. These securities are then repackaged, leveraged and resold many times over. Another pertinent development is the emergence of highly sophisticated derivative products, including the credit default snaps (CDSs). The asset-backed securities and derivatives widely spread the risk and prevent catastrophes like GD 1929.

There is no doubt that securitization, derivatives, leveraging and globalisation have made the global economy more volatile and risky than the world of 1930s. In those times, however, the governments had relatively little understanding of the macroeconomic management. Today, the government and central banks have several tools to restore confidence and revive the economy. "The pace at which the US subprime loan defaults snowballed into a global financial crisis was quite astonishing, but so was the speed with which G7 countries and the emerging economies responded. In a period of less than two months after the collapse of Lehman Brothers, the advanced countries and emerging economies had all introduced broadly similar measures to deal with the crisis, a remarkable feature of global coordination without a single formal treaty or agreement."

It is said that out of the Great Depression was born Keynesian economics which encourages government action to increase or decrease demand and output. Keynes' *The General Theory of Employment, Interest and Money,* published in 1936, states that some micro-level actions of individuals and firms can lead to aggregate macroeconomic outcomes in which the economy operates below its potential output and growth. Many classical economists had believed in Say's Law which states that supply creates its own demand, so that a "general glut" would therefore be impossible. Keynes contended that aggregate demand for goods might be insufficient during economic downturns, leading to unnecessarily high unemployment and losses of potential output. Keynes argued that government policies could be used to increase aggregate demand, thus increasing economic activity and reducing unemployment and deflation.

Keynes argued that the solution to depression was to stimulate the economy "through some combination of two approaches: a reduction in interest rates, and government investment in infrastructure. Investment by government injects income, which results in more spending in the general economy, which in turn stimulates more production and investment involving still more income and spending and so forth. The initial stimulation starts a cascade of events, whose total increase in economic activity is a multiple of the original investment."

Many countries have joined hands to tide over the global financial crisis. The UK has taken a leading role in shaping the international response, and ensuring that China and other emerging economies are fully involved in international discussions.

The Future of Capitalism

The leaders of the former bastions of communist block have blamed capitalists for dragging the world into a serious economic crisis. In the opening address of the World Economic Forum at Davos, Switzerland, the Russian Prime Minister, Vladimir Putin spoke of a "perfect storm" that has decimated the old system, rendering it obsolete. He said that the fundamental stability and "the investment banks once considered the pride of Wall Street have virtually ceased to exist." But the damage has gone beyond Wall Street. Putin said, "The entire economic growth system where one regional centre prints money without respite and consumer material wealth, while another regional centre manufactures inexpensive goods and saves money printed by other governments has suffered a major setback." The Chinese premier, Wen Jiabao also blamed the United States for economic slowdown. "Inappropriate macroeconomic policies ...unsustainable model of development characterised by prolonged low savings and high consumption...the blind pursuit of profit and the failure of financial supervision, all have contributed to the present crisis."

The spectre of failure of capitalism is haunting the world. "Suddenly, the invisible hand that is supposed to guide the goods and people in a free market economy has vanished and the visible hand of the government is back in action." Some economists have called the use of taxpayers' money to cover private losses of mega corporations, big banks—considered to be the backbone of the market system—a strange thing to have happened. It seems that Adam Smith's "hand" money has vanished into thin air, and the world is returning to the good old days of big government as recommended by J.M. Keynes. There are even beliefs that Karl Marx's prophecy that "capitalism will be replaced by communism just as feudalism was replaced by capitalism", may come true in the foreseeable future.

Marx saw the power of unbridled capitalism as a kind of myth which became more real than it actually is. In the present era of unchallenged capitalism, the only reality is money and its purchasing power. People want money in their pockets and their accounts, and the liberty to buy what they want to. That is how they understand the system. People believe in capitalism as it talks about profits, incentive and consumers' sovereignty.

According to Paul Krugman, the Nobel laureate for economics in 2008, communism failed, not because of some technical problem, but because people lost faith in it. But he argues that a market system works whether people believe in it or not: "You may dislike capitalism, even feel that as a system it will eventually fail, yet do your job well because your family needs the money you earn. Capitalism can run, even flourish in a society of selfish cynics. But a non-market economy cannot."

There is no question that the global financial crisis has crippled economic growth around the world. But there is a lesson in this crisis. The rumours about the demise of capitalism may be exaggerated but the warning signs are clear and scary. In the present age of globalisation, an unregulated market—which is susceptible to manipulation by a few rogue characters—can plummet and send out strong ripples. Capitalism may have an in-built self-correcting mechanism, but how painful such mechanism is, can be realized from the present global economic conditions which have jolted the entire world.

Conclusion

"The financial crisis roiling the world today is the result of serious shortcomings in domestic financial governance that have exposed gaps in the global governance of institutional finance and capital." Its immediate roots lie in the excessive and not so transparent leverage of complex securities and derivatives that inflated the real economy to excessive proportions. The US regulatory regime governing its financial and banking worlds—which had far-reaching repercussions for the entire globe—can be euphemistically described as light, incomplete and fragmentary. Thus, the need for efficient, effective and transparent regulatory and surveillance instruments and institutions is quite obvious. The role of global governance institutions, now more than ever before, is to contain the contagion. Only a new regulatory regime will reassure the world at large that the balance has been restored between the risks and the benefits of integrating with an open world economy.

The comity of nations has joined hands to take short-term emergency measures to deal with the financial crisis. There is a growing recognition that the system to manage the modern world of banking, capital and finance has to be redesigned. The corporations, markets and financial flows are global, but regulatory and financial systems are national—or in a few cases like Europe—regional. The world at this juncture needs "some sort of visionary internationalism" like Bretton Wood in 1944.

It is also being felt that the existing political or economic institutions like IMF and G7 have not proved equal to the task of coordinating an adequate response to global crisis. The way things are, it is hard to imagine that any major global challenge can be effectively addressed without involving all three Asian giants—China, India and Japan. But two of the them, viz. India and Japan are not permanent members of the UN Security Council, and two, viz. China and India are not part of the G7. These anomalies need to be removed to give these countries more say in international affairs. The decision to base the initial crisis summitry on the G20, at the Beijing Summit has been hailed as an evidence of changing global equation. The G20, which has effectively replaced G8 (G7 + Russia) brings China, India, Brazil, Mexico and Indonesia together with the major industrial powers and the EU. It is likely to become the architect of global governance and an effective tool of restoring and maintaining a durable economic world order.

The G20 meeting of 2 April 2009, held in London, can be termed as landmark in many ways. The member countries—which are virtually world's main financial powers—pledged more than $1 trillion for emergency loans to reverse the recession.

Emerging markets and developing countries, which have been the engine of recent world growth, are also now facing challenges which are adding to the current downturn in the global economy. It is imperative for global confidence and economic recovery that capital continues to flow to them. This will require a substantial strengthening of the international financial institutions, particularly the IMF. G20 members have therefore agreed to make available an additional $850 billion of resources through the global financial institutions to support growth in emerging markets and developing countries by helping to finance counter-cyclical spending, bank recapitalisation, infrastructure, trade finance, balance of payments support, debt rollover, and social support. They not only decided to reject protectionism but also to bring tighter financial regulation. Positive results can be expected sooner than later.

1

The Global Financial Turmoil and Challenges for the Indian Economy*

D. Subbarao

....

2. The global financial crisis is now the staple of front page news. Banks around the world, including those in India, are in the forefront of managing the challenge of crisis resolution. Since it is so topical, ...on the current global turmoil, its impact on India, the outlook for the Indian economy and the challenges that lie ahead for the Indian banking system, in particular.

Global Financial Outlook

3. The global financial situation continues to be uncertain and unsettled. What started off as a sub-prime crisis in the US housing mortgage sector has turned successively into a global banking crisis, global financial crisis and now a global economic crisis. Textbook economics often cites housing as a prime example of a non-tradable good. It is paradoxical that a quintessentially non-tradable good as housing has triggered a crisis of global dimensions. This crisis is also the first of a kind in the sense that it is the first financial crisis since the Great Depression that originated in the advanced economies and rapidly engulfed the whole world. Such is the depth and sweep of financial globalisation. By far, the most frequently asked question (FAQ) today is whether the worst—in terms of the

---

* *Courtsey*: www.rbi.org.in

financial sector meltdown, and in particular, failure of financial institutions—is behind us. No one is really willing to take a definitive call on this, which is a sign of the increasing number of unknown unknowns.

4. Even as recently as six months ago, there was a view that the fallout of the crisis will remain confined to the financial sector and that, at the most, there would only be a shallow recession in the advanced economies. These expectations, as it now turns out, have been belied. The contagion has traversed from the financial to the real sector; and it now looks like the recession will be deeper and the recovery longer than earlier anticipated.

Global Economic Outlook

5. Many economists are now predicting that this 'Great Recession' of 2008/09 will be the worst global recession since the 1930s. The IMF made its customary forecast for global growth in the *World Economic Outlook* published in October 2008. By early November, the IMF had revised its forecast for global growth downwards—from 3.9 per cent to 3.7 per cent for 2008, and from 3.0 per cent to 2.2 per cent for 2009. There are two inferences that follow from this. First, that the global situation has deteriorated rapidly, in a space of less than two months. Second, that 2009 is going to be a more challenging year than 2008.

Emerging Economies

6. Ironically, even as late as six months ago, it was intellectually fashionable to subscribe to the 'decoupling theory'—that even if advanced countries went into a downturn, emerging economies will, at worst, be affected only marginally, and will largely steam ahead on their own. In a rapidly globalising world, the decoupling theory was never very persuasive; given the evidence of the last few months—capital flow reversals, sharp widening of spreads between sovereign and corporate debt, and abrupt currency depreciations—the decoupling theory has almost completely lost credibility. Growth prospects of emerging economies have

most definitively been undermined by the ongoing crisis with, of course, considerable variations across countries.

Impact of the Crisis on India

7. India too is having to weather the negative impact of the crisis. As the impact on India unfolds, there are two frequently asked questions: First, how is that India is affected when it came out of the Asian crisis relatively unscathed? Second, why is India affected even when its exports account for only 15 per cent of its GDP? The answer to both the questions lies in globalisation. We are certainly more integrated into the world economy today than ten years ago at the time of the Asian crisis. Integration into the world implies more than just exports. Going by the common measure of globalisation, India's two-way trade (merchandise exports plus imports), as a proportion of GDP, grew from 21.2 per cent in 1997-98, the year of the Asian crisis, to 34.7 per cent in 2007-08. If we take an expanded measure of globalisation, that is, the ratio of total external transactions (gross current account flows plus gross capital flows) to GDP, this ratio has increased from 46.8 per cent in 1997-98 to 117.4 per cent in 2007-08. These numbers are clear evidence of India's increasing integration into the world economy over the last 10 years.

8. We must also note another important difference between the crisis in the advanced countries and the developments in India. While in the advanced countries the contagion spread from the financial to the real sector, in India, the slowdown in the real sector is affecting the financial sector, which in turn, has a second-order impact on the real sector.

The Indian Banking System

9. The Indian banking system is not directly exposed to the sub-prime mortgage assets. It has very limited indirect exposure to the US mortgage market, or to the failed institutions or stressed assets. Indian banks, both in the public sector and in the private sector, are financially sound, well capitalised and well regulated. The average capital to risk-weighted assets ratio (CRAR) for the Indian banking system, as at end-March 2008, was 12.6 per cent, as against the

regulatory minimum of nine per cent and the Basel norm of eight per cent. Even so, India is experiencing the knock-on effects of the global crisis, through the monetary, financial and real channels—all of which are coming on top of the already expected cyclical moderation in growth. Our financial markets—equity market, money market, forex market and credit market—have all come under pressure mainly because of what we have begun to call 'the substitution effect' of: (i) drying up of overseas financing for Indian banks and Indian corporates; (ii) constraints in raising funds in a bearish domestic capital market; and (iii) decline in the internal accruals of the corporates. All these factors added to the pressure on the domestic credit market.

10. Simultaneously, the reversal of capital flows, caused by the global de-leveraging process, has put pressure on our forex market. The sharp fluctuation in the overnight money market rates in October 2008 and the depreciation of the rupee reflected the combined impact of the global credit crunch and the de-leveraging process underway.

Outlook for India

11. The outlook for India, going forward, is mixed. There is evidence of a slow down in the economic activity. The real GDP growth has moderated in the first half of 2008-09. Industrial activity, particularly in the manufacturing and infrastructure sectors, is decelerating. The services sector too, which has been our prime growth engine for the last five years, is slowing, mainly in the construction, transport and communication, trade, hotels and restaurants sub-sectors. For the first time in seven years, exports have declined in absolute terms in October 2008. Recent data indicate that the demand for bank credit is slackening despite comfortable liquidity in the system. Higher input costs and dampened demand have dented corporate margins while the uncertainty surrounding the crisis has affected business confidence.

Inflation

12. On the positive side, headline inflation, as measured by the wholesale price index, has fallen sharply, and the decline

has been sustained for the past four weeks, pointing to a faster-than-expected reduction in inflation. Largely, the falling commodity prices have been the key drivers behind the disinflation; however, some contribution has also come from slowing domestic demand. The reduction in prices of petrol and diesel announced last week, and a cut in the excise duties should further ease the inflationary pressures. To be sure, consumer price inflation for the months of September and October 2008 did increase. This is possibly owing to the firm trend in food-articles inflation and the higher weight of food articles in the measures of consumer price inflation. Historically, there has been a positive correlation between wholesale and consumer price inflation, and given this correlation, consumer price inflation too can be expected to soften in the months ahead.

RBI's Policy Stance

13. The Reserve Bank's monetary policy stance has consistently been to balance growth, inflation and financial stability concerns. When inflation surged earlier this year, the RBI had moved quickly to tighten policy. Then again, reflecting the unfolding global situation and expectation of decline in inflation, RBI has adjusted its monetary stance over the last couple of months. The endeavour of our monetary stance has been to manage liquidity—both domestic and forex liquidity—and to ensure that credit continues to flow for productive activities.

Measures Taken So Far

14. The RBI has taken several measures aimed at infusing rupee as well as foreign exchange liquidity and to maintain credit flow to productive sectors of the economy. Measures aimed at expanding the rupee liquidity included significant reduction in the cash reserve ratio (CRR), reduction of the statutory liquidity ratio (SLR), opening a special repo window under the liquidity adjustment facility (LAF) for banks for on-lending to the non-banking financial companies (NBFCs), housing finance companies (HFCs) and mutual funds (MFs), and extending a special refinance facility, which banks can access without any collateral. The Reserve Bank is also

unwinding the Market Stabilisation Scheme (MSS) securities, roughly synchronised with the government borrowing programme, in order to manage liquidity.

15. Measures aimed at managing forex liquidity include upward adjustment of the interest rate ceilings on the foreign currency non-resident (banks) [FCNR(B)] and non-resident (external) rupee account [NR(E)RA] deposits, substantially relaxing the external commercial borrowings (ECB) regime, allowing the NBFCs and HFCs access to foreign borrowing and allowing corporates to buy back foreign currency convertible bonds (FCCBs) to take advantage of the discount in the prevailing depressed global markets. The Reserve Bank has also instituted a rupee-dollar swap facility for banks with overseas branches to give them comfort in managing their short-term funding requirements.

16. Measures to encourage flow of credit to sectors which are coming under pressure include extending the period of pre-shipment and post-shipment credit for exports, expanding the refinance facility for exports, counter-cyclical adjustment of provisioning norms for all types of standard assets (except in case of direct advances to agriculture and small and medium enterprises which continue to be at 0.25 per cent) and risk weights on banks' exposure to certain sectors which had been increased earlier counter-cyclically, and expanding the lendable resources available to the Small Industries Development Bank of India (SIDBI), the National Housing Bank (NHB) and the Export-Import Bank of India (EXIM Bank).

17. To improve the flow of credit to productive sectors at viable costs so as to sustain the growth momentum, the Reserve Bank signalled a lowering of the interest rate structure by reducing its key policy rate, viz. the repo rate by 250 basis points from 9.0 per cent as on October 19 to 6.5 per cent by December 8, 2008.

18. Although, we remain vulnerable to global financial and economic developments, the measures taken so far have eased the liquidity and credit flow situations considerably. ...that in managing the impact of the global crisis, we have been mindful that no policy initiative is totally costless. Managing this

delicate balance between costs and benefits has been one of our challenges.

19. The measures taken by the RBI have been appreciated and criticised. ...While some of the criticism has been fair and value adding, some of it stems from an inadequate appreciation of the RBI perspective....

20. Everyone is now agreed that the way forward on this crisis at the present time is too uncertain. Even today, it is not possible to clearly see the path of the crisis and its resolution over the coming months. It is just not possible to have a precise road map all laid out to be unleashed in one go. This crisis does not allow us that luxury. And, ...India is not unique in this respect. Almost every country, whether or not directly affected, is having to manage under uncertainty. There are simply too many unknown unknowns.

21. In the circumstances, the stance of the RBI has been to respond to the evolving situation swiftly and effectively, and to the extent possible, in anticipation of immediate developments. We do have a road map that is comprehensive and practical. It would be our endeavour to adapt this road map to the evolving global developments and implement it flexibly and pragmatically. Our approach, as indeed of every prudent central banker around the world, has been to "cross the river by feeling the stones". The RBI will continue to be on vigil and do everything possible within its mandate to mitigate the impact of the crisis on the Indian economy.

The Challenges Ahead

22. ...the major challenges facing the banking system in the country, particularly in the wake of the global financial crisis.

The First Challenge: Maintaining the Credit Flow

23. The outlook, both for the world and for India, continues to remain uncertain. The future trajectory of the global crisis is not yet clear. ...the year 2009-10 will be more challenging than the current one. There was a noticeable decline in the credit demand in the month of November 2008 but it is not yet clear if it was a one off episode or it reflects a trend. If it is indicative of slowing economic activity, it would

be a major challenge for the banks to ensure healthy flow of credit to the productive sectors of the economy. ...economic growth, even in normal times, requires efficient financial intermediation. An economic downturn, therefore, requires even more efficient financial intermediation—and this is a major challenge that the banking community has to address. There is a need to ensure a steady credit flow to the real sector of the economy in order to sustain demand even while maintaining credit quality.

24. There are two aspects to lending, viz. availability and cost of credit. While the availability of credit should not be an issue, the cost of credit seems to be an issue at the current juncture. There seem to be two reasons inhibiting the banks from extending credit: first, a high weighted-average cost of funds because of high interest rates on deposits; and second, concerns about credit quality, which makes the banks risk averse, particularly in lending to certain segments. During the last one month, there has been a sharp reversal in trend and, as noted earlier, credit demand seems to be slackening. The reduced funding demand on the banks should enable them to reduce the interest rates on deposit and thereby reduce the overall cost of funds. In addition, from a macro perspective the decelation of headline inflation noticed so far and the expectations of softening of inflation in the months ahead should enable a reduction in nominal interest rates. These developments in turn, would facilitate lending at lower interest rates, making fresh lending more viable and, at least partly obviating the risk aversion of the banks.

25. ...that the RBI, on its part, will continue to maintain adequate liquidity in the system to enable the flow of credit to the economy.

The Second Challenge: How Do We Reform Financial Sector Regulation?

26. By far, the most contentious and most voluble debate triggered by the crisis has been about the flaws in the regulatory architecture of the financial sector. Several issues have come to the fore. ...How can complex derivative products, which transmitted risks across the system, be made

more transparent? What are the financial stability implications of structured products like credit derivatives? Are exchange traded derivatives better than over-the-counter (OTC) derivatives? How do we eliminate the drawbacks of the 'originate-to-distribute' model? Is universal banking, the model that the United States has now turned to, appropriate? Can we apply the same regulatory regime for both wholesale and retail banks?

27. The burden of all the above questions is to identify the drawbacks in the present regulatory regimes and indicate possible solutions. There is no doubt that we must pursue all these questions. In doing so, I would urge that we remember two things. The first thing to remember is that no one size fits all. For example, universal banking may be good in some of the countries and in some of the situations, and not so in others. The second thing to remember is that some regulations, arguably, have been behind the curve. There is no denying that regulations have to keep pace with innovations in the financial markets but in doing so, we must be mindful of the risks of over-tightening the regulations lest they stifle innovation.

The Third Challenge: Regulatory Forbearance and Relaxing Regulatory Norms

28. There has been a sustained demand from various quarters for exercising regulatory forbearance in regard to extant prudential regulations applicable to the banking sector. As a part of counter-cyclical package, we have already made several changes to the current prudential norms. These include: (a) reduction in the risk weights for claims on unrated corporates and commercial real estate to 100 per cent; (b) reduction in the provisioning requirement for all standard assets to 0.40 per cent; (c) permitting housing loans to be restructured even if the revised payment period exceeds ten years; (d) making the restructured commercial real estate exposures eligible for special treatment if restructured before June 30, 2009.

29. There are demands for further regulatory forbearance. For example, there has been a demand to relax the asset classification norms by increasing the period of delinquency

beyond the current norm of 90 days after which the loan asset is required to be classified as non-performing. The objective underlying the demand is to permit the banks to avoid recognising non-performing loans (NPLs) for a longer period. Is it desirable to change the NPL norm by relaxing the 90-day rule? The demand is presumably premised on the argument that the relaxation in the norm will make the banks' financials look better, allow them to reserve less, conserve capital, and may even allow them to offer more credit (or at least not cut back on credit). However, there are several forceful arguments against the relaxation sought. Let me mention a few:

(i) Delay in recognition of NPL removes pressure on the banks to deal promptly with the problem. History suggests that delayed recognition of impairment in the value of the assets makes the problems only worse. The sooner banks restructure the loan (through, say, CDR mechanism) or, where appropriate, send the loan for collection, the better.

(ii) This global downturn is likely to be a prolonged one. If banks do not recognise their problem loans here and now, and deal with them expeditiously, the problem will only get compounded with the passage of time and will keep haunting them in future.

(iii) The prudential regulatory norms ought not to be changed lightly, especially when markets are on edge. If the impression gains ground that the modified norms under-state the extent of impairment and over-state the asset quality in the banking sector, the markets could suspect the worst and needlessly penalise the banks through market discipline.

30. These are the issues we need to reflect on in moving towards further regulatory forbearance.

The Fourth Challenge: Effective Implementation of Basel II Framework

31. As you are aware, a part of the Indian banking system has already migrated to the Basel II Framework effective March 31, 2008 and the remaining commercial banks are

slated to do so by March 31, 2009. However, having regard to the state of preparedness of the system, we have, for the present, adopted only the simpler approaches available under the Framework. The RBI is yet to announced the timeframe for adoption of the Advanced Approaches in the Indian banking system but the migration to these Approaches is the eventual goal—for which the banking system will need to start its preparations in all earnestness.

32. The migration to the Advanced Approaches poses several significant challenges to the bankers and, as the banking regulator and supervisor, also to the RBI. The first challenge is the availability of long time-series data for computing the risk parameters required under the Advanced Approaches. Good-quality, consistent and reliable data and information relating to the loan portfolios of the banks as also sophisticated IT resources are critical to the proper risk assessment under the Basel II Framework. Data limitation is a key impediment to the design and implementation of credit risk models. This may prove to be a major challenge for us in India, given the widespread branch network—though the increasing computerisation in the banking industry should prove to be of great help.

33. The second challenge is that the Advanced Approaches for credit risk and operational risk envisaged under the Basel II Framework also require use of risk models by the banks. This, in turn, requires internal validation of these models by the banks themselves as also by the supervisors before the models can be permitted to be used for regulatory capital purposes. Such a validation process demands expert skills which need to be developed and nurtured.

34. Third, since Basel II Framework is primarily about ensuring robust risk management in the banks, its effective implementation, particularly the Advanced Approaches, will demand rapid and significant upgradation of skills—both at the level of the banking system as also within the RBI. In this context, the challenge that banks are likely to face will be multi-faceted, *viz.*, assessing skill requirements, identifying and bridging the gaps, identifying talents, putting the available

talents to optimum use, attracting fresh talents, retention of talents, and change management. Banks would, therefore, need to pay special attention to strengthening their risk management infrastructure, in all its dimensions, including the human resources. We, in the RBI, are mindful of our part of the challenges in this regard and are taking necessary measures.

35. The implementation of Basel II requires closer cooperation, information sharing and co-ordination of policies among sectoral supervisors, specially in the context of financial conglomerates. The existence of separate supervisory authorities to regulate different segments of the markets within a jurisdiction may create challenges in implementation of Basel II not only within a jurisdiction but also across jurisdictions—which would require effective cross-border supervisory cooperation and co-ordination.

The Fifth Challenge: The Challenge of Banking Development and Financial Inclusion in Eastern India

36. Banking development in the eastern region of the country, as measured by several parameters, is lagging behind the national average. Let me give some evidence to illustrate this.

- In March 2008, the all-India per branch population coverage was 15,400. For the eastern region, the figure varied from 25,000 in Bihar to 9,600 in Sikkim.
- In March 2007, at the all-India level, the per capita deposit was Rs. 28,600. The corresponding figure for the eastern region was Rs. 14,400. Similarly, as against the per capita credit of Rs. 28,600 at the all-India level, the corresponding figure for the eastern region is only Rs. 7,200.
- In March 2007, at the all-India level, the population of people having bank accounts was 41 per cent. The corresponding population for the eastern region was only 30.7 per cent, ranging from 21.1 per cent for Bihar to 39.6 per cent for West Bengal.

- In March 2007, at the all-India level, the credit-deposit ratio was 74.5 per cent. For the eastern region, the ratio was just 50 per cent.

37. In terms of infrastructure coverage and other development indicators, the eastern region is not as developed as other regions of the country. Admittedly, this affects the credit absorption capacity and may also explain some of the lagging parameters mentioned above. However, this cannot be an excuse for inaction. It should be impetus for vigorous action.

38. Finance can lead development just as much as it can be led by it. This is specially true for the poor. Nearly a third of the people of Bihar and West Bengal are below the poverty line. Through greater financial inclusion it should be possible to provide savings, loan and insurance products at affordable prices and this can generate income and employment in a very significant measure.

39. We must recognise that the opportunity cost of formal finance for the borrower is so high that mere financial inclusion can unlock value that today is accruing to rentiers and informal finance providers. This apart, transaction costs can be reduced through the kind of scale of operations that only banks are capable of achieving and this itself become a source of value creation.

40. Financial inclusion cannot be reduced to a mere number game. The actual impact of financial inclusion and expanded banking coverage must be felt at the grass-root level. I find that a number of measures have been initiated to deepen the banking penetration in the region. For example, in West Bengal, a Task Force for extending banking facilities in unbanked Gram Panchayats (GP) was constituted by the State Level Bankers' Committee in December 2007. The task force has identified 511 GPs at which bank branches will be opened in next three years and at 427 GP-centres in the following three years. I understand that the State Government has agreed to provide premises adjacent to the GP offices and extend other facilities like road connection and power at such centres.

41. Where a full-fledged branch cannot be opened immediately, banks could look at covering the unbanked areas through satellite offices, weekly branches, or use the business correspondent model for ensuring greater coverage within a shorter period. Information Technology (IT) solutions should also be explored for providing a backbone of credit information, customer information apart from facilitating more efficient credit delivery and reducing cost of payments and remittances.

42. I understand there has been an interesting and innovative experiment undertaken in West Bengal for promoting financial inclusion. A Financial Inclusion/Literacy Campaign was launched in an urban slum area viz., the Basanti Colony, Ultadanga, Kolkata in mid-October 2008 in association with six commercial banks. These banks are the State Bank of India, United Bank of India, UCO Bank, Allahabad Bank, Bank of India and Bank of Baroda—which had branches in the vicinity of the slum area. All six banks were allotted separate counters for opening of accounts as well as to campaign for their bank-specific products. Free photo facility for account holders was provided and the cost was shared by all the participating banks. The initiatives such as this should be pursued and the full range of financial services provided to these areas. I understand that the Local Council extended support for obtaining identity documents required for opening of bank accounts. This experiment demonstrates what banks can do if only they are responsive, sensitive, proactive and result oriented.

43. Coming to sectoral flow of credit, while the share of agriculture in the State's SDP is higher than at the all-India level, the share of agricultural credit in total credit is roughly the same for the State. This points to the need to look at bankable schemes in the agriculture sector. Also, NABARD has a very significant role to play in this region. As the micro and small enterprises account for 7.2 per cent of total credit in the region, SIDBI too, as a development finance institution, has to play a prominent role in accelerating and catalysing the flow of bank credit to the MSE sector in the region.

44. Although not often acknowledged, effective financial intermediation has been one of the important factors behind India's recent growth episode. Efficient financial intermediation is a formidable challenge where poverty and disadvantage are high. You, as senior bank managers in the eastern region of the country, have a bigger challenge and greater opportunity. A bigger challenge because you have to be even more efficient than elsewhere, and a greater opportunity because by being responsive and sensitive, you can make "a bigger difference".

Conclusion

45. Going forward, developments in the real economy, financial markets and global commodity prices point to a period of moderation in growth with declining inflation. What is heartening though is that the fundamentals of our economy continue to be strong. Once calm and confidence are restored in the global markets, economic activity in India will recover sharply. But a period of painful adjustment is inevitable. It is our collective challenge—for you, the bankers, and for us at the RBI—to respond to this extraordinary situation effectively and return India to its path of growth and poverty reduction.

2

Global Financial Crisis and Key Risks: Impact on India and Asia*

*Rakesh Mohan***

The turmoil in the international financial markets of advanced economies, that started around mid-2007, has exacerbated substantially since August 2008. The financial market crisis has led to the collapse of major financial institutions and is now beginning to impact the real economy in the advanced economies. As this crisis is unfolding, credit markets appear to be drying up in the developed world. With the substantive increase in financial globalisation, how much will these developments affect India and other Asian emerging market economies (EMEs)?

India, like most other emerging market economies, has so far, not been seriously affected by the recent financial turmoil in developed economies..., I will, first, briefly set out reasons for the relative resilience shown by the Indian economy to the ongoing international financial markets' crisis. This will be followed by some discussion of the impact till date on the Indian economy and the likely implications in the near future. I then outline our approach to the management of the exposures of the Indian financial sector entities to the collapse of major

---

* *Courtsey*: www.rbi.org.in

** Based on remarks by Dr. Rakesh Mohan, Deputy Governor at IMF-FSF High-Level Meeting on the Recent Financial Turmoil and Policy Responses at Washington DC on October 9, 2008. The assistance of Meena Hemachandra, Chandan Sinha, R.K. Pattnaik, Amitava Sardar and Muneesh Kapur in preparation of the remarks is gratefully acknowledged.

financial institutions in the US. Orderly conditions have been maintained in the domestic financial markets, which is attributable to a range of instruments available with the monetary authority to manage a variety of situations. Finally, I would briefly set out my thinking on the extent of vulnerability of the Asian economies, in general, to the global financial market crisis.

Financial Globalisation: The Indian Approach

The Indian economy is now a relatively open economy, despite the capital account not being fully open. The current account, as measured by the sum of current receipts and current payments, amounted to about 53 per cent of GDP in 2007-08, up from about 19 per cent of GDP in 1991. Similarly, on the capital account, the sum of gross capital inflows and outflows increased from 12 per cent of GDP in 1990-91 to around 64 per cent in 2007-08.[1] With this degree of openness, developments in international markets are bound to affect the Indian economy and policy makers have to be vigilant in order to minimize the impact of adverse international developments on the domestic economy.

The relatively limited impact of the ongoing turmoil in financial markets of the advanced economies in the Indian financial markets, and more generally the Indian economy, needs to be assessed in this context. Whereas the Indian current account has been opened fully, though gradually, over the 1990s, a more calibrated approach has been followed to the opening of the capital account and to opening up of the financial sector. This approach is consistent with the weight of the available empirical evidence with regard to the benefits that may be gained from capital account liberalisation for acceleration of economic growth, particularly in emerging market economies. The evidence suggests that the greatest gains are obtained from the opening to foreign direct investment, followed by portfolio equity investment. The benefits emanating from external debt flows have been found to be more questionable until greater domestic financial market development has taken place (Henry, 2007; Prasad, Rajan and Subramanian, 2007).

Accordingly, in India, while encouraging foreign investment flows, especially direct investment inflows, a more cautious, nuanced approach has been adopted in regard to debt flows. Debt flows in the form of external commercial borrowings are subject to ceilings and some end-use restrictions, which are modulated from time to time taking into account evolving macro-economic and monetary conditions. Similarly, portfolio investment in government securities and corporate bonds are also subject to macro ceilings, which are also modulated from time to time. Thus, prudential policies have attempted to prevent excessive recourse to foreign borrowings and dollarisation of the economy. In regard to capital outflows, the policy framework has been progressively liberalised to enable the non-financial corporate sector to invest abroad and to acquire companies in the overseas market. Resident individuals are also permitted outflows subject to reasonable limits.

The financial sector, especially banks, is subject to prudential regulations, both in regard to capital and liquidity (Mohan, 2007b). As the current global financial crisis has shown, liquidity risks can rise manifold during a crisis and can pose serious downside risks to macro-economic and financial stability. The Reserve Bank had already put in place steps to mitigate liquidity risks at the very short-end, risks at the systemic level and at the institution level as well. Some of the important measures by the Reserve Bank in this regard include, first, restricting the overnight unsecured market for funds to banks and primary dealers (PD) as well as limits on the borrowing and lending operations of these entities in the overnight inter-bank call money market. Second, large reliance by banks on borrowed funds can exacerbate vulnerability to external shocks. This has been brought out quite strikingly in the ongoing financial crisis in the global financial markets. Accordingly, in order to encourage greater reliance on stable sources of funding, the Reserve Bank has imposed prudential limits on banks on their purchased inter-bank liabilities and these limits are linked to their net worth. Furthermore, the incremental credit deposit ratio of banks is also monitored by the Reserve Bank since this ratio indicates the extent to which banks are funding credit with borrowings from wholesale markets (now known as purchased funds). Third, asset liability management guidelines for dealing with overall asset-liability mismatches take into account both on and off balance sheet items. Finally, guidelines on securitization of standard assets have laid down a detailed policy on provision of liquidity support to Special Purpose Vehicles (SPVs).

In order to further strengthen capital requirements, the credit conversion factors, risk weights and provisioning requirements for specific off-balance sheet items including derivatives have been reviewed. Furthermore, in India, complex structures like synthetic securitisation have not been permitted so far. Introduction of such products, when found appropriate, would be guided by the risk management capabilities of the system.

The Reserve Bank has also issued detailed guidelines on implementation of the Basel II framework covering all the three pillars with the guidelines on Pillar II being issued as recently as on March 27, 2008. In tune with RBI's objective to have consistency and harmony with international standards, the Standardised Approach for credit risk and Basic Indicator Approach for operational risk have been prescribed. Minimum capital-to-risk-weighted asset ratio (CRAR) would be 9 per cent, but higher levels under Pillar II could be prescribed on the basis of risk profile and risk management systems. The banks have been asked to bring Tier I CRAR to at least 6 per cent before March 31, 2010. After analyzing the global schedule for implementation, it was decided that all foreign banks operating in India and Indian banks having a presence outside India should migrate to Basel II by March 31, 2008 and all other scheduled commercial banks encouraged to migrate to Basel II in alignment with them but not later than March 31, 2009.

In addition to the exercise of normal prudential requirements on banks, the Reserve Bank has also successively imposed additional prudential measures in respect of exposures to particular sectors, akin to a policy of dynamic provisioning. For example, in view of the accelerated exposure observed to the real estate sector, banks were advised to put in place a proper risk management system to contain the risks involved. Banks were advised to formulate specific policies covering exposure limits, collaterals to be considered, margins to be kept, sanctioning authority/level and sector to be financed. In view of the rapid increase in loans to the real estate sector raising concerns about asset quality and the potential systemic risks posed by such exposure, the risk weight on banks' exposure to commercial real estate was increased from 100 per cent to 125 per cent in July 2005 and further to 150 per cent in April 2006. The risk weight on housing loans extended by banks to individuals against mortgage of housing properties and investments in mortgage backed securities (MBS) of housing finance companies (HFCs) was increased from 50 per cent to 75 per cent in December 2004, though this was later reduced to 50 per cent for lower value loans. Similarly, in light of the strong growth of consumer credit and the volatility in the capital markets, it was felt that the quality of lending could suffer during the phase of rapid expansion. Hence, as a counter-cyclical measure, the Reserve Bank increased the risk weight for consumer credit and capital market exposures from 100 per cent to 125 per cent.[2]

An additional feature of recent prudential actions by the Reserve Bank relate to the tightening of regulation and supervision of Non-banking Financial Companies (NBFCs), so that regulatory arbitrage between these companies and the banking system is minimized. The overarching principle is that banks should not use an NBFC as a delivery vehicle for seeking regulatory arbitrage opportunities or to circumvent bank regulation(s) and that the activities of NBFCs do not undermine banking regulations. Thus, capital adequacy ratios and prudential limits to single/group exposures in the case of NBFCs have been progressively brought nearer to those applicable to banks. The regulatory interventions are graded: higher in deposit-taking NBFCs and lower in non-deposit-taking NBFCs. Thus, excessive leverage in this sector has been contained.

Various segments of the domestic financial market have been developed over a period of time to facilitate efficient channelling of resources form savers to investors and enable the continuation of domestic growth momentum (Mohan, 2007a). Investment has been predominantly financed domestically in India—the current account deficit has averaged between one and two per cent of GDP since the early 1990s. The Government's fiscal deficit has been high by international standards but is also largely internally financed through a vibrant and well developed government securities market, and thus, despite large fiscal deficits, macro-economic and financial stability has been maintained. Derivative instruments have been introduced cautiously in a phased manner, both for product diversity and, more importantly, as a risk management tool. All these developments have facilitated the process of price discovery in various financial market segments.

The rate of increase in foreign exchange market turnover in India between April 2004 and April 2007 was the highest amongst the 54 countries covered in the latest Triennial Central Bank Survey of Foreign Exchange and Derivatives Market Activity conducted by the Bank for International Settlements (BIS). According to the survey, daily average turnover in India jumped almost 5-fold from US $ 7 billion in April 2004 to US $ 34 billion in April 2007; the share of India in global foreign exchange market turnover trebled from 0.3 per cent in April 2004 to 0.9 per cent in April 2007. There has been consistent development of well-functioning, relatively deep and liquid markets for government securities, currency and derivatives in India, though much further development needs to be done. However, as large segments of economic agents in India may not have adequate resilience to withstand volatility in currency and money markets, our approach has been to be increasingly vigilant and proactive to any incipient signs of volatility in financial markets.

In brief, the Indian approach has focused on gradual, phased and calibrated opening of the domestic financial and external sectors, taking into cognizance reforms in the other sectors of the economy. Financial markets are contributing to efficient channelling of domestic savings into productive uses and, by financing the overwhelming part of domestic investment, are supporting domestic growth. These characteristics of India's external and financial sector management coupled with ample forex reserves coverage and the growing underlying strength of the Indian economy reduce the susceptibility of the Indian economy to global turbulence.

Impact of the Crisis on India

While the overall policy approach has been able to mitigate the potential impact of the turmoil on domestic financial markets and the economy, with the increasing integration of the Indian economy and its financial markets with rest of the world, there is recognition that the country does face some downside risks from these international developments. The risks arise mainly from the potential reversal of capital flows on a sustained medium-term basis from the projected slow down of the global economy, particularly in advanced economies, and from some elements of potential financial contagion. In India, the adverse effects have so far been mainly in the equity markets because of reversal of portfolio equity flows, and the concomitant effects on the domestic forex market and liquidity conditions. The macro effects have so far been muted due to the overall strength of domestic demand, the healthy balance sheets of the Indian corporate sector, and the predominant domestic financing of investment.

As might be expected, the main impact of the global financial turmoil in India has emanated from the significant change experienced in the capital account in 2008-09 so far, relative to the previous year (Table 1). Total net capital flows fell from US$17.3 billion in April-June 2007 to US$13.2 billion in April-June 2008. Nonetheless, capital flows are expected to be more than sufficient to cover the current account deficit this year as well. While Foreign Direct Investment (FDI) inflows have continued to exhibit accelerated growth (US$ 16.7 billion during April-August 2008 as compared with US$ 8.5 billion in the corresponding period of 2007), portfolio investments by foreign institutional investors (FIIs) witnessed a net outflow of about US$ 6.4 billion in April-September 2008 as compared with a net inflow of US$ 15.5 billion in the corresponding period last year.

Similarly, external commercial borrowings of the corporate sector declined from US$ 7.0 billion in April-June 2007 to US$ 1.6 billion in April-June 2008, partially in response to policy measures in the face of excess flows in 2007-08, but also due to the current turmoil in advanced economies. With the existence of a merchandise trade deficit of 7.7 per cent of GDP in 2007-08, and a current account deficit of 1.5 per cent, and change in perceptions with respect to capital flows, there has been significant pressure on the Indian exchange rate in recent months. Whereas the real exchange rate appreciated from an index of 104.9 (base 1993-94 = 100) (US$1 = Rs. 46.12) in September 2006 to 115.0 (US$ 1 = Rs. 40.34) in September 2007, it has now depreciated to a level of 101.5 (US$1 = Rs. 48.74) as on October 8, 2008.

Table 1: Trends in Capital Flows

(US $ million)

Component	Period	2007-08	2008-09
Foreign Direct Investment to India	April-August	8,536	16,733
FIIs (net)@	April-September 26	15,508	-6,421
External Commercial Borrowings (net)	April-June	6,990	1,559
Short-term Trade Credits (net)	April-June	1,804	2,173
Memo:			
ECB Approvals	April-August	13,375	8,127
Foreign Exchange Reserves (variation)	April-September 26	48,583	-17,904
Foreign Exchange Reserves (end-period)	September 26, 2008	247,762	291,819

Note: Data on FIIs presented in this table represent inflows into the country and, thus, may differ from data relating to net investment in stock exchanges by FIIs.

With the volatility in portfolio flows having been large during 2007 and 2008, the impact of global financial turmoil has been felt particularly in the equity market. The BSE Sensex (1978-79 = 100) increased significantly from a level of 13,072 as at end-March 2007 to its peak of 20,873 on January 8, 2008 in the presence of heavy portfolio flows responding to the high growth performance of the Indian corporate sector. With portfolio flows reversing in 2008, partly because of the international market turmoil, the Sensex has now dropped to a level of 11,328 on October 8, 2008, in line with similar large declines in other major stock markets.

As noted earlier, domestic investment is largely financed by domestic savings. However, the corporate sector has, in recent years, mobilized significant resources from global financial markets for funding, both debt and non-debt, their ambitious investment plans. The current risk aversion in the international financial markets to EMEs could, therefore, have some impact on the Indian corporate sector's ability to raise funds from international sources and thereby impede some investment growth. Such corporates would, therefore, have to rely relatively more on domestic sources of financing, including bank credit. This could, in turn, put some upward pressure on domestic interest rates. Moreover, domestic primary capital market issuances have suffered in the current fiscal year so far in view of the sluggish stock market conditions. Thus, one can expect more demand for bank credit, and non-food credit growth has indeed accelerated in the current year (26.2 per cent on a year-on-year basis as on September 12, 2008 as compared with 23.3 per cent a year ago).

The financial crisis in the advanced economies and the likely slowdown in these economies could have some impact on the IT sector. According to the latest assessment by the NASSCOM, the software trade association, the current developments with respect to the US financial markets are very eventful, and may have a direct impact on the IT industry and likely to create a downstream impact on other sectors of the US economy and worldwide markets. About 15 per cent to 18 per cent of the business coming to Indian outsourcers includes projects from banking, insurance, and the financial services sector which is now uncertain.

In summary, the combined impact of the reversal of portfolio equity flows, the reduced availability of international capital both debt and equity, the perceived increase in the price of equity with lower equity valuations, and pressure on the exchange rate, growth in the Indian corporate sector is likely to feel some impact of the global financial turmoil. On the other hand, on a macro basis, with external savings utilisation having been low traditionally, between one to two per cent of GDP, and the sustained high domestic savings rate, this impact can be expected to be at the margin. Moreover, the continued buoyancy of foreign direct investment suggests that confidence in Indian growth prospects remains healthy.

Impact on the Indian Banking System

One of the key features of the current financial turmoil has been the lack of perceived contagion being felt by banking systems in EMEs, particularly in Asia. The Indian banking system also has not experienced any contagion, similar to its peers in the rest of Asia.

A detailed study undertaken by the RBI in September 2007 on the impact of the sub-prime episode on the Indian banks had revealed that none of the Indian banks or the foreign banks, with whom the discussions had been held, had any direct exposure to the sub-prime markets in the USA or other markets. However, a few Indian banks had invested in the collateralised debt obligations (CDOs)/bonds which had a few underlying entities with sub-prime exposures. Thus, no direct impact on account of *direct exposure* to the sub-prime market was in evidence. However, a few of these banks did suffer some losses on account of the mark-to-market losses caused by the widening of the credit spreads arising from the sub-prime episode on term liquidity in the market, even though the overnight markets remained stable.

Consequent upon filling of bankruptcy under Chapter 11 by Lehman Brothers, all banks were advised to report the details of their exposures to Lehman Brothers and related entities both in India and abroad. Out of 77 reporting banks, 14 reported exposures to Lehman Brothers and its related entities either in India or abroad. An analysis of the information reported by these banks revealed that majority of the exposures reported by the banks pertained to subsidiaries of Lehman Bros Holdings Inc. which are not covered by the bankruptcy proceedings. Overall, these banks' exposure especially to Lehman Brothers Holding Inc. which has filed for bankruptcy is not significant and banks are reported to have made adequate provisions.

In the aftermath of the turmoil caused by bankruptcy, the Reserve Bank has announced a series of measures to facilitate orderly operation of financial markets and to ensure financial stability which predominantly includes extension of additional liquidity support to banks.

RBI Response to the Crisis

The financial crisis in advanced economies on the back of sub-prime turmoil has been accompanied by near drying up of trust amongst major financial market and sector players, in view of mounting losses and elevated uncertainty about further possible losses and erosion of capital. The lack of trust amongst the major players has led to near freezing of the uncollateralized inter-bank money market, reflected in large spreads over policy rates. In response to these developments, central banks in major advanced economies have taken a number of coordinated steps to increase short-term liquidity. Central banks in some cases have substantially loosened the collateral requirements to provide the necessary short-term liquidity.

In contrast to the extreme volatility leading to freezing of money markets in major advanced economies, money markets in India have been, by and large, functioning in an orderly fashion, albeit with some pressures. Large swings in capital flows—as has been experienced between 2007-08 and 2008-09 so far—in response to the global financial market turmoil have made the conduct of monetary policy and liquidity management more complicated in the recent months. However, the Reserve Bank has been effectively able to manage domestic liquidity and monetary conditions consistent with its monetary policy stance.

This has been enabled by the appropriate use of a range of instruments available for liquidity management with the Reserve Bank such as the Cash Reserve Ratio (CRR) and Statutory Liquidity Ratio (SLR)[3] stipulations and open market operations (OMO) including the Market Stabilisation Scheme (MSS)[4] and the Liquidity Adjustment Facility (LAF). Furthermore, money market liquidity is also impacted by our operations in the foreign exchange market, which, in turn, reflect the evolving capital flows. While in 2007 and the previous years, large capital flows and their absorption by the Reserve Bank led to excessive liquidity, which was absorbed through sterilisation operations involving LAF, MSS and CRR. During 2008, in view of some reversal in capital flows, market sale of foreign exchange by the Reserve Bank has led to withdrawal of liquidity from the banking system. The daily LAF repo operations have emerged as the primary tool for meeting the liquidity gap in the market. In view of the reversal of capital flows, fresh MSS issuances have been scaled down and there has also been some unwinding of the outstanding MSS balances. The MSS operates symmetrically and has the flexibility to smoothen liquidity in the banking system both during episodes of capital inflows and outflows. The existing set of monetary instruments has, thus, provided adequate flexibility to manage the evolving situation. In view of this flexibility, unlike central banks in major advanced economies, the Reserve Bank did not have to invent new instruments or to dilute the collateral requirements to inject liquidity. LAF repo operations are, however, limited by the excess SLR securities held by banks.

While LAF and MSS have been able to bear a large part of the burden, some modulations in CRR and SLR have also been resorted, purely as temporary measures, to meet the liquidity mismatches. For instance, on September 16, 2008, in regard to SLR, the Reserve Bank permitted banks to use up to an additional 1 per cent of their NDTL, for a temporary period, for drawing liquidity support under LAF from RBI. This has imparted a sense of confidence in the market in terms of availability of short-term liquidity. The CRR which had been gradually increased from 4.5 per cent in 2004 to 9 per cent by August 2008 was cut by 50 basis points on October 6[5] (to be effective October 11, 2008)—the first cut after a gap of over five years—on a review of the liquidity situation in the context of global and domestic developments. Thus, as the very recent experience shows, temporary changes in the prudential ratios such as CRR and SLR combined with flexible use of the MSS, could be considered as a vast pool of back-up liquidity that is available for liquidity management as the situation may warrant for relieving market pressure at any given time. The recent innovation with respect to SLR for combating temporary systemic illiquidity is particularly noteworthy. The relative stability in domestic financial markets, despite extreme turmoil in the global financial markets, is reflective of prudent practices, strengthened reserves and the strong growth performance in recent years in an environment of flexibility in the conduct of policies.

Active liquidity management is a key element of the current monetary policy stance. Liquidity modulation through a flexible use of a combination of instruments has, to a significant extent, cushioned the impact of the international financial turbulence on domestic financial markets by absorbing excessive market pressures and ensuring orderly conditions. In view of the evolving environment of heightened uncertainty, volatility in global markets and the dangers of potential spillovers to domestic equity and currency markets, liquidity management will continue to receive priority in the hierarchy of policy objectives over the period ahead. The Reserve Bank will continue with its policy of active demand management of liquidity through appropriate use of the CRR stipulations and open market operations (OMO) including the MSS and the LAF, using all the policy instruments at its disposal flexibly, as and when the situation warrants.

Impact on Asian EMEs

In contrast to the previous episodes of global turmoil, EMEs have exhibited relative resilience, though equity market and exchange rate pressures have intensified in recent days. So far, the investment sentiment is positive for the Asian EMEs reflecting their strong economic performance and, for some countries, favourable investment opportunities associated with elevated commodity prices, though they have adjusted downwards in recent times, while being somewhat volatile.

Credit policy reforms, better structuring of banking sector debt and improved fiscal positions have also played their role making the EMEs resilient from the crisis. In addition, large foreign exchange reserves, particularly in Asia, also provide a degree of protection against possible sudden stops. Another factor that could be of relevance for this favourable situation is the relatively smaller presence of foreign banks in the Asian banking sector. This is evident from the fact that the share of banking assets held by foreign banks in these economies generally lies between 0 and 10 per cent (Global Development Finance, 2008).

The spillovers to the EMEs from the current global financial market crisis have occurred mainly in and through financial markets, reflecting the relatively high level of integration of such markets in the global financial system. In this respect, there have been four major spillovers, *viz.*, (i) a rise in the price of risk; (ii) a reduction in international bond issuance; (iii) a sell-off in equity markets; and (iv) some unwinding of carry-trade positions. The major EMEs in Asia have been recording surpluses on the current account in recent years, with the exception of Korea and India. Thus, the vulnerability of Asia, other than Korea and India, is relatively contained to that extent. It is in this context the foreign exchange markets in India and Korea have experienced greater pressure in recent times.

Despite the fact that no significant macro-economic disruption has taken place in EMEs, some vulnerabilities exist. There are indications that the current crisis will have some implications in terms of higher funding costs and raising external finance, particularly, for lower rated firms. Further, countries with significant foreign bank presence, mostly in East European economies, might be vulnerable to financial stress faced by a parent bank. Similarly, slowdown in advanced countries might impact the remittances to EMEs.

As regards the impact of financial turbulence on the real sector, Asian EMEs may not be entirely immune to slowing growth in developed economies. For East Asian economies, since most of these economies are small and their trade sector (export plus imports) as proportion of GDP varies at a significantly higher level between over 200 per cent and 60 per cent as opposed to the weight of domestic demand as in India, it could be an area of concern for these countries. Therefore, for these set of countries, the crises could be transmitted through the trade channel. While strong regional sources of growth within EMEs may be a mitigating factor, most EMEs still retain substantial trade linkages with developed economies. In Asia, while intra-regional trade has been growing rapidly over recent years, much of this activity is still driven by developed economies as a major destination for final goods.

According to the analysis contained in the IMF's latest Global Financial Stability Report (October 2008) (IMF, 2008a), both domestic and global factors are important in explaining the movement in equity prices in the EMEs. Correlation of equity markets in EMEs with those in the advanced economies has risen, suggesting a growing transmission channel for equity price movements. Amongst the three group of EMEs (Latin America, Asia and Emerging Europe), the spillover from global factors is found to be strongest in Latin American EMEs followed by Emerging Europe and Asia. The wealth effect of stock market changes on consumption and investment, although statistically significant, is found to be weaker in EMEs *vis-à-vis* the advanced economies. Furthermore, such wealth effects tend to play out gradually.

During the financial turmoil, commodity prices may have been pushed higher to some extent by increased demand for commodities as a hedge against a depreciating US dollar and possibly also as a hedge against higher inflation. As global growth slows, a fall in commodity prices represents a downside risk to commodity-exporting EMEs, which is particularly relevant for some Latin American EMEs. In an extreme scenario, where commodity prices fall dramatically, this could have significant implications for economies that have had a heavy reliance on the performance of commodities in recent years, and might furthermore pose some risks to the financial stability in these countries. On the other hand, Asian EMEs which are commodity importers may benefit from the correction in global commodity prices. This may alleviate inflationary pressures in these economies and may provide the necessary flexibility to monetary policy in these countries. However, the beneficial impact of softening commodity prices is getting partly eroded by the depreciation pressures in some of the EMEs, thus, limiting to some extent the manoeuvrability available to the monetary policy.

Overall, while the real sector in the major Asian EMEs has held up relatively well, it needs to be recognised that the financial crisis in the US has deepened significantly over the past couple of months and there are signs of its spreading to the mature economies in Europe. The deepening and widening of the financial crisis is already getting reflecting in elevated volatility in the financial markets of key EMEs and widening of spreads of the EME assets. Although a large amount of liquidity has been injected by the central banks of the major advanced economies, short-term market rates remain well above policy rates. Financing costs for the EMEs have increased over the past few weeks and could thus deteriorate in the coming months. If the financial crisis were to linger longer and the economic activity in these regions slows down significantly, the adverse impact on the real economies in the major EMEs could turn out to be stronger than that has been observed so far. According to the IMF's latest World Economic Outlook (October 2008) (IMF, 2008b), major advanced economies are already in or close to recession and the recovery is likely to be unusually gradual. Global output growth [at purchasing power parity (PPP) exchange rates] is now seen at 3.0 per cent in 2009, down from the likely 3.9 per cent in 2008 and the robust growth of almost 5 per cent each during 2006 and 2007. Growth in advanced economies is projected to decelerate from an average of 2.8 per cent during 2006-2007 to 1.5 per cent in 2008 and only 0.5 per cent in 2009. Policy rates have been cut in a coordinated manner, an unprecedented move, by central banks of major advanced economies on October 8, 2008 in view of the substantial downside risks to growth. Thus, financial headwinds—both through reduced capital flows, widening of spreads and elevated volatility in domestic financial markets of the EMEs and through weakening of demand in major advanced economies—have increased downside risks of the major EMEs, especially for the relatively more open economies in the region.

Concluding Observations

India has by-and-large been spared of global financial contagion due to the sub-prime turmoil for a variety of reasons. India's growth process has been largely domestic demand driven and its reliance on foreign savings has remained around 1.5 per cent in recent period. It also has a very comfortable level of forex reserves. The credit derivatives market is in an embryonic stage; the originate-to-distribute model in India is not comparable to the ones prevailing in advanced markets; there are restrictions on investments by residents in such products issued abroad; and regulatory guidelines on securitisation do not permit immediate profit recognition. Financial stability in India has been achieved through perseverance of prudential policies which prevent institutions from excessive risk taking, and financial markets from becoming extremely volatile and turbulent.

ANNEX I

Financial Stability Forum (FSF) Report: Status

In the wake of the turmoil in global financial markets, the FSF brought out a report in April 2008 identifying the underlying causes and weaknesses in the international financial markets. The Report contains, *inter alia*, proposals of the FSF for implementation by end-2008 regarding strengthening prudential oversight of capital, liquidity and risk management, enhancing transparency and valuation, changing the role and uses of credit ratings, strengthening the authorities' responsiveness to risk and implementing robust arrangements for dealing with stress in the financial system. The Reserve Bank had put in place regulatory guidelines covering many of these aspects, while in regard to others, actions are being initiated. In many cases, actions have to be considered as work-in-progress. In any case, the guidelines are aligned with global best practices while tailoring them to meet country-specific requirements at the current stage of institutional developments. The proposals made by the FSF and status in regard to each in India are narrated below:

1. Strengthened Prudential Oversight of Capital, Liquidity and Risk Management

(i) Capital requirements

Specific proposals will be issued in 2008 to:

- Raise Basel II capital requirements for certain complex structured credit products;
- Introduce additional capital charges for default and event risk in the trading books of banks and securities firms;
- Strengthen the capital treatment of liquidity facilities to off-balance sheet conduits.

Changes will be implemented over time to avoid exacerbating short-term stress.

(ii) Liquidity

Supervisory guidance will be issued by July 2008 for the supervision and management of liquidity risks.

(iii) Oversight of risk management

Guidance for supervisory reviews under Basel II will be developed that will:

- Strengthen oversight of banks' identification and management of firm-wide risks;
- Strengthen oversight of banks' stress testing practices for risk management and capital planning purposes;
- Require banks to soundly manage and report off-balance sheet exposures.

Supervisors will use Basel II to ensure banks' risk management, capital buffers and estimates of potential credit losses are appropriately forward looking.

(iv) Over-the-counter derivatives

Authorities will encourage market participants to act promptly to ensure that the settlement, legal and operational infrastructure for over-the-counter derivatives is sound.

The road-map for the implementation of Basel II in India has been designed to suit the country-specific conditions. The phased implementation process got underway with the Basel II Accord being made applicable to foreign banks operating in India and Indian banks having operational presence outside India with effect from March 31, 2008. All other commercial banks (except Local Area Banks and RRBs) are encouraged to migrate to Basel II in alignment with them but in any case not later than March 31, 2009. The process of implementation is being monitored on an ongoing basis for calibration and fine-tuning.

The minimum capital to risk-weighted asset ratio (CRAR) in India is placed at 9 per cent, one percentage point above the Basel II requirement. Further, regular monitoring of banks' exposure to sensitive sectors and their liquidity position is also undertaken. In India, off-balance sheet vehicles in the form of SPVs for the purpose of securitisation are in existence for which extensive guidelines, in line with the international best practices, have already been issued. Liquidity facilities to such SPVs are subject to capital charge. Banks have been required to put in place appropriate stress test policies and relevant stress test frameworks for various risk factors by March 31, 2008.

In order to further strengthen capital requirements, the credit conversion factors, risk weights and provisioning requirements for specific off-balance sheet items including derivatives have been reviewed. Further, in India, complex structures like synthetic securitisation have not been permitted so far. Introduction of such products, when found appropriate, would be guided by the risk management capabilities of the system.

The Reserve Bank had issued broad guidelines for asset-liability management and banks have flexibility in devising their own risk management strategies as per board-approved policies. However, in regard to liquidity risks at the very short end, the Reserve Bank has taken steps to mitigate risks at the systemic level and at the institution level as well. The Reserve Bank has introduced greater granularity to measurement of liquidity risk by splitting the first time bucket (1-14 days, at present) into three time buckets, *viz.,* next day, 2-7 days and 8-14 days. The net cumulative negative mismatches in the three time buckets have been capped at 5 per cent, 10 per cent, and 15 per cent of the cumulative cash outflows.

The Reserve Bank had recognised the risks of allowing access to unsecured overnight market funds to all entities and, therefore, restricted the overnight unsecured market for funds only to banks and primary dealers (PD). Since August 2005, the overnight call market is a pure inter-bank market. Accordingly, trading volumes have shifted from the overnight unsecured market to the collateralised market.

Greater inter-linkages and excessive reliance on call money borrowings by banks could cause systemic problems. The Reserve Bank has, therefore, introduced prudential measures to address the extent to which banks can borrow and lend in the call money market. On a fortnightly average basis, call market borrowings outstanding should not exceed 100 per cent of capital funds (i.e., sum of Tier I and Tier II capital) in the latest audited balance sheet.

Recognising the potential of 'purchased inter-bank liabilities' (IBL) to create systemic problems, the Reserve Bank had issued guidelines in March 2007 prescribing that IBL of a bank should not exceed 200 per cent of its net worth (300 per cent for banks with a CRAR more than 11.25 per cent).

2. Enhancing Transparency and Valuation

(i) Robust risk disclosures

- The FSF strongly encourages financial institutions to make robust risk disclosures using leading disclosure practices at the time of their mid-year 2008 reports.
- Further guidance to strengthen disclosure requirements under Pillar 3 of Basel II will be issued by 2009.

(ii) Standards for off-balance sheet vehicles and valuations

Standard setters will take urgent action to:

- Improve and converge financial reporting standards for off-balance sheet vehicles;

Develop guidance on valuations when markets are no longer active, establishing an expert advisory panel in 2008.

(iii) Transparency in structured products

Market participants and securities regulators will expand the information provided about securitised products and their underlying assets.

The Reserve Bank has, over the years, issued guidelines on valuation of various instruments/assets in conformity with the international best practices while keeping India-specific conditions in view. In order to encourage market discipline, the Reserve Bank has developed a set of disclosure requirements which allow the market participants to assess key pieces of information on capital adequacy, risk exposure, risk assessment processes and key business parameters which provide a consistent and understandable disclosure framework that enhances comparability. Banks are also required to comply with the Accounting Standard (AS) on Disclosure of Accounting Policies issued by the Institute of Chartered Accountants of India (ICAI).

In recognition of the fact that market discipline can contribute to a safe and sound banking environment and as part of the ongoing efforts to implement the Basel II Accord, the Reserve Bank issued guidelines on minimum capital ratio (Pillar 1) and market discipline (Pillar 3) in April 2007 and guidelines for Pillar 2 (supervisory review process) were issued in March 2008. Under these guidelines, non-compliance with the prescribed disclosure requirements would attract a penalty, including financial penalty.

3. Changes in the Role and Uses of Credit Ratings

Credit rating agencies should:

- Implement the revised IOSCO Code of Conduct Fundamentals for Credit Rating Agencies to manage conflicts of interest in rating structured products and improve the quality of the rating process;
- Differentiate ratings on structured credit products from those on bonds and expand the information they provide.

Regulators will review the roles given to ratings in regulations and prudential frameworks.

The Reserve Bank has undertaken a detailed process of identifying the eligible credit rating agencies whose ratings may be used by banks for assigning risk weights for credit risk. Banks should use the chosen credit rating agencies and their ratings consistently for each type of claim, for both risk weighting and risk management purposes. Banks are not allowed to 'cherry pick' the assessments provided by different credit rating agencies. If a bank has decided to use the ratings of some of the chosen credit rating agencies for a given type of claim, it can use only the ratings of those credit rating agencies, despite the fact that some of these claims may be rated by other chosen credit rating agencies whose ratings the bank has decided not to use. External assessments for one entity within a corporate group cannot be used to risk weight other entities within the same group.

Banks must disclose the names of the credit rating agencies that they use for the risk weighting of their assets, the risk weights associated with the particular rating grades as determined by the Reserve Bank through the mapping process for each eligible credit rating agency as well as the aggregated risk weighted assets as required.

In India, complex structures like synthetic securitisations have not been permitted so far. As and when such products are to be introduced, the Reserve Bank would put in place the necessary enabling regulatory framework, including calibrating the role and capacity building of the rating agencies.

4. Strengthening the Authorities' Responsiveness to Risks

- A college of supervisors will be put in place by end-2008 for each of the largest global financial institutions.

In the Indian context, there has been exchange of supervisory information on specific issues between the Reserve Bank and few other overseas banking supervisors/regulators. Supervisory cooperation has been working smoothly and efficiently.

The Mid-Term Review of October 2007 had announced the constitution of a Working Group to lay down a road-map for adoption of a suitable framework for cross-border supervision and supervisory cooperation with overseas regulators, consistent with the framework envisaged in the Basel Committee on Banking Supervision (BCBS). A Working Group was constituted in March 2008 and is in the process of finalising its Report. A number of overseas regulators of countries such as the USA, the UK, Canada, Hong Kong, Australia and Singapore have been formally approached to share systems and practices, including legal positions, in the matter of supervisory cooperation and sharing of information with overseas regulators. The response from a few countries has been received and is being examined. The 'Supervisory College' arrangement for this purpose is also being examined by the Group.

5. Robust Arrangements for Dealing with Stress in the Financial System

- Central banks will enhance their operational frameworks and authorities will strengthen their cooperation for dealing with stress.

In the Reserve Bank, there is an institutional arrangement in place to oversee the functioning of the financial markets on a daily basis. There is a Financial Market Committee monitoring and assessing the functioning of different financial markets. Based on such an oversight, appropriate and prompt action is taken, whenever necessary.

The Reserve Bank has the necessary framework for provision of liquidity to the banking system, in terms of Sections 17 and 18 of the Reserve Bank of India Act, 1934. The regular liquidity management facilities of the Reserve Bank include the LAF, OMO and MSS besides standing facilities such as export credit refinance (ECR) and the liquidity facility for stand alone PDs. The Reserve Bank can undertake purchase/sale of securities of the Central or State Governments and can purchase, sell and rediscount bills of exchange and promissory notes drawn on and payable in India and arising out of *bona fide* commercial or trade transactions for provision/absorption of liquidity for normal day-to-day liquidity management operations as also for provision of emergency liquidity assistance to the banks under the lender of last resort function.

The Reserve Bank is empowered under the existing legal framework to deal with the resolution of weak and failing banks. The Banking Regulation Act provides the legal framework for voluntary amalgamation and compulsory merger of banks under Sections 44(A) and 45, respectively. The Deposit Insurance and Credit Guarantee Corporation (DICGC) offers deposit insurance cover in India. The mergers of many weak private sector banks with healthy banks have improved overall stability of the system. Not a single scheduled commercial bank in the country has capital adequacy ratio which is less than the minimum regulatory requirement of nine per cent.

Source: Annual Policy Statement for the Year 2008-09, Reserve Bank of India.

ANNEX II

Measures Taken by the Reserve Bank during September-October 2008 in Response to the Global Financial Market Developments

- CRR cut by 250 basis points to 6.5 per cent, effective fortnight beginning October 11, 2008.
- Repo rate cut by 100 basis points to 8.0 per cent.

- As a temporary measure, banks permitted to avail of additional liquidity support under the LAF to the extent of up to 1 per cent of their NDTL.
- The mechanism of Special Market Operations (SMO) for public sector oil marketing companies instituted in June-July 2008 taking into account the extraordinary situation then prevailing in the money and forex markets will be instituted when oil bonds become available.
- Under the Agricultural Debt Waiver and Debt Relief Scheme Government had agreed to provide to commercial banks, RRBs and co-operative credit institutions a sum of Rs. 25,000 crore as the first instalment. At the request of the Government, RBI agreed to provide the sum to the lending institutions immediately.
- Interest rates on FCNR (B) Deposits and NRE(R)A deposits were increased by 100 basis points each to Libor/Euribor/Swap rates plus 25 basis points and to Libor/Euribor/Swap rates plus 100 basis points, respectively.
- Banks allowed to borrow funds from their overseas branches and correspondent banks up to a limit of 50 per cent of their unimpaired Tier I capital as at the close of the previous quarter or US$ 10 million, whichever is higher, as against the existing limit of 25 per cent.
- Special 14 days repo to be conducted every day upto a cumulative amount of Rs. 20,000 crore with a view to enabling banks to meet the liquidity requirements of Mutual Funds.
- Purely as a temporary measure, banks allowed to avail of additional liquidity support exclusively for the purpose of meeting the liquidity requirements of mutual funds to the extent of up to 0.5 per cent of their NDTL.

- Under the existing guidelines, banks and FIs are not permitted to grant loans against certificates of deposits (CDs). Furthermore, they are also not permitted to buy-back their own CDs before maturity. It was decided to relax these restrictions for a period of 15 days effective October 14, 2008, only in respect of the CDs held by mutual funds.
- For fine-tuning the management of bank reserves on the last day of the maintenance period, a second LAF (SLAF) on reporting Fridays, was introduced with effect from August 1, 2008. It was decided to conduct the SLAF on a daily basis till further notice.

NOTES

1. It may be noted that India is more open as compared to the US: the ratio of current receipts and current payments was 41 per cent of GDP in the US in 2007, while capital inflows and capital outflows were around 15 per cent and 10 per cent, respectively.
2. The status in India with regard to proposals in the April 2008 Report of the Financial Stability Forum (FSF) is given in Annex I.
3. At present, banks are required to hold 25 per cent of their net demand and time liabilities (NDTL) in Government (and some other approved) securities. As against this requirement of 25 per cent, banks holdings of SLR securities were 26.7 per cent of their NDTL as on September 12, 2008. Thus, banks held nearly 1.7 per cent excess SLR securities—equivalent to Rs. 700 billion as on September 12, 2008—which could be used by banks to avail of liquidity from the Reserve Bank under the daily LAF operations.
4. In view of sustained large capital flows on the one hand and the finite stock of government securities with the Reserve Bank, and the absence of the option of issuing central bank securities under the RBI Act on the other hand, a new scheme, Market Stabilisation Scheme (MSS), was introduced in April 2004 to manage the large capital flows. Under this scheme, the Reserve Bank has been empowered to issue government Treasury Bills and medium duration dated securities exclusively for sterilization purposes, so as to manage liquidity appropriately. The proceeds collected under MSS auctions are kept in a separate identifiable cash account with the RBI, and can be used only for redemption and/or buy back of securities issued under the MSS. The payments for interest and discount on MSS securities are not made from the MSS Account, but shown in the Union budget and other related documents transparently as distinct components under separate sub-heads. The MSS securities are indistinguishable from normal government Treasury Bills and dated securities. The introduction of MSS has succeeded broadly in restoring

LAF to its intended function of daily liquidity management [see Mohan (2006)].

5. On a review of the evolving liquidity situation in the context of the abrupt changes in the international financial environment subsequent to the October 6th announcement, it was decided to reduce the CRR by 250 basis points to 6.50 per cent of NDTL with effect from the fortnight beginning October 11, 2008 (instead of the 50 basis points reduction announced on October 6, 2008). As a result, an amount of about Rs. 1000 billion would be released into the system (instead of the injection of Rs. 200 billion announced earlier). A number of other measures were also announced on various occasions during September-October 2008 (see Annex II).

REFERENCES

Henry, Peter Blair (2007), "Capital Account Liberalization: Theory, Evidence, and Speculation", *Journal of Economic Literature*, Vol. XLV, December.

International Monetary Fund (2008a), "Global Financial Stability Report", October.

——— (2008b), "World Economic Outlook", October.

Mohan, Rakesh (2006), "Coping With Liquidity Management in India: A Practitioner's View", *Reserve Bank of India Bulletin*, April.

——— (2007a), "Development of Financial Markets in India", *Reserve Bank of India Bulletin*, June.

——— (2007b), "India's Financial Sector Reforms: Fostering Growth While Containing Risk", *Reserve Bank of India Bulletin*, December.

Prasad, Eswar S., Raghuram G. Rajan and Arvind Subramanian (2007), "Foreign Capital and Economic Growth", Brookings Papers on Economic Activity, 1.

Reserve Bank of India (2008), Annual Policy Statement for the Year 2008-09, April.

World Bank (2008), "Global Development Finance 2008", June.

3

Mitigating Spillovers and Contagion Lessons from the Global Financial Crisis*

D. Subbarao

...

Global Financial and Economic Outlook

4. The global financial situation continues to be uncertain and unsettled. What started off as a sub-prime crisis in the US housing mortgage sector has turned successively into a global banking crisis, global financial crisis and now a global economic crisis. Textbook economics often cite housing as a prime example of a non-tradeable good. It is paradoxical that a quintessentially non-tradable good as housing has triggered a crisis of global dimensions. Such is the depth and sweep of financial globalisation. By far, the most dominant FAQ today is whether the worst in terms of the financial sector meltdown, in particular, failure of financial institutions, is behind us. No one is really willing to take a definitive call on this, which is a sign of the increasing number of unknown unknowns.

5. The global economic outlook has deteriorated sharply over the last two months. Many economists are now predicting the worst global recession since the 1970s. In its *World Economic Outlook*, published in early October, the IMF forecast global growth of 3.9 per cent in 2008, and of 3.0 per cent in 2009. The IMF has since revised its forecast for global

---

* *Courtsey*: www.rbi.org.in

growth downwards to 3.7 per cent for 2008, and 2.2 per cent for 2009. Notably, advanced economies, as a group, are projected to contract by 0.3 per cent in 2009. If this gloomy outcome were indeed to come true, 2009 will mark the first year on record when emerging economies will account for more than 100 per cent of world growth.

Emerging Economies

6. Emerging economies may be the sole contributors to global growth in 2009, but they too are hit hard by the crisis. Ironically, even as late as six months ago, it was intellectually fashionable to subscribe to the 'decoupling theory'—that even if advanced countries went into a downturn, emerging economies will at worst be affected only marginally, and can largely steam ahead on their own. In a rapidly globalising world, the decoupling theory was never totally persuasive; given the evidence of the last few months—capital flow reversals, sharp widening of spreads on sovereign and corporate debt, and abrupt currency depreciations—the decoupling theory has almost completely lost credibility. Growth prospects of emerging economies have most definitively been undermined by the ongoing crisis with, of course, considerable variations across countries. The IMF revised its growth forecast for emerging economies for 2009 from its early October figure of 6.1 per cent to 5.1 per cent. Clearly emerging economies have a painful adjustment to make.

Impact of the Crisis on India

7. India too is having to weather the negative impact of the crisis. Even as consumption and domestic investment continue to be the key drivers of our growth, India's integration into the world has been on the increase. Going by the common measure of globalisation, India's two way trade (merchandise exports plus imports), as a proportion of GDP, grew from 21.2 per cent in 1997/98, the year of the Asian crisis, to 34.7 per cent in 2007/08. If we take an expanded measure of globalisation, that is the ratio of gross current account and gross capital flows to GDP, this ratio has increased from 46.8 per cent in 1997/98 to 117.0 per cent in 2007/08. These numbers are clear evidence of

India's increasing integration into the world economy over the last 10 years.

8. No revolution in human history has been totally benign. So, it is the case with globalisation; globalisation comes with costs and benefits. Managing globalisation requires that we minimize the costs and maximize the benefits. India has undoubtedly benefited from integrating into the world. By corollary, we also need to manage the downside ramifications of integrating into the world, as indeed evidenced by the current context.

9. The Indian banking system is not directly exposed to the sub-prime mortgage assets. It has very limited indirect exposure to the US mortgage market, or to the failed institutions or stressed assets. Indian banks, both in the public sector and in the private sector, are financially sound, well capitalised and well regulated. Even so, India is experiencing the knock-on effects of the global crisis, through the monetary, financial and real channels. Our financial markets—equity markets, money markets, forex markets and credit markets—have all come under pressure mainly because of what we have begun to call 'the substitution effect'. As credit lines and credit channels overseas went dry, some of the credit demand earlier met by overseas financing is shifting to the domestic credit sector, putting pressure on domestic resources. The reversal of capital flows taking place as part of the global de-leveraging process has put pressure on our forex markets. Together, the global credit crunch and de-leveraging were reflected at home in the sharp fluctuation in the overnight money market rates in October 2008 and the depreciation of the rupee.

10. The outlook for India, going forward, is mixed. There is evidence of economic activity slowing down. At the same time, headline inflation, as measured by the wholesale price index, has fallen sharply, and the decline has been sustained for the past three weeks, pointing to a faster than expected reduction in inflation. Clearly, falling commodity prices have been the key drivers behind the disinflation; however, some contribution has also come from slowing domestic demand. To be sure, consumer price inflation for the months of September

and October did increase. This is possibly owing to the firm trend in food articles inflation and the higher weight of food articles in measures of consumer price inflation. Historically, there has been a correlation between wholesale and consumer price inflation, and given this correlation, consumer price inflation too can be expected to soften in the months ahead.

11. The Reserve Bank's monetary policy stance has always been to balance growth, inflation and financial stability concerns. When inflation surged earlier this year, the RBI had moved quickly to tighten policy. Then again, reflecting the unfolding global situation and expectation of decline in inflation, RBI has adjusted its monetary stance over the last couple of months. The endeavour of...monetary stance has been to manage liquidity—both domestic and forex liquidity—and to ensure that credit continues to flow for productive activities.

12. ...we have instituted both aggregate measures as well as sector-specific measures. Although, we remain vulnerable to global financial and economic developments, the measures taken so far have eased the liquidity and credit flow situations considerably. ...in managing the impact of the global crisis, we have been mindful that no policy initiative is totally costless. Managing this delicate balance between costs and benefits has been one of our challenges.

13. Going forward, developments in the real economy, financial markets and global commodity prices point to a period of moderation in growth with declining inflation. The fundamentals of our economy continue to be strong. Once calm and confidence are restored in the global markets, economic activity in India will recover sharply. But a period of painful adjustment is inevitable.

14. The Reserve Bank's policy endeavour will be to ensure an orderly adjustment, and to minimise the pain of its impact. In particular, we will try to maintain a comfortable liquidity position, see that the weighted average overnight money market rate is maintained within the repo-reverse repo corridor and ensure conditions conducive for flow of credit to

productive sectors, particularly the stressed export and small and medium industry sectors....

Lessons from the Crisis

15. The crisis is by no means over. Drawing lessons may, therefore, appear a bit premature. There may yet be surprises. Even so, it will be instructive to put our minds together to understand how we got here and how we may avoid the mistakes and excesses in the future....

1st Debate: How do we Manage Global Imbalances?

16. In popular perception, the collapse of Lehman Brothers on 15 September 2008 will remain as the trigger for the global crisis. At one level, that many well be true. Indeed, for several years ahead, ...furiously debating the famous counterfactual, "If Lehman had not been allowed to fail,...."

17. However, if only we look a little deeper, we will trace the origins of the crisis to the build up of global imbalances during the 90s and this first decade of this century. There is, of course, a separate debate on what caused the build up of imbalances? Is it excess consumption of the US, or is it the savings glut in emerging Asia with the US helping out as the 'consumer of the last resort'?

18. Be that as it may, there is little disagreement over the mega trends that lead to the imbalances. First, there was the globalisation of labour. Emerging Asia added nearly three billion to the world pool of labour as it integrated into the world through the 90s. What this did was to reduce production costs at the aggregate level and increase Asia's comparative advantage. In a manner of speaking, Asia produced and America consumed. Asian economies ran up huge surpluses on their trade accounts which were mirrored by current account deficits in the US. This geographical savings—consumption imbalance was inherently fragile, but we refused to acknowledge it. Instead, we lulled ourselves into believing that we have entered, what Mervyn King of Bank of England famously called, NICE era—'non-inflationary consistently expansionary' era. It is these imbalances that generated easy

liquidity and low interest rates which in turn encouraged under-pricing of risk and deterioration in credit quality.

19. So, the debating issue is, can we prevent global imbalances from building up in the future? There is an argument that global imbalances are inevitable given the demographic profile of the world. Emerging economies typically have younger populations with a higher marginal propensity to save. Conversely, advanced countries with ageing populations have a higher marginal propensity to consume. If the demand for, and supply of, savings at the global level is structurally so well matched, how do we prevent a recurrence of global imbalances?

2nd Debate: Is Self-insurance a Viable Option for Emerging Economies?

20. Writing in the *Business Standard* last week, Arvind Subramanian of the Peterson Institute for International Economics had raised the issue of self-insurance—accumulation of foreign reserves—as a buffer against financial crises. Following the Asian crisis, East Asian countries built up huge reserves as a deliberate policy of self-insurance. China and India too built up reserves, with an important difference though. China's reserves derive from current account surpluses and are, therefore, an unencumbered asset, whereas India's reserves have been built up from capital flows, and are, therefore, encumbered by liabilities. It is this war chest of reserves that has given the muscle to the emerging economies to withstand the worst impact of the ongoing crisis.

21. Self-insurance, of course, is not costless, as Subramanian himself argues. Reserves should ideally be built through current account surpluses. This implies greater reliance on the external sector, particularly exports. But such reliance on exports can become a liability if export demand shrinks which can happen for reasons exogenous to the emerging economy. There is obviously a trade off here. Self-insurance, as defined by reserve build up through aggressive exports, offers protection against financial contagion, but it also makes the economy vulnerable to trade contagion. How do we balance

this trade off between vulnerability to financial contagion and vulnerability to trade contagion?

22. Another relevant issue is that self-insurance may not be necessary, indeed may be redundant, if international collective arrangements—regional or multilateral—can provide easy, quick and unconditional liquidity during a crisis. For example, the motivation for self-insurance will be less compelling if the recently instituted IMF's Short-term Liquidity Facility for Market Access Countries or the swap facility offered to select countries by the US Federal Reserve become more common and can be accessed with relatively low transaction costs.

23. So, the second debating issue…is the following: Is self-insurance a viable policy option for emerging economies?

3rd Debate: How do we Reform Financial Sector Regulation?

24. By far the most contentious and most voluble debate triggered by the crisis has been about the flaws in the regulatory architecture. Several issues have come to the fore. …How can complex derivative products which transmitted risks across the system be made more transparent? What are the financial stability implications of structured products like credit derivatives? Are exchange traded derivatives better than over the counter (OTC) derivatives? How do we eliminate the drawbacks of the "originate-to-distribute" model? Is universal banking, the model that the United States has now turned to, appropriate? Can we apply the same regulatory regime for both wholesale and retail banks?

25. The burden of all the above questions is to identify the drawbacks in the present regulatory regimes and indicate possible solutions. There is no doubt that we must pursue all these questions. In doing so, …we remember two things. The first thing to remember is that no one size fits all. For example, universal banking may be good in some countries and in some situations, and not so in others. The second thing to remember is that some regulations arguably have been behind the curve. There is no denying that regulations have to keep pace with innovations. But in doing so, we must be mindful of the risks

of over tightening regulations so much that they stifle innovation.

26. While on the subject of reforming regulation, there is also the larger question of risk modelling. True, the probability of risk follows a normal distribution—popularly called the bell curve. But our regulatory regimes have been tailored to respond to the central, higher probability portion of the bell curve. Typically, we ignored the black swan lying in the long tail of the curve. We now know from the benefit of hindsight that this was a fatal flaw. The black swan represents the low probability, high risk events that pose systemic risk. While our regulatory regimes were tailored to address institutional failures, they were not equipped to address systemic failures.

27. So, the issues for debate are the following: What are the flaws of the current regulatory regimes? How do we fix them? In what ways can international cooperation be fostered in this regard? How do we address the black swan systemic risk events?

4th Debate: How do we Address Regulatory Arbitrage?

28. Around the world, regulations governing the banking system have typically been quite stringent on the premise that the interests of the depositors need to be protected. But under the very nose of the regulators grew a very extensive and complex network of a 'shadow banking system', comprising hedge funds, broker-dealers, private equity funds, structured investment vehicles and conduits and money market funds. This shadow banking system was typically highly leveraged, and had an extensive nexus with the banking system. However, the shadow banking system suffered much lighter regulation. This 'regulatory arbitrage' encouraged loose practices, hunt for quick yields and non-transparent and risky financial products. When the systems began to unravel, it was realised that many of these institutions in the shadow banking system pose as much of a systemic risk as banks. The moral of the story is that if an institution is 'too big to be allowed to fail', it is also too big to be let off with loose regulations.

29. So, the question for debate is, how do we address the problem of regulatory arbitrage?

5th Debate: How do we keep the Financial Sector in Line with the Real Sector?

30. Last, and perhaps most important, ...the efficiency gains of financial engineering. We got ourselves into believing that significant value could be created by slicing and dicing securities. Illustratively, we believed that financial alchemy could turn the 'lead' of sub-prime mortgages into gold and platinum of 'AAA' securities. In many ways, the malady was worse. We failed to learn from earlier crises. We should have learnt that the modern financial system with its deregulated markets, highly leveraged players and large capital flows was dangerously fragile. We should have seen the crisis incubating behind the dazzle of financial alchemy. We should have noticed the regulatory systems getting lax and behind the curve. Instead what happened was just the opposite. The complexity, sophistication and finesse associated with it gave the financial sector a larger than life profile. Lulled by the seemingly benign economic environment, we deluded ourselves into believing that for every real life problem, no matter how complex, there is a financial sector solution.

31. Forgotten in the euphoria of financial alchemy is the basic tenet that the financial sector has no standing of its own; it derives its strength and resilience from the real economy. It is the real sector that should drive the financial sector, not the other way round.

32. So, the issue for debate is, how do we keep the financial sector in line with the real sector?

Summary and Conclusion

33. That brings...to the close of the five debates relating to the lessons from the global financial crises. To summarize, the five debates...are the following:

(i) How do we manage global imbalances?

(ii) Is self-insurance a viable option for emerging economies?

(iii) How do we reform financial sector regulation?

(iv) How do we address regulatory arbitrage?

(v) How do we keep the financial sector in line with the real sector?

....

4

Obama's Economic Solutions are Contractionary*

John Tamny

> "The man, that lives upon the production of other people, originates no demand for those productions; he merely puts himself in the place of the producer, to the great injury of production."
>
> —*Jean-Baptiste Say,* A Treatise on Political Economy

With President Barack Obama now in control in Washington, it's time to ask how his economic plan might affect the real economy.

Obama has stated that "We are in one of those periods in American history where we don't have Republican or Democratic problems, we have American problems." Obama and his economic team have released a broad outline of the way they intend to fix an economy that some say is on the verge of falling into a second Great Depression. But Obama's solutions meant to aid the economy—at least on paper—won't fix anything. Indeed, if implemented it's easy to see how they might actually cause the economy harm.

Eager to attract support from the Republican side of the aisle, Obama has expressed a high degree of willingness to include tax cuts in his post-inauguration legislation. At first blush, tax cuts sound appealing and speak positively about a

---

* *Courtesy*: www.realclearmarkets.com

politician who's been up front with his belief that a "monopoly on good ideas does not belong to a single party".

Good political theater for sure, but we might add that neither party has a monopoly on bad ideas either. Reading the fine print, we see that the definition of a tax cut in Washington is far more nuanced than what we might be used to. The tax cuts Obama has in mind might attract votes, but they have very little to do with economic growth.

First up are income credits described as tax cuts. The latter are meant for low-income families, and as the *Wall Street Journal* described them, they will allow "more families that earn too little to pay income taxes to claim at least some of the $1,000-per-child tax credit". At present, a household must have income of $12,500 per year to be eligible for tax credits, but under the Obama plan, the cutoff will be reduced to $3,000.

So what Obama and his advisors call a tax cut is really only a transfer payment from one set of hands to another. Such redistribution fosters no new production, and with that, no subsequent demand.

For at least two reasons, the credit will be an economic retardant. Productive workers will see more of their earnings taxed or borrowed in order to stimulate immediate consumption. When we consider that all profits in society result from past parsimony, we can see that the productive economy will be weakened if this form of alleged stimulus is put in place.

Most important, Obama should not run from the basic truth that economic growth is always and everywhere the result of productive work effort. To the extent that low-income families are plied with yet another form of welfare, this will reduce the individual incentives within impoverished households to engage in more work.

Put simply, the tax credits masked as cuts will reduce the work incentives for those redistributed from, all the while making real work less necessary for the alleged beneficiaries of the credit.

On the taxation front for top earners, the story gets worse. The late Warren Brookes once wrote that "We are all blessed by the genius of the relatively few." What Brookes meant was that thanks to the frequently innovative and entrepreneurial efforts of a vital few in this country, all Americans are able to enjoy better jobs and better products.

That is far from Obama's mind. He has made plain that he intends to return the tax rate on top earners to the Clinton-era level of 39.6 per cent, and the capital gains rate on investment success will move from 15 to 20 per cent. Higher tax rates in the Obama model are meant to pay for the aforementioned credits, along with yet another stimulus package.

Assuming Obama's plan to soak the rich works, it has to be said that increased revenues for the federal government will reduce the amount of capital available for the business sector to fund the wages of the poor. Whether the government is borrowing or taxing in order to redistribute, capital is being removed from the private pool of available funds meant to create new industries, new companies, and new jobs.

And when it comes to Brookes's vital few, the poor and the middle class alike will be made worse off if the successful among us choose to remove their skills from the productive economy due to higher penalties on work.

Jean-Baptiste Say once noted that the heavily taxed "are seldom regular in their payments", but it seems he actually downplayed the negatives that come with penalizing the successful. If they were merely irregular in their payments to the tax man the economy would be fine, but the real threat is perhaps the unseen. Indeed, it's tax distortions which cause the rich to be irregular in their work and investment habits that lead to economic degradation.

With regard to corporate taxation, according to another *Wall Street Journal* account, a key provision of Obama's plan is to "allow companies to write off huge losses incurred last year, as well as any losses from 2009, to retroactively reduce tax bills dating back five years." Translated, failing companies will write their losses off on the backs of successful individuals and companies alike.

When we consider what actually causes economies to grow, the corporate tax provision is creating incentives for something quite the opposite. In his *Theory of Economic Development*, Joseph Schumpeter wrote that "development consists primarily in employing existing resources in a different way". But if failing companies are kept alive not by a simple reduction in the tax rate on their profits, but rather thanks to a bailout of the non-financial variety, entrepreneurs waiting in the wings to redeploy mismanaged physical and human capital will be hampered in their efforts to bring the economy out of its slump.

In the end, entrepreneurs can only innovate to the extent that they're able to purchase the assets of failed business combinations with visions of more profitable future combinations. So when governments prop up failed or dying businesses, far from saving the economy, they only hurt it by delaying the process whereby people and capital are managed productively.

All of which brings us to the jobs portion of the Obama corporate tax plan. For the companies that make new hires or forgo layoffs, the Obama administration is set to offer a one-year tax credit in return. Once again, the incentives here are backwards, and if heeded, will surely stimulate the opposite of growth. Indeed, if there's one certain rule when it comes to business success, it has to do with producing as much as possible with as little labor as possible. Far from a job killer, when companies do more with less they free up the very capital that allows them to expand into other potentially profitable areas previously out of reach due to a lack of funds.

To the extent that businesses keep workers employed for non-productive reasons, the economy will surely be rendered poorer in time. Workers are like capital. When either labor or capital is wasted, the end result is less growth.

The tax portion of the Obama package includes write-offs for business expenditures, and it's safe to assume here that companies producing business equipment will be the beneficiaries of this new rule. Equipment write-offs recall a frequent Wainwright theme over the years that when the

Federal Reserve moves around its target interest rate, it merely reschedules economic growth, as opposed to fostering new economic activity. Write-offs should be viewed in much the same way. Businesses will simply move up equipment purchases in the near-term; those purchases will detract from capital spending over the long-term.

It's also important to remember that as a mature economy, U.S. economic growth has very little to do with spending on capital equipment, but quite a lot to do with spending on human capital. Using Google as an example, its growth over the years has been the result of heavy investment in the best minds, as opposed to the best equipment. Equipment write-offs at best address a past version of the U.S. economy that most Americans would no longer recognize.

Sadly, the tax portion of Obama's recovery plan was only put in place to give Republicans the political cover necessary to vote for the various spending initiatives that the new administration envisions. This is the alleged "stimulus" part of Obama's economic package, and as Wainwright publications have emphasized over the years, government spending can in no way stimulate economic growth.

Beyond the negative work incentives created by wealth redistribution, the basic reality is that no one—least of all government—can profit from the same transaction twice. That's the assumption the government is making when it claims it can grow the economy through the transfer of wealth already created. In a sense, the very notion of stimulus turns routine economics on its head.

But to address arguably the worst aspect of Obama's proposed $775 billion spending package, we must once again bring in the notion of the entrepreneur waiting in the wings. It's tautological to say that entrepreneurs cannot innovate without capital. When the federal government is borrowing at relatively low rates from the private sector, there's necessarily less capital at higher rates for entrepreneurs to access in order to utilize human and physical capital more effectively.

At its core, Barack Obama's economic recovery plan is anti-entrepreneur, and as such, anti-growth. So while we should expect to read quite a lot about how "change" in Washington will enhance our economic well-being, we shouldn't be fooled. The new administration plans to engage in feverish activity. It may be meant to make us better off, but it would be charitably naïve to mistake it for any real prescription for economic recovery.

5

Lessons from the Global Financial Crisis with Special Reference to Emerging Market Economies and India*

D. Subbarao

1. Since the collapse of the leading US investment banks in August-September 2008, there has been a breakdown of trust in inter-bank and inter-institutional lending. Given that this kind of extreme risk perception will be reversed only slowly, the full resolution of the crisis will inevitably take time.

2. Additionally, there is the problem of contagion—across markets, across institutions and across countries. Each day, there is news of the crisis spreading to a newer part of the world or to a newer institution. What we are going through is an unprecedented crisis; and we will be failing the world if we do not draw lessons from the crisis to prevent its recurrence....

3. First, financial supervision has drawn widespread critique. The stereotype perception is that risk management and supervisory practices lagged behind financial innovations and emerging new business models. The present crisis underscores the need for regulation staying ahead of the curve, and for continually upgrading the skills and instruments for financial regulation and supervision. However, there is need for a note of caution here. There is a distinct risk that in trying to stay ahead of innovation, regulation may get so stringent that it stifles innovation. This is a risk we must guard against.

---

* *Courtsey*: www.rbi.org.in

4. The second lesson relates to the inter-agency coordination. The origins of the current crisis can be traced to both the build up of macro-global imbalances as well as the mispricing of risks in the financial system, which in turn, was encouraged by prolonged easy monetary policy and excess liquidity. We endorse the IMF view that the respective roles of central banks, regulators, supervisors, and fiscal authorities regarding financial stability needs to be revisited. Central banks should play a central role in maintaining financial stability and should have the necessary informational base to do so effectively. This implies close co-operation among all the agencies entrusted with the task of maintaining financial stability.

5. The third lesson is that the large scale bail-out packages will have implications for the regulatory architecture of the financial system and for the fisc of countries. Besides, the rescue packages offered by one country could have ramifications for other countries, even when they are far from the epicentre of the crisis. A relevant issue in this context is the efficacy and coverage of deposit insurance. What should deposit insurance cover? How are small deposits to be defined? Apart from small deposits, should we, in a crisis situation like this, consider extending guarantees to the money markets and mutual funds?

6. Fourth, the unfolding crisis has revealed the weaknesses of structured products and derivatives in the credit markets. This throws up questions about the appropriateness of various structured product like credit derivatives and their financial stability implications. Are exchange traded derivatives superior to over the counter (OTC) derivatives? Do we need to focus on prescribing and instituting appropriate clearing and settlement practices even for OTC products? In what way can we eliminate the shortcomings of the "originate-to-distribute" model?

7. Finally, the near meltdown of the US financial sector is seen by some as evidence that markets and competition do not work. This is clearly the wrong lesson to draw. The right lesson to draw is that markets and institutions do succumb

occasionally to excesses, which is why regulators have to be vigilant, constantly finding the right balance between attenuating risk-taking and inhibiting growth.

....

9. India, with its strong internal drivers for growth, may escape the worst consequences of the global financial crisis. Indian banks have very limited exposure to the US mortgage market, directly or through derivatives, and to the failed and stressed financial institutions. The equity and the forex markets provide the channels through which the global crisis can spread to the Indian system. The other three segments of the financial markets—money, debt and credit markets—could be impacted indirectly. Risk aversion, deleveraging and frozen money markets have not only raised the cost of funds for Indian corporates but also its availability in the international markets. This will mean additional demand for domestic bank credit in the near term. Reduced investor interest in emerging economies could impact capital flows significantly. The impending recession will also impact on Indian exports.

10. To sum up, even EMEs which do not have direct or significant exposure to stressed financial instruments and troubled financial institutions are experiencing the indirect impact of the financial crisis, and this impact is by no means insignificant or trivial. Indeed, it could intensify in the months ahead.

11. It is heartening that there is coordination among developed countries in the management of the crisis. That is welcome and necessary, but not sufficient. In as much as emerging and developing economies are likely to be increasingly impacted by the crisis, going forward two things are necessary. First, in managing the crisis, the implications of that management for emerging and developing economies should be explicitly factored in. Second, emerging and developing economies should be taken into confidence and consulted whenever the policies and actions of the developed countries have implications for them.

6

Latin America and the Financial Crisis*

Jorge Heine

For the first time in a century, Latin America has managed to at least partially "cushion" itself from the seismic waves of economic turmoil in the US and Europe.

The United Kingdom will face a 2.8 per cent negative growth rate in 2009, the worst economic performance since World War II (in fact, the British economy has already shrunk by 2.7 per cent since last April). In Spain, unemployment has reached 14 per cent, and the government is offering a "golden handshake" to recent immigrants to leave the country for three years. Ireland, so often held up as an example for the developing world because of its relentless tax-cutting, is in dire straits, and Iceland is bankrupt.

In the United States, Dow Jones slipped below 8000 in the very week President Barack Obama took office, the automobile industry continues its downward spiral (Toyota has already displaced GM as the world's largest automaker) and in one day in January, some leading companies announced shedding 72,000 jobs. In California, unemployment is just below 10 per cent, and the State faces a staggering deficit. In Canada, which lost 34,000 in December, Ontario, the nation's industrial heartland (40 per cent of Canada's GDP), is in trouble and looking for ways to renegotiate existing financial arrangements with Ottawa.

---

* *Courtesy*: www.hinduonnet.com

Projections indicate that the developed world will have a negative growth in 2009. What about Latin America?

The standard line is that "when the United States sneezes, Latin America catches a cold." And that was exactly what happened in the past. The Great Depression had a devastating effect on Latin America—so much so that in the late 1930s and early 1940s, it begot the import-substitution-industrialisation (ISI) strategy, as governments realised that in times of global slowdowns they could not be left at the mercy of having enough hard currency to buy essential goods from the industrialised North; they needed some installed capacity of their own.

Something similar happened in the early 1980s when rising interest rates in the US pushed the region into its worst debt crisis and a "lost decade," in which countries like Chile saw 14 per cent negative growth in 1982 and unemployment rates of 30 to 35 per cent for several years. According to the conventional wisdom, Latin American economies should be in the doldrums, with the Northern recessionary waves hitting Southern shores with a multiplier effect leading to an even deeper economic downturn there.

Yet, this isn't happening. Yes, this is a global recession and the region has not been spared. Growth will be cut in half; commodity prices have dropped and so have export volumes, thus affecting regional exports which reached a record $902 billion in 2008. International credit has tightened, and some projected FDI is not materialising. Remittances to the region, which also reached a record ($67 billion) in 2008, will take a hit.

After six consecutive years of over 4 per cent economic growth rates, the region is projected to grow 1.9 per cent in 2009. Unemployment, at 7.5 per cent in 2008, is projected to rise to between 7.8 and 8.1 per cent. Whatever else it may be, this is not a recession.

Countries like Peru, the star economic performer over the past few years, may grow as much as 5 per cent in 2009, with smaller economies like Cuba, Panama and Uruguay clocking 4 per cent or more. And the larger economies like Argentina

(2.6 per cent), Brazil (2.1 per cent), Chile (2 per cent) and Venezuela (3 per cent) should perform quite respectably. In fact, South America as a whole, according to ECLAC, will grow at 2.4 per cent. It is Mexico (0.5 per cent) and many Central American and Caribbean nations that will be especially affected by the drop in tourism and in remittances and by lower demand in the US market.

This does not mean that if the financial meltdown continues to wreak havoc on the North and the economic wreckage is extended over time, it will not eventually have a greater impact in Latin America. My point is a different one. For the first time in a century, Latin America has managed, if not totally, to "decouple," at least to partially "cushion" itself from the seismic waves of economic turmoil in the US and Europe, markets on which it traditionally depended. The fact that several countries from the region (Brazil, Mexico and Colombia) are placing bonds in international markets in these difficult times speaks for itself.

That this should happen at a time when eight of ten countries in South America are ruled by Left or Left-of-Centre parties is ironic. For much of this decade, we have repeatedly been told how Latin America, by veering towards the Left, was once again "missing the boat" on economic development, and how it risked being caught in a time warp, left behind by the twin imperatives of globalisation and economic interdependence, beholden to outmoded ideologies at a time of the end of ideology.

Instead of dollarising their economies (as Ecuador did in 2000, much to its subsequent chagrin) and opening themselves up to whatever Washington demanded, many countries (led by Brazil) preferred a different path, one that turned out to be not so misguided after all. If anything, many Latin American governments seem to have shown a better understanding of the perils of unfettered globalisation and "casino capitalism" than several of their counterparts in the North.

What does the Latin American Left stand for today and what has it done in government?

Far from the "populism" so much of the Western media labels it with, the modern Left in the region today embodies a set of beliefs very different from the mid-20th century populist movements associated with this term.

It is fully democratic, believing in free and fair elections, having strongly opposed the military regimes supported by the Right in the 1970s and 1980s; it is secular, standing apart from the integrista Catholicism of so many conservative forces in the region; it is committed to greater social equality in a region with the dubious distinction of having the highest economic inequality; it believes in diversifying trading and investment partners, as well as the number and variety of export products, thus moving away from the *econom'a monoexportadora* syndrome of the past; finally, it is fiscally responsible—starting from the premise that only by having macroeconomic equilibria (that is, if the government balances the books) and tackling inflation will you be able to make progress. Prudent economic policies combined with aggressive social programmes—like Brazil's Bolsa de Familia or Chile's recent pension reform—are at the heart of this approach.

It is these principles and the policies that flow from them that have allowed the countries in the region to bring down their foreign debt from 37 per cent of the GDP in 2000 to 20 per cent today. They have permitted Brazil to start a $48-billion infrastructure programme, and Chile to launch a $4-billion stimulus package to deal with the global slowdown.

But the region being partially cushioned from the worst effects of the latter is also due to something else. For large export-oriented economies today, diversifying their export markets means targeting Asia. This is what South America's leading economies have done. China, Japan, South Korea and India are the prize markets. For Chile, in 2007, China was its number one export market (displacing the US), Japan was number three, South Korea six and India 10 (displacing Germany). Asia received 43 per cent of Chile's exports that year; not surprisingly, a dip in the US market, which gets a little over 20 per cent of Chilean exports, is not a major blow to its economy. Though Chile, because of its Asia-Pacific orientation, is a bit of an extreme case, for Argentina, Brazil and Peru the pattern is not too different.

In this context, a critical question is whether the "Asian giants," China and India, will also be dragged down by the recession in North America and Western Europe. Initial indications are that they have already been, with their growth projections going down from double digits to 6-7 per cent. A second question is to what extent this growth will be export- or internal demand-driven. China's $600-billion stimulus package is designed to pump up domestic demand in an economy that until now has been largely driven by exports. India, on the other hand, has based its high growth mostly on its internal market.

These are, make no mistake about it, perilous times, and the treacherous waters of the world economy need to be navigated with a steady compass. Nonetheless, it is refreshing to see, for once, that Latin America may well grow its way through a global recession, as opposed to being once again the region most seriously affected by it.

7

Global Financial Crisis

Uma Narula

The factors of global financial crisis of Sept 08 onwards can slow economic growth and can impact the transformation speed in India as its transformation is affected by the globalize factors playing role in growth of business enterprises and economic growth in general and by the spillover of the global financial crisis.

Financial crises are terrifying when underlying economic fundamentals are out of line with established theory, leading to bursts of unjustified optimism and/or pessimism. It is the responsibility of the powers that be to bring sense to the market. Every financial crisis is different, but they do all end. The Lehman Brothers bankruptcy and Merrill Lynch's acquisition by Bank of America is yet another stage in the progression of the financial crisis in Sept 08 onwards that had its roots in the US sub-prime mortgage market and in Nov 08 Citibank massive failure.

Key features of this crisis that started in the middle of 2007 has been the lack of clarity on both the nature and number of financial institutions that have indirect exposure to sub-prime assets, as well as, cross-product problems involving movement from sub-prime to prime mortgages with final spillover into derivatives, structured products and counterparty risks.

These are days of extreme and often irrational pessimism. The way to survive this crisis is to stay focused on the fundamentals. From a fundamental perspective, India's financial system has a lot going for it. Indian banks have no direct exposure to G7 mortgage markets and their indirect exposure is minuscule relative to the size of their balance sheet. This has protected India in the past and will continue to insulate it to a significant degree from the turmoil in global markets. As this phase of extreme pessimism abates a bit, global investors are likely to reward India for the robustness of its system.

De-coupling theory is proving wrong with the emerging economies including India and China being hit hard by the economic recession in US, UK, Japan and Europe. Many major emerging economies are facing capital flow reversals, export contractions and resultant large scale job losses. China has cut production and trying to sell the export goods to Non-western countries where also there is consumption slow down in the aftermath of global crisis. The governments of both China and India are giving fiscal support to their economies in a bid to offset the negative impact of the export slowdown.

The emerging markets may be the sole contributors to the global growth in 09. The lessons for emerging markets is to learn how to manage the global imbalances, following the Asian crisis, East Asian countries built up huge reserves as deliberate policy of self-insurance. China and India too have built up their reserves. It is this war chest of reserves that has given the emerging economies muscle to withstand the worst impact of the crisis. Emerging economies with younger population have higher marginal propensity to save. Conversely, advanced countries with ageing population have higher propensity to consume. If the demand for and supply of savings at the global level is so well matched how do we prevent recurrence of global imbalances. (Seminar Mitigating Spillovers and Contagion: Lessons from the Global Financial Crisis, Mumbai, Dec 08.)

The enormity of the global crisis disaster sparked distrust among high-street banks, which refused to lend to each other, and panic among investors who sold fearing the worst, forcing some of the central banks to swing into action. People's Bank of China cut interest rate for the first time in six years and lowered reserve requirements for smaller banks, while the US Fed made it easier for bond houses to borrow. It offered bail out packages to Lehman Brothers and Merrill Lynch. It is actually need not be a bailout proposal at all. It's in fact a proposal to try to re-liquefy markets by reducing leverage, by increasing transparency, and by increasing liquidity and by establishing a set of pricing processes that involve the private market.

According to Standard & Poor's monthly stock market review 'The World by Numbers', world's emerging markets have fared even worse than its global peers falling 7.09 per cent in August 08 and 19.40 per cent over the past three months. With the credit crisis casting its shadow on the international market, developed and emerging equity markets lost ground in August, and have now produced double-digit negative returns over the past three months, it said.

Post-mortems of what went wrong with the global financial system highlight new global economic truths: First rich countries were never rich at all; they were living off the debt generated by growth of powerhouse economies like China. Secondly, the new wisdom that China and at time India saves too much. The analysts and economists suggest that real solution to the problem will be if India and China start spending all that they earn instead of saving and financing the debts of Americans and Britons. China and India are not amused at this suggestion.

USA is managing the Global financial crisis by offering bail out, financial stimulus packages, rate cuts even to zero level and lower taxes. It has offered $1 trillion package again in Dec 08 to salve its economy and jobs. May be USA—the super-power is in decline. It can feed, clothe and be self-sufficient and is still capable of those 'dirty' jobs like manufacturing and others that are outsourced to China and India. It has to take the decision on that though decline in outsourcing and offshoring may hit India, China and other emerging countries.

India Financial Scenario Regarding Global Financial Crisis

Earlier than 90s India faced the challenges of low economic growth, and close economic policies. Since 90s the expectations have been rising because of economic liberalization, economic reforms and economic policies opening gradually which paved the way to globalization participation and economic growth. India faced multiple urgent challenges when its economic policies opened in 90s. In 2008, global financial is impacting its economic growth and slowing it down due to those global factors which were boosting its higher growth.

Globalization did create challenges for India from various perspectives and it does face more and more challenges as the process, the structure, the dimensions and face of globalization changes *vis-à-vis* India. India's transformation challenges are impacted by external global factors. The factors accelerating or slowing economic growth can impact the transformation speed in India.

It is being assumed that we in India are experiencing the spillover effects of what is happening in the advanced countries. We are not the cause of the problem but we are being invited to be part of the solution to the problem.

Capital flows is one important factor for Indian economy. Indian policymakers will now have to face up to the challenge of slowing capital flows, which could slide further after the latest developments on Wall Street. The turmoil in the global financial and credit markets had led to capital flowing out at a faster pace. Between April and July 2008, foreign portfolio investors have taken out close to $4.5 billion, going by RBI data. According to SEBI figures, foreign investors have pulled out close to $400 million in August and September so far. For the full year, foreign portfolio investors have sold stocks worth over $7 billion.

Much of India's current economic problems relate to external sector—exports, rupee depreciation and capital inflows. What has began as financial crisis is now a crisis in the real economy affecting growth outlook of all economies of the world and India is not exception.

The slowdown in capital flows this fiscal year is in sharp contrast to the scenario over a year ago when the Indian central bank was struggling to manage inflows. The new RBI governor D. Subbarao now has the challenge of stemming outflows unlike his predecessor, Y.V. Reddy who had to manage the copious flow of capital for a good part of his tenure. The prime minister's economic advisory council in its outlook for the economy for 2008-09 has already warned that policymakers "may have to be prepared to face a situation of greater volatility in capital inflows on account of the uncertain external environment".

The prime minister's advisory council report, however, adds that even if capital inflows are lower this year, it will be adequate to finance the enlarged CAD, leaving about $29 billion to accrue in the foreign exchange reserves of the RBI. Of all the major sources of foreign capital inflows such as foreign direct investment (FDI), foreign portfolio investment, overseas borrowings by Indian corporate (ECBs) and NRI deposits, only FDI inflows have been strong this fiscal. At the policy level, there may well be measures to boost flows.

Over the next few months, the challenge for the RBI would be to handle outflows. Just as excessive inflows are not good for the economy, even excessive outflows will have an adverse affect on markets. As for other policy measures, it is time to take a look at certain capital controls. The end-use norms on foreign borrowings and the rate cap at Libor plus 200 could be revisited; even the Participatory Note (PNs) norms could be diluted to encourage capital flows. The government in order to invite FDI is relaxing some of the norms and regulations such as about Participatory Note. However, assuming that the foreign borrowings' window is opened up again, there may not be much of an impact considering that there is hardly any global appetite for debt paper from emerging markets, said an analyst with a private bank.

The problem of capital flows is not confined to the Indian markets alone. According to a recent report by Fitch Ratings, capital flows to Asia have started slowing down given the heightened risk aversion of global investors and the deteriorating economic fundamentals of the region; and to that extent, the central bank should be less worried about the weak currency and its competitive advantage/disadvantage.

Stock Markets to bring liquidity in the market. Money market is volatile and there is liquidity crunch. Emerging economies are bearing the brunt of global meltdown, giving double-digit negative returns in the past three months, even as Indian stocks have managed to perform the best among BRICs in August. Three steps need to be taken: stabilize the markets, fix the problem, and finally prepare long-term rehabilitation. Those three tasks must be accomplished in order.

The economic slump may have slow down the private equity (PE) investments but more PE deals are being stuck in emerging businesses. Earlier most of the PE investments were in venture capital (VC) deals. Analysts say pre-IPO placements by FDI have dried up as many IPOs (initial public offering of stocks) are not coming up due to slump. FDI used to invest in a company through pre-IPO placements and made money by offloading the stake when the investee company goes public. A number of FDI funds are now adopting the VC way of investing and working in close tandem with the company to make it grow and creating values so that good returns accrue when they exit.

Tightening Outsourcing and Offshoring by developed countries to India can be another significant factor for slow economic scenario. India's outsourcing industry will likely face pricing pressure and a slowdown in volume growth. Still new deals come as the competence and cost effectiveness of outsourcing through India cannot be ignored. Infosys bags mega deal in multimillion dollar agreement from UKs AstraZeneca in Dec 08 to offer applications maintenance services to its global operations including manufacturing, supply chain finance and human resources. Wall Street firms have long dominated the client lists of India's top outresourcers who are now diversifying revenue streams from these troubled financial clients. Infosys has been trying to wean from US clients which account for its 62 per cent revenue.

Global crisis is likely to impact the business scenario and employment. The government is taking adequate steps to bring cash liquidity in the market and avoid credit crunch. As government warns we have to be cautious in investments and business dealings; the growth will slow down.

The government does not want the country to go into economic recession, people to lose jobs and to make them face credit crunch in taking bank loans for housing and vehicles and other non-durables. It is urging the business employers not to fire people with knee-jerk as that can adversely affect the economy as well employee's morale. Businesses have agreed not to fire people but also they are not ready to hire people; thus not generating employment.

On the business front the joint ventures with foreign partners are put on hold and even they are deferring projects on domestic front to consolidate their financial position. DLF has deferred its Mega mall project in Gurgaon, and Mergers and Acquisitions are also put on hold for better times.

Industry posted negative growth in Oct 08 quarter; this is first in the 15 years. The industrial output decline for October is down 0.4 per cent. Manufacturing, Capital goods, consumer spending is worst hit and recorded negative growth. Meltdown is hitting India harder than anticipated. The consensus among analysts and economists is that the trend is likely to continue for sometime. Nobody is sure whether stimulus packages announced in bit and packages by government will be able to trigger significant recovery.

Institutes that sprung up a few years ago to fill the talent gap such as Aviation, retail, fashion designing and retailing, finance, banking, insurance etc. are changing their business model to align themselves with the market realities and ensure that students passing out manage to finds jobs. They are lowering their student intake, diversifying their curriculum, broadening their course focus, targeting foreign and non-traditional recruiters such as recruiters from Middle East, and delay student's entry into the job market.

Risk Management in Global Financial Crisis

India is trying to manage its economic crisis in a way as not to thwart economic growth in a big way. Agriculture is managed well and should grow, adequate liquidity is provided to industry, credit is actually delivered to industry, and individuals, and credit crunch has to be avoided; for that confidence has to be infused in banks to give credit at affordable rates. It is important to pull down inflation rates to single digits.

Finance Minister P. Chidambaram (Nov 08) speaking on the effects of the current global crisis on India said that there have been global recessions in the past but added that the current recession threatens to last longer and deeper than before. He said that India does not have a problem but is bearing the brunt of the spillover of this global recession. The world economy has changed more rapidly in the last sixty days than it has over a long time. But this is not the first time in which industrialized countries are going into a recession. There have been recessions in the past in Japan, in Europe and in the United States. This recession of course threatens to be a longer and deeper affecting more industrialized countries notably USA, Japan and some European countries. We in India are experiencing the spillover effects of what is happening in the advanced countries. We are not the cause of the problem but we are being invited to be part of the solution to the problem.

The crisis will end some day. We must take note of the structure of economy and the manner in which most Indians live and work. 60-65 per cent of India's workforce depends on agriculture and he expects a bumper crop this year and feels it will continue to grow at a robust pace.

"In the last sixty days both the government and the Reserve Bank of India (RBI) have moved swiftly to take steps that will ensure adequate liquidity is provided to industry. However, providing liquidity is not the panacea for the current crisis. Providing liquidity is only the first step, the second is ensuring appropriate price and the third step is ensuring that at that price credit is actually delivered to industry."

Other scenarios are volatile money market that may erode banks profitability. ICRA says that Net interest margins for banks in the country are likely to come under pressure and may vary across entities. The firm attributed this to extreme volatility in inter-bank and money market rates.

Government would also try to return to growth trajectory of 9 per cent once the stock market stabilizes. On the whole the general outlook continues to be one of cautious optimism. Economists agree with the finance minister's projections and expects economic growth to improve from the second quarter of next (2009) fiscal year. The global economic scenario will also improve towards the second quarter next year.

Government is borrowing more than originally planned, spending more on welfare schemes and is open to further cut taxes. 'Since there is increased expenditure, government may take one more year of fiscal responsibility management targets', FM said.

The housing industry in India may be going through one of the worst phases but in such times there are enough reasons for making affordable housing a priority. The focus has been in mainly in upper-end urban housing and commercial malls and office spaces. But there is greater need for low-end urban housing and rural housing. The additional low-end urban housing free up rental dwellings for migrant populations at affordable rents and thus preventing slumps and ensuring supply of human capital for city's growth. Experts say that to fulfil the unmet demand for affordable housing we need innovative techniques to make lesser use of resources of cement, aluminum and steel, etc. Government is also urging banks to give housing loans at affordable low interest rates. Softening global commodity prices coupled with good domestic harvest could pull down is pulling down inflation rates to single digits.

It is suggested that trade within Asia should be taken to tackle down slow down. India will do well to make use of free trade pact with ASEAN countries in certain sectors—automobiles, pharmaceuticals, electronic components. It should not be merely a transient option but could well be long term strategy.

Montek Singh Ahluwalia's (Dec 08) addressing the press highlights efforts to mitigate the crisis effects. He advocates that a set of measures should be taken to minimize the impact of the weak global economy on the Indian economy. RBI announced the monetary and the credit side of the package, there is a significant effort to give a stimulus on the expenditure side. We have tried to look at what additional expenditure, particularly in key infrastructure, rural infrastructure, etc. is possible in the rest of this year and we think that it may be possible to authorize and to implement additional expenditure up to about Rs. 20,000 crores. In addition to this additional expenditure, a very strong effort is being made to make sure that the expenditure that has been budgeted already actually takes place. One of the problems we have had in the past for many reasons is that expenditure that is in the budget tends to be underutilized. It is a very important spending boost to the economy.

In addition to the planned expenditure side, there are actions that have been taken on the revenue side. There is an across the board reduction of four percentage point in the Cenvat rate except for some one or two items that would be across the board and that will be an important example of fiscal stimulus. A number of measures have been taken to respond to the concerns of the exporter community. Exporters faced a weak global demand situation. Most of our exporters are also small and medium enterprises, so a number of initiatives have been taken which in our view will make it a lot easier for exporters in the remaining months of the year. We are also putting in place significant new initiatives in housing. On 7th Dec, the Governor of Reserve Bank announced the special refinance facility of Rs. 4,000 crores for the National Housing Bank. On the government side, we are looking at what can be done to expand expenditure in the Indira Awas Yojana. That will be part of the expenditure stimulus I mentioned earlier. Public sector banks are coming out with attractive and affordable package for homeowners wishing to take loans to purchase flats or houses.

He mentioned the small medium and micro sector—this is a very critical sector of the economy. Most of the employment in industry comes from this sector and we are very concerned that the weakening of the growth stimulus should not leave this sector high and dry. So, in quantitative terms, announcement on 6th Dec, of a refinance facility of Rs. 7,000 crores that will go to Small Industries Development Bank of India (Sidbi) and be available for incremental lending by Sidbi or for refinance for incremental lending by the commercial banks. It is a very major step to help the medium and small sector.

In addition, several other steps have been taken like expanding the guarantee cover and also giving instructions to the central public sector enterprises that they should ensure prompt payment of bills for the small scale sector. This is a very important area in the sense that when there is a tightness of credit, the bigger units delay payments to the smaller units. We are in fact taking steps to make sure that the banks will lend and that public sector enterprises should have no difficulty in getting their credit needs met by the banks and we want to make sure that they, in turn, pass on the benefits of this to the SME. There is a package for the textile sector where another Rs. 1,400 crores is being made available to clear the backlog in TUF scheme of the textile sector and also expanding the coverage of the Vishesh Krishi and Gram Udyog Yojana.

A major area for the government to focus on is infrastructure financing. Prime Minister had said several weeks ago that we need to give a contra-cyclical thrust to infrastructure investment. We are doing that in the public sector through some of the measures being taken on the budget side. In addition, many initiatives are underway promoting infrastructure investment in the public-partner mode, particularly, in the area of roads and ports. I know that a large number of projects have now gone through the various clearance processes and are pretty much being put up for invitation to bid. It is very important that the financing environment for infrastructure is supportive.

What is being proposed is that the India Infrastructure Finance Company Limited (IIFCL) which was setup just over a year ago, is being given additional resources of about Rs. 10,000 crores in the form of permission to mobilize tax-free bonds and depending on need, government will in fact expand this permission. The resources mobilized will be used by the IIFCL to refinance bank lending to infrastructure. This will be in addition to what it normally does, which is to provide direct financing. The point about refinancing is that it doubles. If they provide 50 per cent refinancing then it means that this Rs. 10,000 crores will actually come to Rs. 20,000 crores going out into the infrastructure sector. On the whole, taking a longer view, all this cannot be done in the next 3 or 4 months but we are really trying to build up an entire program for infrastructure investment. We think, for example, in the highway sector alone, it would be possible over the next 18 months to support or to clear to total investment program of almost Rs. 100,000 crores. That doesn't mean that all that money will be spent in 18 months but we will start and bring to financial closure projects which would get implemented over a period of 2-3 years but which would have a total value of almost Rs. 100,000 crores.

There are some other measures also, like for example, government departments being allowed to take up replacement of government vehicles within the existing budget which is relaxation of economy instructions, reduction in import duty of naphtha and also a reduction in the export duty on iron ore lumps and an elimination of the export duty on iron ore fines that would basically provide a stimulus for exports for this sector.

The overall position really is that like all countries, we are facing a world economy that is not in good shape. Fortunately, the Indian economy is in much better shape than most others. But we cannot be complacent. We want to take action in advance of any problems arising so that factors that would otherwise weaken our growth performance are minimized. It may not be possible to eliminate them completely. Growth in the current year (08) will be less than it was last year but the steps that we have taken will make sure that the impact is minimized and also this must be emphasized that this is not necessarily the only thing we are going to do. We watch the situation closely both on the monetary and on other sides and would take additional action if necessary.

In the global meltdown of 08, government is taking stock of India growth story. India story has been road to growth and it must be sustained. There is liquidity crunch. RBI and government are coming forth to reduce the liquidity crunch. Banks have lost confidence in public. But they should not freeze the financial system by their fear factor. They should give credit/loans for investments to individuals and Corporates.

Government has been concerned about the impact of the global financial crisis on the Indian economy and a number of steps have been taken to deal with this problem. The forward looking policies of the government and its intervention inputs will counter fiscal crunch. It suggests corporate focus on customers through inter-factoring and micromanaging domestic demand and finance flows back to banks. Government has to reduce cost of transactions and improve infrastructure. It must energize business leadership to improve strength and capability, and deliver high in global meltdown.

The fiscal stimulus package is expected to boost demand. Fiscal policy is an important instrument to stimulate demand. Dec 7th, 08, the government has announced Rs. 20,000-crore fiscal stimulus package to industries, banks, textiles to boost the morale of the market. The crucial focus of fiscal stimulus package is on expenditure stimulus, consumer consumption stimulus, creating demand by consumers to produce goods and services and thus sustain employment. The focus is on creating housing demands and credit through housing loans by banks thus helping the Real estate sector. The other sectors are infrastructure financing, and stimulus for exports. As RBI governor Subbarao commented, when there is upswing, confidence is restored and world economies start recovering. India will be the first to recover.

Experts opinions: Narula (09) advocates that three new concepts of global structure which focus on expansion of businesses and development of human, intellectual and financial capital, dimensions of global transformation and transformation challenges for countries participating in the globalization process may be undermined by the global meltdown. The transformation success and failure of India along with its challenges and the rate of transformation is dependent on the planning, policies and actions of the governance and its people re global meltdown scenario.

Current situation in India is going to get better as India is going through slower growth (Peter Hendal, Dale Carnegie Training), India will see higher growth rate once the current situation settles down i.e. by end 2009 (research analyst Gartner), India's exposure to global trade is low which will help soften the adverse affects of slowdown. Given the favourable demographics and long-term growth potential we expect India to attract significant foreign investments particularly in infrastructure, which should help improve productivity and competitiveness of Indian industry (Joel Pelman, Copal Partners). There will be significant change in the verticals. The focus will be on the domestic market than exports. In the short run, revenues and margins will be affected but in the long time it will lead to good industry practices as bad practices will be weeded out (Anil Kumar, Quinnox).

Experts are predicting that once India gets back to its feet, things will get better for industries as well for organizations and their employees. This will be also the time when other industries will also gain in value in terms of availability of other job opportunities for potential gain strength and there will be shift in the focus to core sectors like power, construction, manufacturing and retail Growth will be stronger in government and industrial sector wherein they would like to leverage competitive advantage through technology.

Education sector is likely to gain momentum as many people will retool themselves to adapt to the changes resulting from crisis. The pressing need will be to make qualified the right talent by looking at pre-hire assessments and other tools to improve the selectivity of the recruits (Diwakar Nigam, Newgen Software, Esawaran, Dexterity).

This will also give Indian organizations and entrepreneurs to expand more in terms of value and supply as they will be entering and playing, in a more mature field. There has been tremendous downsizing of the employees because of meltdown but experts say that by the end of this period employees will be better off as organizations will come with rampant policies to help them get better suited to their jobs though salary increases will be modest. Most companies will reduce their HR budgeting by snipping increments, outsourcing work to cut costs and increasing proportion of variable component and performance linked pay.

Infosys CEO said, the company is focusing on additional training and education for employees to prepare them better for the growth and recovery after global financial meltdown (Nov 08).

Shankar Acharya, Member, Board of Governors and Honorary Professor, ICRIER, (Dec 08) sees FY09 GDP growth at 7 per cent. "We will be lucky to see 6 per cent growth in FY10. He feels the speed of the global recession and the huge uncertainty increases risks. The severity of the global recession is not yet fully seen in India. The recession is likely to be longer than that seen in the last few decades. A turnaround in the global economy is likely only by 2010. Commenting on the recent Government and Reserve Bank measures, Acharya felt both entities have reacted promptly and effectively. The effects of the recent fiscal package will kick in next year. There is more room for fiscal stimulus in FY 10 only if commodity prices stay low. We will see more RBI action in the form of refinancing CRR, repo and reverse repo cuts."

India being cautious at this stage will be cautious to invest FDI in USA, UK through M&A and Joint ventures.

It is presumed that rural spend and housing may rescue growth. India may buck the global crisis largely based on the buying power of the bottom 80 per cent of population that accounts for 67 per cent of he consumption. These are also the people who are not affected by the negative wealth effect caused by the stock market crunch. Schemes like NREGA, pay commission handouts and farm loan waivers may revive consumption and even boost the stock markets (M.K. Venu).

These are the few steps to be taken immediately in the current financial crisis scenarios. Government is boosting up the morale of the businesses, banks and investors and people in general by taking various steps to safeguard the economic and financial health of the country and assuring that India is not in recession state. Call it prediction or hope—this global financial crisis will end. It had domino effect across the globe. For India it may be sooner than the rest, it will be among the very few countries to emerge mostly unscathed and also with a positive outcome.

What would you rather do, continue to discuss the economic meltdown or focus on strategic solutions with innovation gurus.

REFERENCES

Montek Singh Ahluwalia, Deputy Chairman of Planning Commission India address to the press. Dec 2008.

Narula Uma, *Rising Expectations: India's Transformation* (in press), Atlantic Publishers and Distributors (P) Ltd., New Delhi, 2009.

Seminar Mitigating Spillovers and Contagion: Lessons from the Global Financial Crisis, Mumbai, Dec 08.

8

The False Death of Trickle-Down Economics*

John Tamny

It's fashionable in certain economic circles to mock the notion of trickle-down economics, the process whereby success enjoyed by the wealthy accrues to those not wealthy. As recently as August economist Jared Bernstein wrote that "Trickle-down economics died yesterday at 10 AM", and in a column last year recent Nobel Laureate Paul Krugman asked "Where's My Trickle?"

It turns out the "trickle down" theory that Krugman et al. dismissed so jubilantly is alive and well; the certain and positive truth when it comes to trickle-down sadly showing up in reverse. Indeed, newspaper headlines and articles amid our ongoing economic struggles make plain that its deniers wrote too soon in celebrating its demise. As it turns out, when those with money (meaning the rich) are hurting, their pain is often transferred to those who need money even more.

In a *New York Post* story dated September 25, the proprietor of Soho-based Five-Point Fitness spoke of his inability to attain financing for his popular workout facility. According to owner Kevin McGrath, "The guys [from the bank] said if this was a year ago, it would have been a slam dunk." But as the *Post* story noted, as "the economy continues to tailspin, scores of small-business owners are struggling to get

---

* *Courtesy*: www.realclearmarkets.com

tightfisted banks to dole out loans for much needed expansion plans".

It turns out McGrath is not alone. Four days later a *Wall Street Journal* account of major food franchisees found that they too are facing troubles with regard to finance. As the *Journal* put it, the tough financing environment for Panera Bread, Yum Brands and Sonic (employers of those who'd like to be rich one day) is "a sign of how the turmoil on Wall Street is spreading to large companies and small business owners".

Seeking out other lower-income individuals impacted by problems on Wall Street, *USA Today* reporter Charisse Jones traveled to Greenwich Avenue in Greenwich (CT), a street famous for its fancy shops and restaurants. While it's safe to say its shopowners and employees have traditionally earned microscopic fractions of what their customers have traditionally brought home, they've not been immune to the financial downturn that has plagued the elite of Greenwich.

Josè Candray, manager of Village Bagels in Greenwich told Jones that "tips are smaller" these days, while Greenwich resident (and investment banker) Bob Jermain referenced the fact that his kids no longer "need 20 sweaters", which means sales at Greenwich Avenue clothing stores are set to fall. Are layoffs of the lower-wage workers these businesses employ not too far off?

It turns out yes, because as an October 14th *USA Today* story noted, with "stores doing all the cost cutting they can to preserve profit margins", this "will mean fewer salespeople available to help shoppers". It's also notable that while those who make $100,000 or more only account for 10 per cent of the U.S. population, according to a study conducted by the Harrison Group, those in the $100,000 income bracket account for *50 per cent of retail spending.*

The Harrison Group study dovetails well with a *Bloomberg* story from last month which detailed a looming financial shortfall when it comes to efforts "to combat hunger, poverty and disease". Bill Gates was featured in the *Bloomberg* piece, and owing to his desire for "rich-world" governments to free up funds for poverty programs alongside his private efforts, Gates fears that "Rich-world budgets may not have room for increased generosity".

The above is interesting when we consider whose economic efforts regularly fill rich-country coffers with so much cash. Not only do the rich account for the majority of retail sales, but as countless studies have shown, they similarly account for the vast majority of tax revenues taken in by governments. So if the economy continues to falter, tax authorities worldwide will collect less from the rich, and this will soon enough reveal itself through less in the way of government funding for poverty programs here and around the world. This is probably a good thing considering the persistent failure of government-led poverty initiatives, but the point is still valid.

A recent *Washington Post* story, "Crisis sparks search for new aid sources", showed yet again how the poor hurt the most when the "dastardly" rich see their fortunes turn south. It turns out Lehman Brothers, as part of its expansive charity program, was until recently a $50,000 dollar donor to Habitat for Humanity. Dollar fifty thousand may not seem like much, but those funds paid for the construction of over 100 one-room houses that put a roof over the heads of 500 citizens of New Delhi. According to the *Post* account, previously those 500 "had been living in shanties of tarpaulins and old clothes". With Lehman no longer with us, it's fair to say that the beneficiaries of its charitable activities will have to get by on less.

Looked at from the perspective of private, non-charitable economic activity, an October 6 *USA Today* story wrote about taco vendor Jorge Flores in Nuevo Laredo, Mexico. While previously he would sell 300 tacos per day to laborers reliant on our robust economy, thanks to economic problems stateside, he now only sells 180. What's that they say about a rising tide lifting all boats? A subsiding tide evidently *lowers* all boats if Mr. Flores's story is at all indicative.

More generally, in 2007 charitable donations from Americans hit a record of $300 billion. But a recent newspaper headline noted that "Nonprofits Brace for Slowdown in Giving". Sure enough, nonprofits frequently only exist thanks to the generosity of the rich. And with the rich in many cases hurting in this uncertain economic climate, the ability of charitable organizations to continue their missions will be severely compromised.

What these various accounts tell us is that whether due to pure profit motive through which the rich supply capital to businesses, or through perhaps simple vanity that causes them to give to all manner of charities, it is thanks to the wealthy that job-creating businesses are funded, and it is also thanks to the rich that societal ills are addressed with ample funds.

So to deny the reality of trickle-down economics is the equivalent of denying that the sun sets in the west. It does, and trickle-down economics *is*. In short, politicians can dream up all sorts of tax plans and programs to harm the rich, but in doing so, they should make no mistake about who in fact will pay in the end.

9

The Global Financial Crisis: What Caused it, Where it is Heading?*

Ravi Batra†

Two thousand eight was year extraordinaire. It started off in a rather nonchalant way, but ended with a bang. Its myriad and breathtaking events caught the world off guard, but please allow me to say, arrogant as it sounds, that they did not surprise me, including the epoch-making victory of Barack Obama in the US presidential election. I had anticipated them all in two books more than two years ago. The first, *Greenspan's Fraud*, was written in 2005, and the second, *The New Golden Age: The Coming Revolution Against Political Corruption and Economic Chaos*, was finished before October 2006. In fact, the title of the second work itself reveals that I had anticipated an Obama-like revolution in the United States.

It now appears vain to remind the people of my forecasts, but see what I had to endure after I made them. Both books had served to reinforce my reputation as a crack pot, who sought public attention with bogus claims and phony prophecies that occasionally came true. *Greenspan's Fraud* was especially galling to my fellow economists, even some of my colleagues. Alan Greenspan was still the chairman of the Federal Reserve in the United States, and had been so for the past 18 years. Some people regard the Fed chairman, with his

---

* Prepared for St. Stephen's College, Delhi.

† www.ravibatra.com

all-encompassing ability to influence interest rates globally, as the most powerful man in the world.

This is perhaps an exaggeration, but Greenspan, who had actually been in the limelight for over three decades, was more than just a Fed chairman. Investors around the world came to worship him in the 1990s, as share markets broke record after record in many nations. Best-selling author Bob Woodward, who achieved celebrity writing about the Watergate scandal, declared Greenspan as the Maestro in 2000 in a book with the same title. Others were equally euphoric about him. Some called him a rare genius, the best economist ever; even Queen Elizabeth chipped in and knighted him in 2002 as Sir Alan Greenspan. Here I was, a mere professor at Southern Methodist University, who had the temerity not just to criticize him but call his policies self-serving and fraudulent. My book's title shocked the people, who in turn mocked me without reading my facts and arguments. But sometimes one has to bear insults to bring out the truth.

Where did I learn my economics? The question makes me nostalgic and takes me back into the 1960s, when I was a masters' student at the Delhi School of Economics. There I studied under luminary professors such as K.N. Raj, Jagdish Bhagwati, Amartya Sen, and India's current prime minister, Manmohan Singh. They were great teachers and taught me the fundamentals of modern economics.

However, there was one other teacher, whose theories were remarkably different and unknown. He was not even at the Delhi School. I met him in Lucknow, at the time a rather small town in India. He was Shri Prabhat Ranjan Sarkar, a wonderful man of vast knowledge in many different areas. He had written books on history, economics and philosophy among others. Two points stood out in his theories. First, the foundation of prosperity is people's purchasing power; second, rising inequality eventually destroys any economy.

I left India for the United States in 1966 to do a Ph.D., but Sarkar's ideas stayed with me and followed me wherever I went. I studied classical economics, Keynesian thought, and numerous other schools, but none focused on what Sarkar had stressed. Finally, I decided to write about his ideas and introduce them to the world, because few paid attention to the gems he had offered. I wrote a number of books based on his theories, starting in 1978, but here I want to emphasize how his ideas enabled me to see through the vacuity and deception of Greenspan's policies.

The Wage-Productivity Gap

Greenspan focused on company profits and labor productivity as the main engines of economic growth and prosperity. He believed that high profits generate high employment and high wages lead to joblessness. I will now show how this view is myopic and the sole cause of most of the economic travails afflicting the world.

Let me start with a universally acceptable statement. A healthy economy requires that there is a balance between supply and demand. Here supply means the production of goods and services offered to entire society, and demand means society's demand for such things. Thus, economic balance requires that

Supply = Demand

Without this balance, there is either high unemployment or high inflation. The main source of supply is labor productivity, whereas the main source of demand is the real wage, or people's purchasing power in Sarkar's nomenclature. When productivity rises, production or supply goes up and when the real wage increases, consumer spending, and hence investment spending, go up. Because of this investment and new technology, productivity grows over time, which means supply rises over the years. Therefore, demand must also grow proportionately to maintain the economic balance, implying that the real wage must rise in proportion to productivity. However, Greenspan loved to see the rise in productivity but hated the rise in the real wage. He even wanted to abolish the minimum wage, and always argued against its rise, although relentless price increases in the United States had all but demolished its purchasing power. In this respect, the maestro had a lot of company, including the support of President

George W. Bush and economic establishment. As a result, the US minimum wage, which peaked at $10 per hour in 1969 in terms of 2008 prices, is now less than $7. Incidentally, the unemployment rate in 1969 was just 3.5 per cent, among the lowest in US history.

If the real wage fails to grow as fast as productivity, then over time, a wage-productivity gap develops and

Supply > Demand

Then how do you maintain the indispensable economic balance? This is where the special genius of Greenspan, along with that of conventional economics, came into play. This is where liberal and conservative economists alike, some of them Nobel Laureates, preached their gospel and in the process failed the world.

There is another way through which demand can be raised—new debt. It is an artificial way, and cannot be used forever, but it can postpone the problem for a long time, while the potential economic imbalance builds and cumulates. From 1981 on, U.S. budget deficits, with Greenspan and company advising President Reagan, grew apace. Economists called it fiscal policy, but in reality it was a debt-creating policy. This is how the supply-demand balance was maintained in the presence of the rising wage gap. Thus, for a while, economic balance occurs when

Productivity growth = growth of the real wage plus debt

and

new debt = supply – demand

The Profit and Stock-Market Bubbles

Once productivity outpaces the real wage and debt fills the supply-demand gap, company profits skyrocket, because the entire fruit of rising productivity goes to capital income. However, these are debt-supported profits, because without this debt goods will be unsold and profits will fail to materialize. With rocketing profits come rocketing share prices, so everybody becomes happy and begins to dance. This is how Greenspan won the world's adulation, and no one looked at the magical role played by debt.

Once federal debt began to sore in the United States from 1981 on, it took barely a year, before the Dow Jones Index (the Dow in short) began to rise. The Dow ended the year around 800, but climbed above 2,000 by mid-1987. It had taken the ballyhooed index about 100 hundred years to go past 1,000, but the next 1,000 came in merely two years. A grateful Reagan appointed Greenspan as the Fed chairman in August 1987, but two months later the maestro had to face the music of his own handiwork. The debt-built stock market bubble, founded by that debt-built profit bubble, crashed in the month of October. Greenspan had no idea of how the rising wage gap generates the supply-demand gap. Instead of focusing on wages, he turned to the other way of creating debt. He flooded the world with money and trimmed the interest rate to lure consumers into borrowing. New debt was now created with the help of fiscal policy as well as what economists like to call monetary policy. However, such euphemisms only mask the truth, which is that these policies solve the problem only by generating new debt.

With increasing use of computers and the Internet, productivity began to rise faster than before, while government policies restrained wage growth. So the wage gap continued to rise and actually accelerated. Not surprisingly, new debt played an even larger role during the 1990s. The government did not borrow as much as before, but the public did more than its share. The mushrooming US trade deficit also made a contribution in this regard, because the rest of the world bought American government bonds with its trade surplus that resulted in its dollar hoard. Consequently, American interest rates remained low for a long time and lulled Greenspan and the fawning world into believing that his policies were actually responsible for the surface prosperity.

So the debt-and-stock-market party that had been derailed by the 1987 crash returned with a gusto. This time the world got drunk on the dot.com boom that took share markets to stratosphere, with the Dow crossing 10,000 in 1999. Still no one realized the crucial role played by new debt in the ever growing mania. For a variety of reasons, the US federal government enjoyed a budget surplus in 1999. Since the wage gap continued to rise, I became convinced that the budget surplus would soon generate a supply-demand gap and hence a crash in profits and share prices. That is when I wrote my book, *The Crash of the Millennium*, predicting that share markets would collapse in 2000 and beyond. This is exactly what happened, because in an environment of the growing wage gap, the moment debt stops growing, supply exceeds demand, over production results, profits tumble and share prices sink. The stock-market crash of 2000-2001 was the worst since the great crash of 1929.

The Housing Bubble

Somehow Greenspan loves bubbles. As the stock market plummeted in 2000, he panicked and slashed interest rates to depths that had not been seen since the depression of the 1930s. He knew consumer demand was inadequate but did not attribute it to the stagnant real wage. He would rather have the public spend money through borrowing than through higher salaries. Greenspan also encouraged people to use their home equity to secure loans and asked banks to lower their lending standards. The banks dutifully followed as they and their CEOs began to make bushels of money. Add to this his deregulation spree that freed banks to trade in the stock market, and bubbles started to emerge in home prices and credit markets. Soon the new bubbles bested even the dot.com balloon of the 1990s. Greenspan still had not realized that since debt cannot grow exponentially all bubbles burst in the end, and when they do the consequences are very painful.

I have just given you a capsule of Greenspan's follies and policies; there is much more that cannot be presented in a brief article. But the main point is that the maestro succeeded in hiding the true consequences of his actions and tailored his advice to the ideology of whoever became the American president. In the process Greenspan contradicted his earlier policies, mainly to secure his reappointment as the Fed chairman by the incoming president. Today people realize that Greenspan is mostly to blame for the global crisis. In fact, the cable television channel CNN recently included him among the top 10 culprits responsible for the spreading fiasco, but the same CNN had once idolized the maestro.

Greenspan retired in January 2006 and was replaced by Ben Bernanke, who is no different from the former chairman. Mr. Bernanke is also unaware of the role played by sufficiently high wages in restoring economic balance. So he has rehashed Greenspan's policies at even faster place, although it must be added in his defense that the current mess is not entirely of his making.

Where Are We Headed?

In *The New Golden Age*, I predicted that economic chaos would begin in 2007 with a housing meltdown in the United States, followed by a banking crisis and share price declines in 2008 and 2009. I now foresee that this crisis would last at least till 2010, and possibly longer. This is because conventional economists still do not understand the nasty economic effects of the wage-productivity gap, which has grown enormously all over the world. If the doctor does not diagnose the sickness properly, the patient has to suffer for a long time. That is why I am afraid the global financial debacle will turn into a steep recession and be the worst since the Great Depression, even worse than the painful slump of 1980-1982 that afflicted the whole world. I have offered a number of economic reforms deriving from the theory of the wage gap in my two books explored above, and it is possible to come out of the recession within a year, but alas conventional economists would not let us escape the looming disaster so quickly.

Yet all is not lost. There is an effulgent silver lining lurking behind the pal of dark clouds. Sarkar's historical cycles that I have repeatedly used in my forecasts also show that eventually the world will see a wonderfully prosperous era enshrined in the new golden age. This, I feel, could happen by the end of the next decade.

10

US Senate the False Death of Trickle-Down Economics, Part II*

John Tamny

Last October, this column addressed the notion of trickle-down economics. The aforementioned concept has to do with the basic belief that the economic gains made by the rich accrue to those not rich.

Economic thinkers from Paul Krugman to Jared Bernstein to Jonathan Chait (Chait refers to thinking here as the "Big Con") have dismissed the idea that the above is real, but as the referenced column showed, trickle-down economics quite simply is. Indeed, all it took to prove this point was to collect media accounts showing how economic uncertainty for the well-to-do in our midst had greatly impacted those not as well-to-do. This revealed itself everywhere from the retail sector to tips given at restaurants to charity.

Sadly, news accounts since October have yet again shown that when the rich are hurting, the poor hurt even more. The logic underpinning trickle-down economics is difficult to refute, and if the news since the fall is any kind of indicator, the concept's reversal amid our economic decline continues to harm the poor and middle class.

To begin, we can reference a December article by Miriam Jordan in the *Wall Street Journal*. Titled "When the Going Gets Tough, Some People Lay Off the Nanny", Jordan among

---

* *Courtesy*: www.realclearmarkets.com

others profiled Dolores Jacobo, nanny for three-month old twins in an “affluent Malibu, Calif., household.” According to Jordan, Jacobo had “earned her place as an integral member” of the family, but with the family hit hard by this nation’s economic decline, Jacobo was recently informed that her $1,000-a-week position was being eliminated.

Jacobo is not alone in this regard. Jordan observed that “on a recent morning, it was standing room only in the waiting room at DDL Domestic Agency in Los Angeles.” Applicants for new caregiver positions included Alba Monterrosa, a 31-year old single mother of two who had previously earned $600/week caring for the 3 and 5-year old children of Suzanne Sirof. But thanks to the economic downturn, Sirof can no longer afford Monterrosa.

Moving to houses of worship, another *Wall Street Journal* article from last month titled “In Hard Times, Houses of God Turn To Chapter 11 in Book of Bankruptcy”, showed how churches are similarly taking the enervated economy on the chin. As the article noted, during “this holiday season of tough times, not even houses of God have been spared.” According to various accounts, church giving is down as much as 15 per cent, and as a result, some have been forced to file for bankruptcy.

When it comes to charities, a November article from the *Journal* chronicled “Big Players” that have scaled back on charitable donations. Due to losses in the stock market combined with a recessionary outlook, the “pipeline from corporate America to the nation’s charities is starting to dry up.” Formerly big givers such as Bear Stearns, Lehman Brothers and Merrill Lynch have either collapsed or been bought, not to mention the fact that billionaires—including Bill Gates—have said they’ll be scaling back the dollar amount of their grants.

Other billionaires joining Gates when it comes to less giving include renowned philanthropist David Koch, who says he’s “not making new commitments.” Former AIG chief Hank Greenberg’s foundation is heavily weighted in AIG stock, but with the insurer’s shares well down, Greenberg says “You can’t give what you haven't got." Las Vegas casino mogul Sheldon Adelson has watched his Sands' holdings decline by $30 billion, which means the traditional recipients of his largesse will see a decline in the funds they receive, assuming they receive anything at all.

Residents of Palm Beach, the legendary playground of the rich, were in particular hit hard given how many had exposure to the allegedly fraudulent dealings of Bernard Madoff. According to the *Wall Street Journal's* Paulo Prada, if the worst materializes, "Gardeners and dog walkers are likely to lose jobs, along with accountants and lawyers."

For the business owners whose shops and restaurants line Palm Beach's Worth Avenue, they worry that the "alleged fraud will exacerbate what already has been an unusually quite season." That being the case, it's fair to assume that the waiters and waitresses heavily reliant on tips will experience for the first time in a while what it's like to serve relatively impoverished customers.

As for Jewish charities, some have already folded altogether, and some face disastrous shortfalls. According to the *Wall Street Journal's* Eleanor Laise and Dennis Berman, programs "for bone-marrow transplants, death-row inmates and human rights campaigns" have already been threatened "as dozens of philanthropies took stock of their exposure" to Madoff.

Moving to our institutions of higher learning, a *Los Angeles Times* article from Christmas day pointed to donation shortfalls at Syracuse University that if not corrected, would force 400 students to drop out. Thanks to California's budget crisis, student fees at schools in the UC system will rise 10 per cent next year, while the Cal State system will reduce its enrollment by 10,000 students.

Citing losses in its $17.2 billion endowment, Stanford plans to reduce financial aid. President-Barack Obama's former college, Occidental, plans to freeze non-faculty hiring, and the University of Southern California plans the same.

And with retail sales down, Liz Claiborne CEO William McComb now catches various subways and trains to New York City airports in order to shield his shareholders from costs related to cabs and livery drivers. Last month, this writer made a speech in Pittsburgh, and was taken in a cab from downtown to the Pittsburgh airport by cabdriver Jim Marosz. Marosz said the downturn has taken his fares down 30 per cent. In the words of Marosz, "our fares go up and down with the economy."

So while elite economic thinkers turn their noses up to the notion of trickle-down economics, all it takes to confirm the latter's truth is to pick up any major newspaper on any given day. With the US economy struggling, the rich are very much hurting. Sadly, it remains the case that those not rich will feel their pain most acutely.

All of the above will hopefully be remembered the next time a politician posits that economic bliss will result from hurting the rich. Indeed, while the rich surely pay the most in taxes and experience the greatest losses of wealth during tough economic times, it's invariably the poor who truly feel their pain.

11

The Global Meltdown and Business: An HR Perspective

Tapomoy Deb

Recession has impacted every single business firm particularly the small and medium enterprises. Firms are increasingly finding going getting tougher each day and many small and medium firms have become unviable and hence closed down. In this scenario, HR function can carve out a significant role for itself by reviewing, innovating and implementing various core strategies. The paper articulates upon some of the core strategies like performance management system, talent management, succession planning, participation, employee engagement, etc.

The current global recession has taken its toll on most of the countries. The US economic downturn has spelt doom for the developing countries like India. Although the domestic sector is still better than international market, the growth rate projected for India at 8 per cent has virtually fallen down to around 5 per cent. The global economic crisis is affecting everyone and it hurts business all the more. Since last year, following global trends, there has been massive job cuts in India also and Textile, IT and Automotive industry are the worst hit. It is estimated that more than 1.5 lakh jobs have been cut in the Indian textile sector alone in the last couple of months. Although some of the experts comment that perhaps bottom has already been reached and therefore things should improve for Indian business and people in the next 6 months or so. Nevertheless, recession has adversely affected industry, entrepreneurs, employees and consumers as well.

In this current economic meltdown, firms are reviewing their strategies, business plans and workforce. In order to save cost, necessary to stay afloat to tide over bad times, firms are cutting jobs more than anything else. Suddenly, firms have found that a sizeable portion particularly their temporary workers are in excess which they could easily shed. Some other firms are cutting their workforce salaries by at least 20 per cent. Paradoxically, though people are considered to be strategic asset of a firm, but they happen to be the first casualty of economic recession. Commentators argue that most of the CEOs are not seeking any cut in their pay, perquisites, benefits or expenses, but they are cutting their employee's wage bill which often is only a fraction of the CEO's pay. Though there are a few firms like Federal Express, where the CEO and other members of the board has voluntarily offered for pay cuts in order to save some jobs of the employees. However, such instances happen to be limited. Beyond paradox, the ground reality is that people constitute a significant part of operational and product cost of the firms. Therefore, by reducing people cost, firms are striving hard to reduce their product cost so that they continue to be cost-competitive in the market and are able to attract customers. While CEOs are worried about sustainability of business, managers are anxious about meeting their business targets and employees are concerned about their job safety. Nevertheless, the situation is grim; as people's morale is at the lowest ebbs. In such a scenario, the role of human resource management (or HR) function assumes paramount importance.

Surely for long HR has chartered a parallel track for itself along with business. This has led to gradual lowering of its credibility to directly contribute to business outcomes especially the bottom line. With economic recession, HR needs to demonstrate robust business outcomes. As many senior HR professionals agree that this is the right time for effective contribution from HR function both with business perspectives and people orientation. Broadly speaking, the role of HR function needs to be diagnostic and action-oriented at this stage. Diagnostic because it needs to review various people-oriented processes, systems and programmes and also evaluate their connectivity with business. The diagnosis will help to identify areas needing immediate attention and focus and accordingly action plans can be formulated and implemented effectively. Some of the suggested HR strategies for effectively managing human resources in this global meltdown are as follows:

- **Recruitment.** Many firms are not making recruitments as expansion or growth plan has been temporarily suspended. Therefore, HR functionaries should freeze their new recruitment plans and work upon only replacement recruitments in order to replenish the workforce necessary to stay competitive. Such recruitments, wherever possible, should be made internally. If internal recruitment is impossible, then external recruitment should be resorted to. However, for firms creating new work activities and functions, new recruitment should be made very cautiously. Additionally, HR functionaries should be very focused in hiring the right talent as many people are up for hiring in the labour market. They should use best discretion to make effective selection from a large pool of candidates. Hence, HR functionaries should now ensure that all recruitments are bare necessity, strategically relevant, talent driven and a cost efficient proposition for the firms.
- **Performance management system.** Performance management system of the organization is essentially a competency development and talent identification process. Therefore, HR functionaries should ensure renewed emphasis on performance management system, seek involvement of managers and their employees, ensure effective monitoring of results and identify talents for leadership or key positions in the firm. Employees who are not upto the mark should be weeded out irrespective of their tenure or seniority.

Recession in one way accords an opportunity to the firms to evaluate the skills and competencies of their workforce, identify best employees and weed out others in order to stay effective and competitive.

- **Reward and recognition system.** HR functionaries should defer till such time as things improve, all large bonuses, rewards, gifts, holidays, mega-celebrations, etc. However, it needs to focus upon innovative employee benefits, rewards and incentives. In place of cash payments, emphasis on benefits and long-term incentives likes stocks should be utilized. Additionally, recognition programmes must be increasingly used, particularly public recognition of talents. This will help to motivate employees.
- **Talent management system.** In these difficult times, only talents will help firms to tide through difficult times. Therefore, firms must either emphasize or initiate talent-mapping processes internally to identify best employees. The results of performance management system along with various HR interventions like assessment centres, 360 degree feedback, etc. should be fully utilized for identifying talents and ensuring their strategic placement within the firm.
- **Succession planning.** HR functionaries should immediately look at succession plans of the firm. Identifying senior executives drawing fat salary but with limited perspectives and contributions can be considered for replacement with their identified successors. Promoting leadership internally will not only save cost for the firms which is very crucial at this stage, but will also motivate people across the firm to perform exceedingly well. The outcomes of performance management system and talent management system can be relied upon for the purpose.
- **Training and development.** Surely this is not the time for freezing training and development programmes.

This is because skills and competencies of people need to be even better than ever before if the firm intends to sustain itself. HR functionaries should though refrain from expensive training and management development programs, but should carve out those programmes in association with internal business leaders and outside experts that give a competitive edge to the firm. In other words, training and development programs should focus on skills and competencies to thrive in recession-prone marketplace. Moreover, it may be noted that a lot of acclaimed trainers and development facilitators are available at a very competitive fees in current scenario. HR functionaries can therefore negotiate well and make productive use of their skills.

- **Employee engagement.** No firm can ever be competitive if its employees are not truly engaged to their jobs. HR functionaries should focus on various engagement activities at no cost such as open house communication, business presentation quizzes, customer persuasion competitions, etc. HR functionaries must ensure that their firms show commitment to its workforce. As late Shri Aditya Vikram Birla once remarked, "Your men will be as loyal to you as you are to them". Therefore, management commitment is the first step towards engaging employees. Managers should be coached by HR functionaries so that they facilitate the involvement of employees in various functional activities, tasks and jobs. This will renew the sense of ownership employees have towards their firm and jobs.
- **Participation and feedback.** Participation of employees in formulating and implementing strategies to fight recessionary condition is crucial for the continued sustainability of the firms. HR functionaries should immediately embark upon a system and diagnostic survey and interaction with

employees across the firm to ascertain how each one of them can help save costs and ensure sustainability. A textile firm which carried out such a survey brought to light many important points for management's consideration and subsequent implementation as shown in the box below:

Key Performance Indicators for Fighting Recession

Production. Reduce cost through the following measures:

(a) Inventory level.
(b) Energy conservation.
(c) Machine productivity.
(d) Wastage reduction.
(e) Sales of unutilized assets and materials.
(f) Producing saleable materials only.
(g) Suspend all capital expenditures.

Marketing. Initiate the following measures:

(a) Increasing sales through enhanced enquiry.
(b) Reviewing current pricing strategy.
(c) Focus on high margin markets and customers.
(d) Warehousing.
(e) Focusing upon direct sales rather than through commission agents.
(f) Focus with renewed ideas and energy.

Logistics. Initiate the following measures:

(a) Proper vessel scheduling.
(b) Reduce container retention cost by 50%.
(c) Improving logistic support at BB plant.

Finance. Initiate the following measures:

(a) Tight control on expenses.
(b) Speedy collection of funds from institutions and government agencies.
(c) Reduce discrepancies in LC for saving bank charges.
(d) Avoid wastage of cheques.
(e) Realistic and achievable business plan for preventing cash crunch.

Technology/IT. Initiate the following measures:

(a) Effective implementation of SAP.
(b) Controlling license fees through use of Linux.
(c) Reduce AMC fees.

Contd...

HR/Administrative. Initiate the following measures:

(a) Forming special task groups.
(b) No leave encashment.
(c) Control manpower cost.
(d) Control administrative expenses (Conduct why–why analyses).
(e) Five days a week working to save on overheads.
(f) Accountability-oriented work culture.
(g) Freeze all new recruitment except for replacement purposes.
(h) Vendor re-negotiations in view of lower rate of diesel and petrol.

Legal. Initiate the following measure:

(a) Educating/training users on legal aspects to prevent conflicts/disputes.

Engineering. Initiate the following measure:

(a) Improve utilization of utilities and monitoring power/heating/cooling/humidification for cost efficiency.

Thus, it is clear that HR functionaries can ensure that key performance indicators to deal effectively with recession are identified and implemented by the workforce itself. It is then, that the commitment of the employee shall be high and results nothing less than outstanding. This also helps to focus on the specific and distinctive aspects of the business which need immediate action. The following may be noted in this regard:

- **People touch.** Communication is the most crucial human tool of touching lives of people. More than ever before, HR functionaries should now communicate with the employees across the firm and hierarchy to share various strategies put in place to fight recession and assure their job continuity. Once employees have their apprehension regarding job security put to rest by the HR functionaries, their wholehearted participation, engagement and ownership can be effectively leveraged for best organizational outcomes. Additionally, HR functionaries must ensure that their CEOs are communicating often with the employees to boost workforce morale.
- **Change management.** In order to sail through current difficult times, change management is necessary. HR functionaries should take a lead in initiating,

managing and utilizing change management process for sustaining business. They need to undertake careful planning, design meticulous processes, and above all, motivate employees for organizational change necessitated by economic downturn.

- **Employee retention.** It would be the greatest fallacy for the firm's leadership to assume that given recession and subsequent dearth of jobs, talented employees will not leave their firms. The truth is that whether in good times or bad times, talents have immense potential and therefore numerous opportunities. This is even more prevalent during recessionary times because firms are looking for the very best employees and these talented employees will be quickly and easily spotted and hired by other firms. Therefore, HR functionaries should emphasize their talent retention programs to ensure they do not lose control of those who have the ability to steer the firm through troubled waters successfully.
- **Monitoring costs.** HR functionaries must ensure that everyone in the firm is cost savvy and why-why analyses are made before taking a decision to spend even a single penny. Negotiations with vendors, suppliers and service providers should be made to ensure that maximum value is leveraged by the firm. Further, various operational and product innovations must be undertaken to reduce costs.

Hence, we may conclude that recession is a threat to business but an opportunity to HR functionaries to prove their mettle in sustaining the firm through and by the productive contributions and involvement of the employees. While HR strategies enumerated above may have differing shades and styles depending on the leadership, culture and climate, yet the role of employees in steering through difficult times cannot be overemphasized. However, it needs to be clearly understood that the role of leadership in meeting and surpassing downturn is critical. Without an engaging and inspiring leadership, not just the success of HR strategies but the sustainability of the firm as a whole will be questionable.

12

Indian PM's Statement at the Summit of Heads of State or Governments of the G20 Countries on Financial Markets and the World Economy

Washington: 15 November 2008

We are meeting at a time of exceptional difficulty for the world economy. The financial crisis, which a year ago seemed to be localized in one part of the financial system in the US, has exploded into a systemic crisis, spreading through the highly interconnected financial markets of industrialized countries, and has had its effects on other markets also.

It has choked normal credit channels, triggered a worldwide collapse in stock markets around the world. The real economy is clearly affected. Industrialised countries were expected to slow down in 2008. They are now projected to be in a recession in the second half of the year, and there is as yet little prospect of an early recovery. Many have called it the most serious crisis since the Great Depression.

Emerging market countries were not the cause of this crisis, but they are amongst its worst affected victims. Recession will hit the export performance of developing countries and the choking of credit, combined with elevated risk perception, will lead to lower capital flows and reduced levels of foreign direct investment. The combined effect will be to slow down economic growth in developing countries.

India is experiencing this negative impact. After growing at close to 9 per cent per year for four years, our growth rate is expected to slow down to between 7 to 7.5 per cent in the current financial year. The pace of growth next year will depend, in part, upon how long the global recession lasts and how quickly global capital flows return to normal. Much of India's growth is internally driven and I expect we can maintain a strong pace of growth in the coming years, but many developing countries will be harder hit.

A slowing down of growth in developing countries will push millions of people back into poverty, with adverse effects on nutrition, health and education levels. These are not transient impacts but will impact a full generation. If we are to prevent a slide back and ensure that MDGs are achieved, we need to ensure that growth in developing economies is not affected.

Since the crisis is global, it calls for a coordinated global response and this summit is therefore timely. In our discussions, we need to distinguish between the immediate priority, which must be to bring the crisis under control as quickly as possible with as little adverse effect on developing countries, and the medium term objective of reforming the global financial architecture to prevent similar crises in future. I will comment briefly on both.

As far as the immediate priority is concerned, I recognize that a number of important steps have already been taken by countries to inject liquidity into the financial system, recapitalize banks and other systemically important institutions. Some countries have also introduced a number of innovative, even unorthodox, measures to restore confidence so that the financial system could start functioning again. These measures have had some effect, but the crisis is far from over. Credit channels remain clogged and the signs of distress in the real economy suggest that additional measures are needed.

An obvious issue is to consider whether the emergence of recessionary trends calls for some fiscal stimulus. A coordinated fiscal stimulus by countries that are in a position to do so would help to mitigate the severity and duration of the recession. It would also send a strong signal to investors around the world. Resort to fiscal stimulus may be viewed as risky in some situations, but if we are indeed on the brink of the worst downturn since the Great Depression, the risk may be worth taking. We should, therefore, take all possible measures at the national level to complement any coordinated international stimulus.

The international community needs to consider special initiatives to counter the shrinkage of capital flows to developing countries that is almost certain to occur over the next two years. The initiative by the IMF to establish a new liquidity facility is a welcome step. However, we must also consider whether the IMF is adequately funded for the task it will face in managing this global crisis. Looking ahead we must plan for possible additional demands on the IMF if the global recession is pronounced. This suggests that we must activate a process for replenishing IMF resources.

An alternative to the IMF as a source of quick disbursing liquidity is the establishment of short-term swap arrangements. The existence of such arrangements will reduce the burden on the IMF and will add to confidence in the system. Countries in a position to do so should consider the scope for expanding such arrangements.

Depressed conditions in the global economy are likely to produce a downturn in private investment in developing countries which will worsen recessionary trends. It is necessary to take steps to counter this development. Expanding investment in infrastructure by the public sector and also the private sector where possible is an ideal countercyclical device. It has the immediate effect of stimulating demand counter-cyclically and the longer-term effect of laying the conditions for an early return to faster growth. Investment in infrastructure today is perhaps the best signal for reviving private investment, including FDI, tomorrow.

This requires new and innovative ways of solving the financing problems that will restrain infrastructure investment. The World Bank, regional development banks and national governments need to consider measures such as providing additional credit for infrastructure projects, promote new instruments for infrastructure financing and providing capital and liquidity support to banking institutions to lend to infrastructure projects that are underway. The World Bank/ IFC and the Regional Development banks should aim at making an additional $50 billion per year in support of infrastructure development in the public and private sectors. This window can be wound down once normalcy returns to global capital flows.

Industrialized countries can also help to revive trade flows in developing countries by expanding the scale of export credit finance available to these countries. We know there is a temporary market failure in this area with elevated risk perceptions which discourage private flows. There is a need to intervene to overcome market failure. A collapse of trade is the last thing that one wants in the current crisis, with all its implications for growth and employment. Concerted government action in expanding export credit financing on reasonable terms will help support the pace of development in developing countries, which is critical for achieving poverty alleviation and employment objectives.

Our willingness to take specific steps to support developing countries in this period of exceptional difficulty will be a test of our collective leadership. Many developing countries have made strenuous efforts to implement economic reforms to deal with the challenges of an increasingly open and globalised world. This has often required implementation of policies which have aroused domestic fears and uncertainties. We have persevered in this process and have benefited from it. Economic performance in almost all developing countries has improved. In the process, attitudes towards globalisation have begun to change and people all over the world have come to appreciate the enormous benefits that can be derived from global economic integration. It would be a great pity if this growing support for open policies in the developing world is weakened because of a failure to protect developing countries from a recession which is not of their making.

We need to take urgent steps to strengthen the global trading system and forestall any protectionist tendencies which always surface in times of recession. A successful conclusion of the ongoing multilateral trade talks would be an important confidence builder at this stage. We are willing to work constructively with other major players to reach a balanced and mutually beneficial outcome.

While our immediate priority should be to deal with the crisis which is still unfolding, we also need to look ahead to see what changes are needed in the global financial architecture to avoid such crisis from recurring. Much useful work in this area has already been done by Finance Ministers and there is considerable consensus on many areas. I will, therefore, limit my remarks to a few points.

I agree with the general consensus that there are several factors behind the crisis and the future global economic architecture must be designed to deal with these. These include failure of regulatory and supervisory mechanisms, inadequate appreciation and management of systemic risks and inadequate transparency in financial institutions.

The new architecture we design must include a credible system of multilateral surveillance which can signal the emergence of imbalances that are likely to have systemic effects, and also put in motion a process of consultation that can yield results in terms of policy coordination. At this point, I would like to emphasise the importance of broad based multilateral approaches to our efforts. Bodies such as the G-7 are no longer sufficient to meet the demands of the day. We need to ensure that any new architecture we design is genuinely multilateral with adequate representation from countries reflecting changes in economic realities.

The International Monetary Fund is the logical body to perform the task of multilateral surveillance of macro-economic imbalances and their relationship to financial stability. However, it is relevant to ask whether its systems and procedures are adequate to the task. Over the years, the Fund has become marginal to the task of policy analysis and consultations on macro-economic imbalances and related policies in the major countries. That task is now performed in other forums, though it is questionable whether it is being performed well. I believe we need a comprehensive review of the procedures of the IMF leading to recommendations on governance reform which would enable the Fund to perform the role of macro-economic policy coordination.

An important element of longer-term reform is to restructure the representation in the governance levels of the Fund to reflect the current and prospective economic realities. Quota reform is the normal way to effect a change in voting power but it has been contentious and incremental, and what has been achieved thus far has fallen far short of what is needed. The Board of Governors of the IMF should be explicitly charged with exploring alternative modalities to achieve a more legitimate representation.

Looking ahead, we also have to pay attention to the many regulatory gaps in the financial system which allowed the development of excess leverage and the risks associated with it. It is obvious that we need better systems of risk management and better regulation and supervision, especially of institutions that have a global reach and are dealing in financial instruments that are exceedingly complex. Managers of financial institutions, credit rating agencies and regulators have to do a much better job. The structure of incentives in the system has to be aligned to this end. We also need to examine whether the existing forums of regulators that are there are adequate and cover the entire gamut of regulatory and supervisory activities that are required.

These are technical issues that should be tackled in the specialized forums dealing with financial stability, notably the Basle Committee on Banking Supervision and the Financial Stability Forum. However, both these bodies need to have broader representation than they do at present. International co-ordination on regulatory issues would be more easily achieved if the principal forums where these issues are discussed were seen to be more representative. Broad basing the present representation in these forums is much easier to achieve and I hope this Summit will give a clear signal in this direction. It will certainly build confidence in our intention over the longer-term to achieve significant reform in the governance of the global financial system.

Given the fact that this financial crisis has affected growth prospects across the board, we also need to examine the present structures of trade and development finance to consider how to ensure greater stability in these flows in the face of difficult situations such as the current one. This issue could be examined by the expert group I have referred to or by separate group focusing on this issue. Its work could lead to the design of appropriate international mechanisms and instruments for maintaining and enhancing these flows in future.

...The world has certainly changed sufficiently to need a new architecture, but this can only be done on the basis of much greater preparation and consultation. We can however signal that we are serious about starting a process that will, in time, produce an architecture suited to the new challenges and vulnerabilities facing the world economy and reflective of the changes that have taken place in the economic structure. We must also give the world a clear signal of our resolve to take specific coordinated action to handle the current crisis in a manner which restores confidence and which also responds to the needs of developing countries. We need to ensure that the processes we set in motion today safeguard and promote the welfare of our future generations.

13

Remarks by Indian PM on the International Financial Crisis at the ASEM Summit

Beijing: 24 October 2008

The international financial crisis has resulted from three failures:

(a) A regulatory and supervisory failure in major developed countries;

(b) A failure in risk management in private financial institutions;

(c) A failure in market discipline mechanism.

These are not my views but those of the distinguished Managing Director of the IMF, with which I agree.

We must analyse objectively how and why these failures have occurred with such ferocity. This is necessary to put in place a new set of rules which will prevent reoccurrence of such failures.

The sad truth is that in this age of globalisation we have a global economy of sorts but it is not supported by a global polity to provide effective governance.

The resulting crisis of liquidity, accumulation of bad assets, shortage of capital and collapse of confidence threatens to spill over into the real economy by way of reduced demand for goods and services particularly exports, reduced access to trade and suppliers credits superimposed on other crises—food and fuel price rises that have strained budgets and balance of payments leading to rising inflation and living costs in many developing countries.

The President of the World Bank has identified at least 30 developing countries whose balance of payments will experience a severe deterioration in the wake of this financial crisis.

The immediate task is to declog the credit markets the world over. Coordinated global action is essential to restore a measure of confidence in the credit markets.

From the standpoint of developing countries, international financial institutions, particularly the IMF and World Bank, need to put in place exogenous shock facilities to provide assistance to the affected countries more quickly and in larger amounts with less service conditionalities and greater flexibility.

Countries with strong foreign exchange positions could make additional resources available to the international financial institutions on appropriate terms to finance their operations.

As a counter cyclical device, increased infrastructure investments in developing countries, if backed by increased resources flows from multilateral financial institutions such as the IBRD and Regional Development Banks, can act as a powerful stabilizer.

The IMF should revisit the potentially powerful instrument of creating liquidity through fresh allocation of Special Drawing Rights in favour of multilateral development finance institutions.

The reform and reconstruction of the financial system has to be a collective international effort since borders no longer confine financial institutions or can keep out financial turmoil. Given the growth in cross-border investment, trade and banking in the last three decades, the world must ponder over the need for a global monitoring authority to promote global supervision and cooperation in the increasingly integrated world in which we live.

In devising a reform agenda, one must bear the wise saying of John Maynard Keynes regarding the economically damaging role of excessive speculative activity. To quote Keynes:

> "Speculators may do no harm as bubbles on a steady stream of enterprise. But the position is serious when enterprise becomes the bubble on a whirlpool of speculation. When the capital development of a country becomes a byproduct of the activities of a casino, the job is likely to be ill-done."

Clearly, there has been a massive failure of regulatory and supervisory powers. Speculators have had a free run for far too long a period. International institutions like the IMF have also not covered themselves with glory. There has been an unacceptable failure of effective multilateral supervision of major developed economies and in particular of what has been going on in their financial markets.

India's banking system is sound and well capitalized. It is not exposed to the type of assets which have given rise to this crisis. Our real economy will grow at the rate of 7 to 7.5 per cent this year despite the global slowdown of export demand and capital inflows. We have injected fresh liquidity in the system.

We realize that we cannot remain totally unaffected when the global economy and financial system are in deep trouble. Our stock markets and the exchange rate of the rupee are under pressure due to capital outflow of foreign institutional investors. Sooner or later, the real economy is bound to experience the pain.

We are, therefore, sincere in our desire to cooperate and coordinate our actions with the world community to find effective and pragmatic solutions to the formidable challenges the world economy is now faced with.

14

Indian Government's Fiscal Stimulus Package Announced on 7 December 2008

Government Announces Measures for Stimulating the Economy

The Government has been concerned about the impact of the global financial crisis on the Indian economy and a number of steps have been taken to deal with this problem.

The first priority was to re-assure the people of the stability of the financial system in general and of the safety of bank deposits in particular. To this end, steps were taken to infuse liquidity into the banking system and also to address problems being faced by various non-bank financing companies. These steps have ensured that the financial system is functioning effectively without suffering the kind of loss of confidence experienced in the industrialised world.

Having assured stability of the system, the Government has focused its attention on countering the impact of the global recession on India's economic growth. On the monetary side, the RBI has sought to pump sufficient liquidity into the banking system to enable bank credit to meet the expanded requirements of the economy keeping in mind the contraction in credit from non-bank sources. Banks have been provided adequate liquidity through a series of reductions in the CRR and additional flexibility in meeting the SLR requirement. Interest rate reductions have also been signalled by reductions in the repo and reverse repo rates, the most recent of which was announced on Saturday when both the repo rate and the reverse repo rate were cut by 100 basis points. Access to external commercial borrowings has also been liberalised so that borrowers capable of accessing funds from abroad are allowed to do so. The banks are being encouraged to counter what might otherwise become self-fulfilling negative expectations by enhanced lending to support economic activity.

These measures in the area of money and credit are being supplemented by fiscal measures designed to stimulate the economy. In recognition of the need for a fiscal stimulus, the government had consciously allowed the fiscal deficit to expand beyond the originally targeted level because of the loan waivers, issue of oil and fertilizer bonds and higher levels of food subsidy. In addition, the following steps are being taken:

1. Plan Expenditure

In order to provide a contra-cyclical stimulus via plan expenditure, the Government has decided to seek authorisation for additional plan expenditure of upto Rs. 20,000 crore in the current year. In addition, steps are being taken to ensure full utilisation of funds already provided, so that the pace of expenditure is maintained. The total spending program in the balance four months of the current fiscal year, taking plan and non-plan expenditure together is expected to be Rs. 300,000 crore.

The economy will continue to need stimulus in 2009-2010 also and this can be achieved by ensuring a substantial increase in plan expenditure as part of the budget for next year.

2. Reduction in Cenvat

As an immediate measure to encourage additional spending, an across-the-board cut of 4 per cent in the *ad valorem* Cenvat rate will be effected for the balance part of the current financial year on all products other than petroleum and those where the current rate is less than 4 per cent.

3. Measures to Support Exports

(i) Pre- and post-shipment export credit for labour intensive exports, i.e., textiles (including handlooms, carpets and handicrafts), leather, gems & jewellery, marine products and SME sector is being made more attractive by providing an interest subvention of 2 per cent upto 31-3-2009 subject to minimum rate of interest of 7 per cent per annum.

(ii) Additional funds of Rs. 1100 crore will be provided to ensure full refund of Terminal Excise duty/CST.

(iii) An additional allocation for export incentive schemes of Rs. 350 crore will be made.

(iv) Government back-up guarantee will be made available to ECGC to the extent of Rs. 350 crore to enable it to provide guarantees for exports to difficult markets/products.

(v) Exporters will be allowed refund of service tax on foreign agent commissions of upto 10 per cent of FOB value of exports. They will also be allowed refund of service tax on output services while availing of benefits under Duty Drawback Scheme.

4. Housing

Housing is a potentially very important source of employment and demand for critical sectors and there is a large unmet need for housing in the country, especially for middle and low income groups. The Reserve Bank has announced that it will shortly put in place a refinance facility of Rs. 4000 crore for the National Housing Bank. In addition, one of the areas where plan expenditure can be increased relatively easily is the Indira Awas Yojana. As a further measure of support for this sector public sector banks will shortly announce a package for borrowers of home loans in two categories: (1) upto Rs. 5 lakh and (2) Rs. 5 lakh-Rs. 20 lakh. This sector will be kept under a close watch and additional measures would be taken as necessary to promote an accelerated growth trajectory.

5. MSME Sector

The Government attaches the highest priority to supporting the medium, small and micro enterprises (MSMEs) sector which is critical for employment generation. To facilitate the flow of credit to MSMEs, RBI has announced a refinance facility of Rs. 7000 crore for SIDBI which will be available to support incremental lending, either directly to MSMEs or indirectly via banks, NBFCs and SFCs. In addition, the following steps are being taken.

(a) To boost collateral free lending, the current guarantee cover under Credit Guarantee Scheme for Micro and Small enterprises on loans will be extended from Rs. 50 lakh to Rs. 1 crore with guarantee cover of 50 per cent.

(b) The lock in period for loans covered under the existing credit guarantee scheme will be reduced from 24 to 18 months, to encourage banks to cover more loans under the guarantee scheme.

(c) Government will issue an advisory to Central Public Sector Enterprises and request State Public Sector Enterprises to ensure prompt payment of bills of MSMEs. Easing of credit conditions generally should help PSUs to make such payments on schedule.

6. Textiles

(a) An additional allocation of Rs. 1400 crore will be made to clear the entire backlog in TUF Scheme.

(b) All items of handicrafts will be included under 'Vishesh Krishi & Gram Udyog Yojana'.

7. Infrastructure Financing

A large number of infrastructure projects are now being cleared for implementation in the Public Private Partnership mode. These projects may experience difficulty in reaching financial closure given the current uncertainties in the financial world. In order to support financing of such projects, Government has decided to authorise the India Infrastructure Finance Company Limited (IIFCL) to raise Rs. 10,000 crore through tax-free bonds by 31-3-2009. These funds will be used by IIFCL to refinance bank lending of longer maturity to eligible infrastructure projects, particularly in highways and port sectors. In this way it is expected that IIFCL resources used for refinance can leverage bank financing of double the amount. Depending on need, IIFCL will be permitted to raise further resources by issue of such bonds. In particular, these initiatives will support a PPP programme of Rs. 100,000 crore in the highways sector.

8. Others

(a) Government departments will be allowed to take up replacement of government vehicles within the allowed budget, in relaxation of extant economy instructions.

(b) Import Duty on Naphtha for use in the power sector will be eliminated.

(c) Export duty on iron ore fines will be eliminated and on lumps will be reduced to 5 per cent.

The Government is keeping a close watch on the evolving economic situation and will not hesitate to take any additional steps that may be needed to counter recessionary trends and maintain the pace of economic activity.

15

Speech of Finance Minister P. Chidambaram at Economic Editors' Conference 2008

I welcome you to this annual event which brings together well informed economic editors, correspondents and representatives of the media from across the country to a dialogue with the Government. This conference has become a landmark in the annual calendar of events in New Delhi, evolving into an important platform that offers scope for serious discussion between the policy makers and the media, and through the media with the public at large, on critical issues of development and economic policy. Indeed, while it is an added opportunity for us to communicate and explain the Government's thinking, policies and the initiatives being taken to address the issues before us, it is also an opportunity for you to analyze—critically and constructively—the steps taken by the Government and provide feedback for measures to effect course correction, where required, and respond to issues that are yet to be addressed. It is, therefore, a mutually beneficially engagement that I hope you will find the discussions over the next two days useful and meaningful.

2. The United Progressive Alliance (UPA) Government assumed office in May 2004 after a six-year period of modest growth. Memories are short. It would, therefore, be useful to remind ourselves of the state of the economy at the end of

March, 2004. The table below captures the main features of that period of six years.

Year	GDP growth rate	Fiscal deficit	Revenue deficit	Tax to GDP ratio	Savings to GDP ratio	Investment to GDP ratio
1997-98	4.3	4.8	3.0	9.1	23.8	25.3
1998-99	6.7	5.1	3.8	8.2	22.3	23.3
1999-00	6.4	5.4	3.5	8.8	24.8	25.9
2000-01	4.4	5.7	4.1	9.0	23.7	24.3
2001-02	5.8	6.2	4.4	8.2	23.5	22.8
2002-03	3.8	5.9	4.4	8.8	26.4	25.2
2003-04	8.5	4.5	3.6	9.2	29.8	28.2

3. At best, the growth rate during that period was modest. In particular, 2002-03 recorded the lowest growth rate after the beginning of the reforms in 1991-92. As a consequence, the growth rate in 2003-04 appears impressive; but what is important is the average for that period. The average was only 5.7 per cent. The other figures in the table tell their own story. The correction in fiscal deficit was marginal. Revenue deficit became worse. The tax-GDP ratio crawled from 9.1 per cent to 9.2 per cent. Both savings and investment as a proportion of GDP showed moderate increase. I suggest that we put an end to myth-making and spinning make-believe stories about that period.

4. The accurate description of that period would be stasis. This itself begat a crisis—fewer jobs were created, per capita income increased moderately and investment opportunities were lost.

5. I now turn to the record of the UPA Government. Let me create a similar table for the period 2004-05 to 2007-08.

Year	GDP growth rate	Fiscal deficit	Revenue deficit	Tax to GDP ratio	Savings to GDP ratio	Investment to GDP ratio
2003-04	*8.5*	*4.5*	*3.6*	*9.2*	*29.8*	*28.2*
2004-05	7.5	4.0	2.5	9.7	31.8	32.2
2005-06	9.4	4.1	2.6	10.2	34.3	35.5
2006-07	9.6	3.4	1.9	11.4	34.8	35.9
2007-08	9.0	2.8	1.2	12.5		

6. There are several features of this story that deserve to be told and retold. It is for the first time that the Indian economy was able to sustain a growth rate of 9 per cent or more over a period of three-years. Further, in the matter of fiscal correction, India, at the end of 2007-08, was almost near the target. Per capita income during the four-year period increased at an average rate of 7.2 per cent—leading to higher savings and higher investment. I would draw particular attention to the fact that gross capital formation in agriculture as a proportion of GDP improved from 10.2 per cent in 2003-04 to 12.5 per cent in 2006-07.

7. There has been a marked change in the way the Indian economy is viewed both within and outside the country. Increased global competitiveness of Indian enterprises, the resilience of the economy to global shocks, high rates of economic growth, strong macro-economic fundamentals and, above all, a positive economic outlook have contributed to this changing perception.

8. We have been able to demonstrate our capacity to mobilize the resources to meet the growth target of 9 per cent that is set for the Eleventh Five Year Plan. At the beginning of 2008-09, the macro-economic fundamentals continued to inspire confidence and there was general optimism about the medium to long-term prospects of the economy. This is reflected, for instance, in the continued inflows of FDI. Following a record US$32.4 billion of FDI received in 2007-08, FDI flows into India have amounted to US$19.3 billion up to September, 2008. Another example is the growth rate of exports. Following an impressive growth rate of 28.9 per cent (in USD) in 2007-08, exports, at the end of September, 2008, have increased by 30.7 per cent.

9. It is the impressive growth rate in the first four years of the UPA Government that gave us the capacity and the confidence to fund ambitious programmes. The tables below highlight the vastly increased outlays under selected heads of expenditure:

(Amount in Rs. crore)

Sector	Budget allocations in 2003-04	Budget allocations in 2008-09
Agriculture	3,262	9,700
Education	7,024	34,400
Health	6,983	16,534

(Amount in Rs. crore)

Scheme	Budget allocations in 2003-04	Budget allocations in 2008-09
Sarva Siksha Abhiyan	1,951	13,100
Mid-day Meal Scheme	1,175	8,000
Integrated Child Development Scheme	2,356	6,300
Rural Employment Schemes*	4,986	16,000 +10,500*

* Additionality of Rs. 10,500 crore has been provided for NREGS through the 1st Batch of Supplementary Demand for Grants.

10. I must confess that I was looking forward to a rather uneventful year in 2008-09, although I had hinted in my Budget Speech of February 29, 2008 that there were some clouds on the horizon. Let me recall what I said in that Speech:

> "...since August, 2007, the financial markets in the developed countries have witnessed considerable turbulence that has not yet abated. The consequences for developing countries are also not clear.
>
> "There are other downside risks too. World prices of crude oil, commodities and food grains have risen sharply in the period April 2007 to January 2008. The position of crude oil is well-known to this House. Among commodities, the prices of iron ore, copper, lead, tin, urea, etc. are elevated. The prices of wheat and rice have increased in the world market by 88 per cent and 15 per cent, respectively. All these trends are inflationary...."

11. As the year unfolded, we found that the world was hit by three crises at the same time: first, the fuel crisis; second, the food crisis; and third, the financial crisis. Never before did the

world economy face three crises at the same time. Needless to say, India was also affected.

12. During the six-year period 1998-99 to 2003-04, the average price of crude oil was US$ 21.6 a barrel. The highest price was US$ 27.9 a barrel. Unfortunately, the situation changed since 2004-05. A steady and continuous rise in the price of crude oil took it to an unbearable level of US$147 per barrel. Crude oil, in a sense, determined the price of many commodities, especially, energy substitutes, oil derivatives and metals. India has, if I may say, weathered the crisis. No doubt, we paid a price in terms of inflation, but we still recorded high growth. I hope that the worst is over. Crude oil prices have declined since August, 2008. Along with that, prices of many commodities have also moderated.

13. There is one aspect about administered prices which needs to be clarified. There is a popular misconception that, under the UPA Government, the incidence of tax on petrol and diesel is high, or it is higher than what it was under the NDA Government. In May, 2004, the customs duty on crude oil was 10 per cent. It was reduced to 5 per cent on March 1, 2005 and, with effect from June 4, 2008, it was reduced to zero per cent. As regards excise, *ad valorem* duties have been replaced by specific duties. Excise duty as a proportion of the retail price of petrol and diesel has declined since 2003-04. In the case of petrol, it has declined from 34.99 per cent in 2003-04 to 27.20 per cent in 2008-09. Likewise, in the case of diesel, it has declined from 15.82 per cent to 10.66 per cent. Sometimes, I am dismayed by the inaccurate reports appearing in a section of the media on the tax incidence on petrol and diesel that give a totally misleading picture to the consuming public.

14. Regarding the food crisis, we faced two difficult years in 2005-06 and 2006-07 when we had to resort to import of wheat. Thanks to the hard work of our farmers and the incentives provided by way of higher MSP, we are now self-sufficient both in wheat and rice, but we cannot afford to relax our vigil and we must do more. The increase in agricultural production is one of the highlights of the success story of the last four years. In every year under the UPA Government, we

have increased total production of food grains by about 10 million tonnes, as will be evident from the table below:

Year	MSP for wheat (Rs. per quintal)	Production of wheat (in million tonnes)	MSP for paddy (Rs. per quintal)	Production of rice (in million tonnes)	Total food grains production (in million tonnes)
2004-05	640	68.6	560	83.1	198.4
2005-06*	700	69.4	570	91.8	208.6
2006-07*	850	75.8	620	93.4	217.3
2007-08 (AE)	1000	78.4	745**	96.4	230.7

* including incentive bonus

** MSP for paddy was revised

15. There is more encouraging news for Rabi 2008-09. Sown area in most crops has increased significantly as will be seen from the table below. We can, therefore, expect a rich harvest in Rabi 2008-09.

(as on 21-11-2008) (in lakh hectares)

Crop	2007-08	2008-09	Increase over last year
Wheat	84.99	83.78	-1.21
Maize	2.93	3.97	1.04
Jowar	39.12	43.98	4.87
Barley	2.62	3.42	0.80
Pulses	71.56	89.27	17.71
Oil seeds	58.79	72.81	14.02

Growth Performance and Outlook for 2008-09

16. I now turn to the events that have so far marked 2008-09 and the prospects for the remainder of the year.

17. The financial crisis that has enveloped the world since 2007 has become worse. Many developed countries are, officially, in recession. Among them are Germany, Japan, the United Kingdom and the Netherlands. Many more, including the United States and France, are expected to slip into a recession shortly. A recession is defined as two successive quarters of contraction of the GDP. I wish to emphasize that

India is nowhere near a recession. The growth estimate for the first quarter of 2008-09 is 7.9 per cent and the second quarter will, undoubtedly, show high positive growth. Therefore, we must banish the thought of recession. I also urge the media not to use the word "recession" while describing the Indian economy.

18. Nevertheless, we face a difficult situation. From time to time, both the Prime Minister and I have taken the country into confidence on the state of the economy. After the Cabinet reviewed the situation on October 8, 2008, Government made a statement in which we noted that:

> "liquidity conditions in India too have tightened in the last few weeks. Our authorities have responded to the situation. The Reserve Bank of India has taken steps to infuse more liquidity into the market."

19. Again, on October 20, 2008, the Prime Minister made a statement in Parliament in which he said:

> "India, like other developing countries, is experiencing the ripple effects of the financial crisis. However, we have taken a number of steps to minimize the impact.
>
> "The Government is conscious of the fact that it is not enough to infuse liquidity. The liquidity must translate into expanded flow of credit to industry, trade and business.
>
> "Nevertheless, we must be prepared for a temporary slowdown in the Indian economy.... Our effort will be to minimize the negative effect of the financial crisis and, once the global situation stabilizes, to return to the growth trajectory of 9 per cent. I would urge Honourable Members and the people of India to continue to repose faith in the fundamentals of the Indian economy.
>
> "India has faced challenges in the past and has overcome them. We have the strength to overcome the current challenges too."

20. The World Economic Outlook (WEO) of the IMF (October 2008) places the global output growth at 3.9 per cent

in 2008 and 3.0 per cent in 2009. In India, we have already seen the impact of the crisis on the equity and foreign exchange markets. The money, debt and the credit markets have also been affected, albeit indirectly. However, the macro-economic impact of the global financial turmoil has been muted due to the overall strength of domestic demand and the predominantly domestic nature of financing of investment.

21. There is a silver lining in this crisis. While insulating ourselves, to the extent feasible, from the adverse changes in the global economic environment over the next few years, we have to seize the opportunity to review and revisit pending reforms. As and when required, we must introduce measures, particularly in the financial sector, to make our economy more competitive and the economic regulatory and oversight system more efficient, quick and responsive to global developments.

Challenges Facing the Economy

22. Let me now share our assessment of the economic developments in the current year.

23. After three years of plus 9 per cent growth in GDP, the current year has seen some moderation essentially due to external factors. Growth in the first quarter of 2008-09 has been estimated at 7.9 per cent.

24. There are two inter-related macro-economic challenges that we face in maintaining high GDP growth on a sustained basis. These relate to capital inflows and inflation. High GDP growth attracts foreign capital looking for profitable investment opportunities. In a positive cycle this inflow will indeed find profitable investment opportunities that others have missed and lead to even higher growth. In recent years, especially in 2006-07 and in 2007-08, the capital inflows had spurted to an average of around 7 per cent of GDP, far in excess of the current account financing requirements, leading to large accumulation of reserves and a buildup of pressure on prices.

25. In order to curb inflationary expectations, the RBI raised interest rates which had, to some extent, implications for the growth rate from the demand side as well as the supply

side. While inflation has moderated, there is still some distance to go before we can say that the inflation rate has reached a tolerable level. Taking note of the downturn in the inflation rate, RBI has lowered the policy rate as well as the reserve requirements. RBI's policy is now biased towards stimulating growth.

26. We must remember that the current growth phase is primarily investment driven. There has been a significant increase in the growth rate of investment. Private consumption, for the first time, ranks below investment as a driver of growth.

27. In terms of sectoral growth drivers, manufacturing, communications, trade, agriculture and construction have been the major contributors to the spurt in the growth rate. In the current year, there is likely to be moderation of growth in these sectors. The Index of Industrial Production data for April-September 2008 shows an overall growth of 4.9 per cent year-on-year basis compared to a growth of 9.5 per cent in April-September 2007. Deceleration in growth was significant in the manufacturing and electricity sectors, and somewhat moderate in the mining sector.

28. There is still a lot to be done in the infrastructure sectors—both economic and social. More investment and quicker implementation of projects and programmes are required in roads, ports and airports, power, education, health and skill development. Increasing expenditure in the infrastructure sector is an important part of the countercyclical measures that are being contemplated to address the impact of the global slowdown.

29. On the whole, the general outlook continues to be one of cautious optimism. In its review of macro-economic policy for the first quarter of 2008-09, RBI indicated that the median forecast of professional agencies for GDP growth during 2008-09 was 7.9 per cent. In its mid-term review, barring domestic or external shocks, RBI has estimated GDP growth during 2008-09 to be between 7.5 and 8.0 per cent. In our view, we may expect a moderation in growth rate in the

current year to a level between 7 and 8 per cent. India would still be the second fastest growing large economy in the world.

Prices and Inflation Management

30. The weeks ending November 1, 2008 and November 8, 2008 have recorded a significant decline in inflation measured by the WPI. As on November 8, 2008, headline inflation was 8.90 per cent. The monthly de-seasonalized inflation rate has been negative during September and October, suggesting a continuing moderation in WPI inflation in the coming months. These figures indicate that the measures initiated to tackle inflation are bearing fruit.

31. On the fiscal side, Government has given up revenues to the extent of Rs. 31,000 crore post Budget. This has to be viewed in the context of increased expenditure. While the total expenditure was placed at Rs. 750,884 crore in the Budget documents, an additional expenditure of Rs.105,613 crore was approved in the First Supplementary Demands for Grants.

32. In addition to the fiscal measures, monetary instruments were used by the RBI for demand management. These included a gradual increase in the Repo rate to reach 9.0 per cent on August 30, 2008 and an increase in CRR, in steps, by 400 basis points to reach 9.0 per cent effective August 30, 2008. Since then, the direction of policy has changed. The Repo has been brought down to 7.5 per cent effective November 3, 2008 and the CRR has been reduced to 5.5 per cent effective November 8, 2008.

33. If the rate of inflation continues to decline, the policy rates may also moderate and the bias in favour of growth may deepen.

External Sector

34. India's external sector continued to be robust and reflected the strengths of the economy in 2007-08. In the current fiscal, merchandise trade data is available for April-September 2008. Exports and imports have registered an impressive growth of 30.9 per cent and 38.6 per cent, respectively. Oil imports, however, grew faster (59.2 per cent) than non-oil imports (29.3 per cent). There has, however, been

a deceleration in the growth rate of exports in September 2008. India is diversifying its exports to various other countries. For example, during the first quarter of this financial year there has been an increase in the share of India's exports to China, Singapore, Netherlands and Saudi Arabia. China remained the major source of imports followed by UAE, Saudi Arabia and USA in the first quarter of this year.

35. Preliminary BOP estimates released by the RBI for the first quarter of the current year (April—June 2008) point to a moderation in capital inflows and a widening of the trade and current account deficits on a quarter-on-quarter basis. The current account deficit was placed at US$ 10.7 billion primarily due to strong growth of imports (33.3 per cent) *vis-à-vis* exports (22.2 per cent). Net invisibles at US$ 20.9 billion could only partly offset the trade deficit of US$ 31.6 billion. Foreign direct investment (net) inflows remained buoyant at US $ 10.1 billion, while portfolio (net) flows were negative at US $ -4.2 billion in the first quarter of 2008-09.

36. India has evolved a liberal and transparent policy on foreign direct investment (FDI). Except for a small negative list, FDI is allowed mostly on the automatic route. A liberal investment regime is complemented by a tax regime that is moderate and stable. FDI equity inflows during April-September 2008 were US$ 17.21 billion, representing a growth of 137 per cent over the previous year (US$ 7.25 billion). The sectors attracting the highest FDI equity inflows have been the services sector, construction activities including roads and highways, housing and real estate, and computer hardware and software.

Fiscal Consolidation

37. Fiscal consolidation remains a priority of this Government. Although the Fiscal Responsibility and Budget Management Act, 2003 was passed in Parliament during the tenure of the NDA Government, it was only after the UPA Government took over that it was notified on July 2, 2004. Fiscal consolidation has been on course until the end of March, 2008. While buoyant tax revenues have helped, we have also maintained a strict watch over expenditure. However, there

has been a deliberate and conscious shift in expenditure in favour of health, education and the social sector. This expenditure is classified as revenue expenditure. Besides, we have also provided for more expenditure in the current year as a countercyclical measure. As a consequence, we may need one more year to achieve the FRBM target of eliminating the revenue deficit and containing the fiscal deficit to below 3 per cent of GDP.

Social Sector Development and Inclusive Growth

38. Faster economic growth has also begun to get translated into more inclusive growth, both in terms of employment generation and poverty reduction. The 61st Round of the NSSO Survey estimated that 47 million additional work opportunities were created during 1999-2000 to 2004-05, at an annual average of 9.4 million as against an annual average of 4 million job opportunities during 1993-94 to 1999-2000. The proportion of persons below the poverty line declined from around 36 per cent of the population in 1993-94 to 28 per cent in 2004-05 as per the uniform recall period. Based on the mixed recall period, the number of persons below the poverty line declined from 26 per cent in 1999-2000 to 22 per cent in 2004-05.

39. No estimates have been made after the 61st Round of the NSSO Survey. However, the annual GDP growth rate since 2004-05 has been significantly higher by an average of 3 per cent. Hence, on a parity of reasoning, it can be argued that the additional work opportunities created since 2004-05 would have been more every year and the proportion of persons below the poverty line would have declined further. I have no doubt that the next round of the NSSO Survey would vindicate these conclusions.

40. In pursuance of the objective of inclusive growth, Government has been implementing eight flagship programmes supported by sizeable outlays. These include National Rural Employment Guarantee Scheme (NREGS), National Rural Health Mission (NRHM) and Sarva Shiksha Abhiyan (SSA), Mid-day Meal (MMS), Integrated Child Development Services (ICDS), Jawaharlal Nehru National Urban Renewal Mission

(JNNURM), Rajiv Gandhi Drinking Water Mission and the Total Sanitation Campaign. Together, these flagship programmes aim to improve the livelihood of people as well as provide them with easy access to basic facilities like education, health, clean drinking water and sanitation. Besides, Bharat Nirman, which is an important programme to improve the quality of life and mainstreaming of the rural population, has received high priority.

41. The Government can legitimately take some credit for the initiative it has taken in the rapid expansion and universalization of the National Rural Employment Guarantee Programme. In 2007-08, 3.39 crore households were provided employment and 143.5 crore person-days were generated in 330 districts. In 2008-2009 (upto September 2008), 2.93 crore households have been provided employment and 109.30 crore person-days have been generated. The enhanced wage earnings have led to a strengthening of the livelihood resource base of the rural poor in India. This is also reflected in the increased demand for and consumption of wage goods.

42. There are many other initiatives that have been taken by the UPA Government but, in view of the constraints of the time, I shall not dwell on them in my opening remarks. However, I would like to make special mention of the National Action Plan on Climate Change and the Skill Development Programme.

43. It is our endeavour to continue to provide a stable and conducive investment climate, both for the domestic investor and the foreign investor, and to manage the economy in a manner that facilitates inclusive growth driven by enhanced investment and consumption. We believe that our policy of encouraging both the public sector and the private sector and fostering competition has stood us well. It is only an open economy that will bring gains in efficiency and productivity, reward innovation and enterprise, and ensure inclusive growth. I would like to conclude by saying that the five years of the UPA Government—including the current difficult year—will mark a phase of development that put India on a high growth path. It will also mark the starting point of a journey that, say

20 years from now, would have placed India as a middle-income nation that has been successful in eliminating abject poverty and providing a decent standard and quality of life for its people.

16

Statement by Dr. D. Subbarao, Governor, RBI

27 January 2009

....

2. ...With all the advanced economies—the US, Europe and Japan—firmly in recession, the crisis has fully transmitted from the financial sector to the real economy. The loss of confidence in the global financial markets has set off a chain of deleveraging, declining asset values, falling income, contracting demand and rising unemployment. Governments and central banks around the world are responding to the crisis with bold and unconventional initiatives. Even so, there is a contentious debate on whether these measures are adequate and appropriate, and when, if at all, they will begin to have an impact. There is also considerable uncertainty about when we might see the bottom of the asset and business cycle. There is emerging consensus though that there may be no recovery till late 2009; indeed, some analysts believe that recovery may be delayed beyond 2009. Contrary to the expectation of decoupling, which was a commonly held view even till recently, the crisis has spread to the emerging economies too through all the channels—the financial channel, the real channel, and importantly as happens in all financial crises, through the confidence channel.

3. The Indian economy experienced a cyclical moderation in growth accompanied by high inflation in the first half of

2008-09. There is now distinct evidence of further slowdown as a consequence of the global downturn. The knock-on effects of the global financial crisis, economic slowdown, and falling commodity prices are affecting the Indian economy in several ways. Capital flow reversals intensified in September and October 2008 though they have stabilised since then; international credit channels continue to be constrained; capital market valuations remain low; industrial production growth has slackened; export growth has turned negative during October-November 2008; and overall business sentiment has deteriorated. On the positive side, the headline inflation has decelerated, though consumer price inflation is yet to show moderation; and the domestic financial markets are functioning in an orderly manner. Although bank credit growth has been higher than in the previous year, rough calculation shows that flow of overall financial resources to the commercial sector in the current financial year has declined marginally as compared with the previous year. This was on account of decline in other sources of funding such as resource mobilisation from the capital market and external commercial borrowings (ECBs).

4. To manage the impact of the crisis, since mid-September 2008, the Reserve Bank has taken a number of monetary easing and liquidity enhancing measures. The Government has also launched two fiscal stimulus packages to boost aggregate demand....

I. Macro-economic and Monetary Developments

Global Outlook

5. The global economic environment continues to be uncertain. The world economy, which was passing through unprecedented financial turmoil since August 2007, experienced a jolt in September 2008 when the failure of Lehman Brothers led to widespread panic across global financial markets. The liquidity crisis that ensued not only engulfed developed markets but also quickly transmitted to emerging markets, including India. The US Federal Reserve responded by infusing dollar liquidity into large financial centres through currency swap arrangements with major

foreign central banks in addition to massive injection of liquidity in the domestic market through several innovative schemes.

6. Many systemically important commercial banks, investment banks, insurance companies and other financial institutions in the US and Europe have suffered large losses that undermined their capital bases. The credit spreads for corporate paper went up sharply. The US Federal Reserve and other central banks/governments have rescued financial institutions through large bailout packages, but financial markets continue to suffer from a crisis of confidence. The unfolding developments have broader ramifications for both growth and stability in an integrated world where cross-exposures, particularly among banks/financial institutions, and trade links are inextricably large and complex. There is yet no sign of any early resolution as damage to collaterals continues unabated with house prices tumbling in the US and also in parts of Europe.

7. According to the November 2008 update of the World Economic Outlook (WEO) issued by the International Monetary Fund (IMF), global real GDP growth, on a purchasing power parity basis, is projected to decelerate from 3.7 per cent in 2008 to 2.2 per cent in 2009. In market exchange rate terms, the projected deceleration is even sharper from 2.6 per cent in 2008 to 1.1 per cent in 2009. Furthermore, the IMF has cautioned that the downside risks to these global growth projections have further intensified.

8. The US, the UK, the Euro area and Japan, which together accounted for nearly half of world GDP in 2007, are officially in recession. All evidence suggests that contractionary forces are strong: demand has slumped, consumer confidence is at a historic low, production has declined, job losses are on the rise and asset prices continue to fall. Reflecting the slowdown of international demand, crude oil prices declined sharply in the last quarter of 2008. Prices of many other key commodities such as metals, cement, cotton and wheat too have dropped sharply. Consequently, consumer price inflation has declined significantly in many countries including the US, the Euro area,

Japan and the UK. The international financial system continues to remain dysfunctional amidst extreme risk aversion, freezing of money and credit markets, and disruption of international capital flows. In response, central banks in advanced countries have reduced their policy interest rates to historically low levels. The major global concern now is to forestall the worst ever recession since the 1930s. While monetary ammunition has been nearly exhausted in many countries, at least in terms of setting nominal interest rates, measures such as quantitative easing, credit easing and fiscal stimulus are on the policy agenda.

Emerging Market Economies

9. The emerging market economies (EMEs), which showed considerable resilience in weathering the crisis up to September 2008 on the strength of domestic demand supported by sustained export growth, came under strain in the last quarter of 2008 through contagion from trade and financial channels. The slowdown of world trade was deeper than anticipated causing reduction in aggregate demand in the EMEs. In a sign of flight to safety, capital flows from developed countries to the EMEs declined sharply in 2008. Reflecting lower flows through both current and capital accounts, currencies of the EMEs depreciated against the US dollar. EME equity markets suffered large losses in the wake of reversal of portfolio flows. Bank lending to the EMEs declined and credit spreads increased sharply due to the prevailing credit crunch in advanced economies. EME exports declined because of tighter trade credit coming on top of slumping export demand. Going forward, exports to advanced economies are expected to decline further posing a major risk to growth in the EMEs.

10. In evaluating the current and potential problems arising from the crisis, it is important to note some broad differences between the advanced economies of Europe and North America and the EMEs. The crisis originated in the financial sector in the US, which led to the near collapse of their largest financial institutions and banks. Because of linkages across the financial system, the crisis spread almost immediately to Europe with European banks reporting very

large losses. Both the US and European governments responded through large scale infusion of funds into the banking systems. Furthermore, with the erosion of banks' balance sheets, mistrust among banks intensified, as a result of which money markets dried up, and inter-bank markets choked. This engendered a credit squeeze which transmitted to the real economy. The first line of defence in fighting the crisis was aggressive monetary policy action, including rate cuts followed by quantitative monetary and credit easing. These measures were also accompanied by a significant expansion of central banks' direct participation in money markets in several ways.

11. The situation in the EMEs has been quite different. By and large, their financial institutions have not exhibited fragility, inter-bank confidence has been relatively normal and inter-bank money markets have continued to function. Nevertheless, the crisis has affected the EMEs in mainly three ways. The first was the exit of foreign equity which resulted in decline in stock markets, capital flow reversals and pressures on the exchange rate. The second source of impact was the drying up of overseas lines of credit for banks and corporates which shifted demand to the domestic credit market. The third source of impact is the significant deceleration in global trade growth reducing the demand for EME exports. Monetary policy actions by the EMEs have, therefore, been more in response to emerging real economy problems rather than financial sector problems. It is important to keep this distinction in view in designing and evaluating responses to the crisis.

Domestic Outlook

12. Like other EMEs, India too has been affected by the global financial crisis. Real GDP growth moderated to 7.8 per cent in the first half of 2008-09 as against 9.3 per cent in the first half of 2007-08 (Table 1). The third quarter of 2008-09 witnessed signs of further moderation in growth, especially in the industrial sector and some segments of the services sector.

Agriculture and Industry

13. Good sowing and favourable weather conditions suggest that agricultural production during 2008-09 may be close to or better than last year's record production. During April-November 2008, the index of industrial production (IIP) growth decelerated to 3.9 per cent from 9.2 per cent a year ago. Episodes of large inventory build-up, production cuts and temporary closure in some sectors such as automobiles at the beginning of the second half of 2008-09 indicate a period of stress on account of lack of demand.

Table 1: Real GDP Growth (%)

Sector	First Half Year (April-September)	
	2007-08	2008-09
Agriculture	4.5	2.9
Industry	9.1	5.0
Services	10.6	9.9
Overall	9.3	7.8

Corporate Performance

14. During the first two quarters of 2008-09, despite high top-line growth, operating margins of the private corporate sector were eroded by higher input costs and significant drop in 'other' income. In light of the subsequent slowdown, industrial investment plans are slowing down, although ongoing investment projects appear to be continuing. The erosion in pricing power of corporates was reflected in rising inventories as a proportion to sales. While the downside risk to corporate profitability has increased, this may at least be partly offset by falling input prices and a gradual reduction in borrowing costs.

Business Confidence

15. The Reserve Bank's latest round of quarterly Industrial Outlook Survey shows weak and deteriorating business sentiment among private manufacturing companies for the last quarter of 2008-09. The survey indicates weak demand conditions and decline in sentiment for production, order books, capacity utilisation and exports. Corporates also

reported a significant decline in employment expectations for January-March 2009. This picture is consistent with business confidence surveys conducted by other agencies.

Lead Indicators

16. In terms of lead indicators, service sector activity appears to be moderating in several sub-sectors, barring communications and freight movement. On the positive side, sustained performance of the agricultural sector, fiscal stimulus, falling global crude oil prices and softening of domestic input prices such as energy, cement and steel would have a positive impact on industrial production in the coming months.

Inflation

17. Headline inflation, as measured by year-on-year variations in the wholesale price index (WPI), fell by more than half from its intra-year peak of 12.91 per cent on August 2, 2008 to 5.60 per cent by January 10, 2009. While prices of primary articles and manufactured products increased, fuel prices declined (Table 2). In terms of relative contribution to decelerating headline inflation between August 2, 2008 and January 10, 2009, petroleum and basic metals (combined weight of 13.2 per cent in WPI) together accounted for 79.4 per cent, followed by 'oilseeds, edible oils & oil cakes' (16.4 per cent). Clearly, the fall in commodity prices reflecting global trends has been the key driver of the sharp fall in WPI inflation although effective management of domestic demand too has contributed to this moderation.

Table 2: Annual Inflation Rate (%)

Wholesale Price Index (WPI)	January 12, 2008 (y-o-y)	January 10, 2009 (y-o-y)
WPI - All Commodities	4.36	5.60
WPI - Primary Articles	4.49	11.64
WPI - Fuel Group	3.69	-1.32
WPI - Manufactured Products	4.57	5.90
WPI - Excluding Fuel	4.55	7.53
WPI - Excluding Food and Fuel	5.21	6.52

Contd.....

Consumer Price Index (CPI)	December 2007 (y-o-y)	December 2008 (y-o-y)
1. CPI for Industrial Workers*	5.51	10.45
2. CPI for Agricultural Labourers	5.90	11.14
3. CPI for Rural Labourers	5.63	11.14
4. CPI for Urban Non-Manual Employees*	5.06	10.79

* Pertains to November.

18. On the other hand, inflation based on various consumer price indices (CPIs) is still in double digits due to the firm trend in prices of food articles and the higher weight of food articles in measures of consumer price inflation (Table 2). As the decline in input prices percolates over time to the prices of manufactured and other products, consumer price inflation too is expected to soften in the months ahead. For its overall assessment of inflation outlook for policy purposes, the Reserve Bank continues to monitor the full array of price indicators.

Fiscal Scenario

19. As a proportion of the budget estimates (BE), both tax and non-tax revenue receipts of the Central Government for the period April-November 2008 were lower than those in the corresponding period of the previous year. On the other hand, both revenue expenditure and total expenditure, as a proportion to the BE, were higher than a year ago. Consequently, the revenue deficit and the gross fiscal deficit (GFD) were significantly higher during April-November 2008 as compared with the corresponding period of the previous year (Table 3).

Table 3: Fiscal Position of the Central Government

Item		April-November			
		Percentage to Budget Estimates		Growth (%)	
		2007-08	2008-09	2007-08	2008-09
1.	Revenue Receipts	56.5	52.2	24.2	14.7
2.	Gross Tax Revenue	55.5	52.0	25.2	17.5

Contd.....

3.	Tax Revenue (Net)	54.6	50.0	24.5	15.1
4.	Non-Tax Revenue	65.7	64.1	22.7	13.2
5.	Total Expenditure	60.5 *(58.7)*	65.8	22.2 *(11.7)*	20.1 *(31.5)*
6.	Revenue Expenditure	61.8	69.3	12.7	32.4
7.	Capital Expenditure	54.5 *(37.8)*	40.7	116.3 *(1.2)*	-43.4 *(21.0)*
8.	Revenue Deficit	97.9	256.2	-17.2	102.0
9.	Fiscal Deficit	63.8 *(63.0)*	132.4	-11.0 *(-12.2)*	83.3 *(85.7)*

Note: Figures in parentheses are net of transactions relating to transfer of the Reserve Bank's stake in State Bank of India to the Government.

20. For 2008-09, the Central Government had budgeted gross market borrowing of Rs. 1,78,575 crore and net market borrowing of Rs. 99,000 crore. Subsequently, the Government presented two supplementary demands, as a result of which the market borrowing programme of the Central Government was raised to Rs. 2,52,154 crore (gross) and Rs. 1,75,374 crore (net). Against this enhanced borrowing program, market borrowing of the Central Government was Rs. 2,22,154 crore (gross) and Rs. 1,51,697 crore (net) during 2008-09 so far (up to January 23, 2009). The weighted average yield and weighted average maturity of Central Government dated securities issued during 2008-09 (up to January 23, 2009) were at 8.03 per cent and 14.59 years respectively as compared with 8.10 per cent and 14.38 years in 2007-08. The State Governments have borrowed a net amount of Rs. 46,327 crore up to January 23, 2009.

21. The evolving scenario raises some concerns on the extent of stress on the fisc in the current year emanating from several factors. First, the Centre is expected to suffer revenue losses from lower direct tax collection on account of the economic slowdown. Second, the Centre is likely to lose further revenues worth about 0.6 per cent of GDP due to cuts in excise and customs duties. Third, there has been a disproportionate growth in expenditure of the Central Government during April-November 2008, particularly in respect of revenue expenditure arising out of increase in

subsidies, disbursements as well as implementation of the recommendations of the Sixth Pay Commission and the farm debt waiver scheme. The net cash outgo indicated in supplementary demands for grants would be of the order of 2.8 per cent of GDP (Rs. 1,50,310 crore). Thus, additional expenditure coupled with foregone revenue would raise the fiscal deficit from the budget estimate of 2.5 per cent to at least 5.9 per cent of GDP. In addition, special bonds for Rs. 44,000 crore and Rs. 14,000 crore, amounting to 1.1 per cent of GDP, have been issued to oil marketing companies and fertiliser companies respectively during 2008-09 (up to January 23, 2009). In its latest Review of the Economy (January 2009), the Economic Advisory Council to the Prime Minister has placed the consolidated fiscal deficit of the Central Government, including full issuances of oil and fertiliser bonds, at 8.0 per cent of GDP for 2008-09.

22. The consolidated budgeted revenue surplus of the States in 2008-09 may not, in fact, materialise. Consequently, the consolidated fiscal deficit of the States is expected to rise to 2.6 per cent of GDP. While some of the increase in the revenue and fiscal deficits is on account of post-budget expenditure commitments such as payment of arrears resulting from the Sixth Pay Commission Award, a substantial increase is also due to the economic downturn arising from the impact of the global financial crisis. Although the fiscal stimulus packages have meant deviation from the roadmap laid out by the Fiscal Responsibility and Budget Management (FRBM) Act, reversing the consolidation process of the last several years, they were warranted under the prevailing circumstances. It is critically important, however, that the Centre and States re-anchor to a revised FRBM mandate once the immediacy of the crisis is behind us.

Monetary Conditions

23. Growth in key monetary aggregates—reserve money and money supply (M3)—in 2008-09 so far has reflected the changing liquidity positions arising from domestic and global financial conditions and the monetary policy response to the evolving macro-economic developments. Reserve money

variations during 2008-09 have largely reflected increase in currency in circulation and reduction in the cash reserve ratio (CRR) of banks.

24. Reduction in the CRR has three inter-related effects on reserve money. First, it reduces reserve money as bankers' required cash deposits with the Reserve Bank fall. Second, the money multiplier rises. Third, with the increase in the money multiplier, M_3expands with a lag. While the initial expansionary effect is strong, the full effect is felt in 4-6 months. Reflecting these changes, while the year-on-year increase in reserve money as on January 2, 2009 was lower, it was significantly higher when adjusted for the first round effect of CRR reduction. The annual M_3 growth as on January 2, 2009 though lower compared with last year, was higher than the trajectory projected in the Annual Policy Statement (Table 4).

Table 4: Annual Variations in Monetary Aggregates (%)

Item	Annual Variations (y-o-y)	
	January 4, 2008	January 2, 2009
Reserve Money	28.8	7.4
Reserve Money (adjusted for CRR changes)	18.1	19.4
Currency in Circulation	15.6	16.6
Money Supply (M_3)	22.6	19.6
M_3 (Policy Projection)*	17.0-17.5	16.5-17.0
Money Multiplier	4.66	5.20

* Policy projections are for the financial year as indicated in the Annual Policy Statements of the respective financial years.

25. Since September 2008, monetary conditions have been evolving following changes in monetary policy in response to global developments and also due to slackening of domestic demand conditions. As the Reserve Bank had to provide dollar liquidity, its net foreign exchange assets (NFEA) contracted. The Reserve Bank sought to compensate the fall in NFEA by expanding its net domestic assets (NDA) through: (i) buy-back of securities held under the market stabilisation scheme (MSS); (ii) purchase of oil bonds; (iii) enlargement of the refinance window; and (iv) repo operations under the liquidity

adjustment facility (LAF). Thus, a notable feature of monetary operations during the third quarter of 2008-09 was the substitution of foreign assets by domestic assets to keep the overall liquidity conditions comfortable. Liquidity conditions have indeed improved since mid-November 2008 as reflected in daily absorption under the LAF reverse repo and moderation in market interest rates.

Credit Conditions

26. The year-on-year (y-o-y) growth in non-food bank credit at 23.9 per cent as on January 2, 2009 was higher than that of 22.0 per cent as on January 4, 2008 (Table 5). Increase in total flow of resources from the banking sector to the commercial sector (*i.e.*, non-food bank credit together with investments in shares/bonds/debentures and commercial papers issued by public sector/private sector companies) was also higher at 23.4 per cent as compared with 21.7 per cent a year ago. Despite the expansion in bank credit, there was a perception of lack of credit availability. This could be attributed to reduced flow of funds from non-bank sources, notably the capital market and external commercial borrowings.

Table 5: Annual Variations in Banking Indicators (%)

Item	January 4, 2008 (y-o-y)	January 2, 2009 (y-o-y)
Aggregate Deposits	25.1	21.2
Bank Credit	21.4	24.0
Non-food Bank Credit	22.0	23.9
Total flow of Resources from Banks to the Commercial Sector	21.7	23.4
SLR Investments	25.8	19.2
Incremental Credit-Deposit Ratio	63.1	81.4

27. During 2008-09 so far, the total flow of resources to the commercial sector from banks and other sources was marginally lower than in the previous year reflecting contraction of funds from other sources (Table 6).

Table 6: Flow of Financial Resources to the Commercial Sector

		(Rs. crore)
Item	2007-08 (Up to January 4, 2008)	2008-09 (Up to January 2, 2009)
From Banks	2,24,921	2,93,243
From Other Sources*	2,74,563	1,91,470
Total Resources	4,99,484	4,84,713

* Includes borrowings from financial institutions and NBFCs as well as resources mobilised from the capital market and by way of ECBs, FCCBs, ADRs/GDRs, FDI and short-term credit as per the latest available data, adjusted for double counting.

28. At a disaggregated level, the year-on-year increase in bank credit to industry as of December 2008 was sharply higher than that in the previous year reflecting the substitution effect of other sources of funding by bank credit (Table 7).

Table 7: Annual Sectoral Flow of Credit

Sector	As on December 21, 2007 (y-o-y)		As on December 19, 2008 (y-o-y)	
	Amount (Rs. crore)	Variations (%)	Amount (Rs. crore)	Variations (%)
Agriculture	38,139	19.3	53,612	22.7
Industry	1,56,192	24.9	2,36,064	30.2
Real Estate	13,621	35.8	24,827	48.1
Housing	31,780	14.6	21,989	8.8
NBFCs	22,953	59.6	24,668	40.1
Overall Credit	3,54,802	21.8	4,90,199	24.8

29. There has been a noticeable variation in credit expansion across bank groups. Expansion of credit by public sector banks was much higher this year than in the previous year, while credit expansion by foreign and private sector banks was significantly lower. The relatively slower pace of credit expansion by foreign and private sector banks has also added to the perception of inadequate credit flow in the system. There has also been perceptible deceleration in growth of deposits with private and foreign banks (Table 8).

Table 8: Bank Group-wise Deposits and Credit

Bank Group	Annual Growth (y-o-y) (%)	
	As on January 4, 2008	As on January 2, 2009
Deposits		
Public Sector Banks	24.2	24.2
Foreign Banks	34.1	12.1
Private Sector Banks	26.9	13.4
Scheduled Commercial Banks *	25.1	21.2
Credit		
Public Sector Banks	19.8	28.6
Foreign Banks	30.7	16.9
Private Sector Banks	24.2	11.8
Scheduled Commercial Banks *	21.4	24.0

* Including regional rural banks (RRBs).

30. Commercial banks' holdings of SLR securities became more liquid on account of two factors. First, banks were permitted to use SLR securities to the tune of 1.5 per cent of their net demand and time liabilities (NDTL) under the LAF to meet the funding requirements of mutual funds, non-banking finance companies (NBFCs) and housing finance companies (HFCs). Second, the reduction in SLR by one percentage point to 24.0 per cent of NDTL in November 2008 released funds for credit deployment. Commercial banks' SLR holdings declined from 27.8 per cent (28.4 per cent adjusted for LAF) of NDTL in March 2008 to 25.8 per cent (28.1 per cent adjusted for LAF) in mid-October 2008 reflecting the banks' reliance on the repo facility under the LAF as liquidity conditions tightened. Reversing this trend by early January 2009, banks' SLR holdings increased to 28.9 per cent of NDTL (27.1 per cent adjusted for LAF) reflecting improved liquidity conditions and increased government market borrowings.

31. Bank deposit and lending rates, which had firmed up during the current financial year up to October 2008, started easing from November 2008. Between November 2008 and January 2009, all public sector banks, several private sector banks and some foreign banks reduced their deposit and

lending rates. The magnitude of reduction by public sector banks was larger than that by foreign and private sector banks (Table 9).

Table 9: Deposit and Lending Rates of Banks (%)

Bank Group/Maturity Domestic Deposit Rate	October 2008	January 2009
Public Sector Banks		
61-90 days	5.25-6.00	5.25-6.00
180 days – 1 year	8.00-8.75	7.25-8.00
1-3 years	9.50-10.50	8.00-9.00
> 3 years	8.75-9.75	8.25-8.50
Private Sector Banks		
61-90 days	4.00-6.25	4.00-5.50
180 days – 1 year	8.00-9.00	7.75-8.00
1-3 years	9.00-10.10	8.00-9.00
> 3 years	8.50-9.75	8.00-8.75
Foreign Banks		
61-90 days	6.00-8.50	5.25-7.00
180 days – 1 year	7.00-9.50	7.50-9.00
1-3 years	7.50-9.00	7.50-8.50
> 3 years	7.50-10.00	7.50-7.75
Benchmark Prime Lending Rate (BPLR)		
Public Sector Banks	13.75-14.00	12.00-12.50
Private Sector Banks	15.25-17.25	14.75-16.75
Foreign Banks	14.25-15.50	14.25-15.50

Note: Data relate to five major public sector banks, four private sector banks and three foreign banks.

32. The interest rate response to monetary policy easing has been faster in the money and bond markets as compared to the credit market because of several structural factors. First, the administered interest rate structure on small savings could potentially constrain the reduction in deposit rates below some threshold. Second, a substantial portion of bank deposits is mobilised at fixed interest rates with an asymmetric contractual relationship. During the upturn of the interest rate cycle, depositors have the flexibility to prematurely terminate the existing deposits and re-deposit the funds at higher interest rates. However, in the downturn of the interest rate cycle, banks have to necessarily carry these deposits at higher rates of interest till their maturity. Third, competition among banks for

wholesale deposits for meeting the higher credit demand in the upswing leads to an increase in the cost of funds. Fourth, linkage of concessional lending rates to banks' BPLRs makes overall lending rates less flexible. Fifth, persistence of the large market borrowing programme of the government hardens interest rate expectations. Sixth, with increase in risk aversion, lending rates tend to be high even during a period with falling credit demand. From the real economy perspective, however, for monetary policy to have demand inducing effects, lending rates will have to come down.

33. Notwithstanding the various factors that impede monetary transmission, market interest rates do respond to changes in policy interest rates. As such, current deposit and lending rates have significant room for further reduction. Interest rates in the money and bond markets have already declined perceptibly since their peaks in October 2008 (Table 10). Major public sector banks have also reduced their term deposit rates in the range of 50-150 basis points. Benchmark prime lending rates (BPLRs) of major public sector banks have come down by 150-175 basis points. Major private sector banks have reduced their BPLRs by 50 basis points, while major foreign banks are yet to do so. As a result of several measures initiated by the Reserve Bank since mid-September 2008, banks' cost of funds would come down. This should encourage banks to reduce their lending rates in the coming months.

Financial Markets

34. The overnight interest rates generally ruled above the ceiling of the LAF rate corridor at the beginning of October 2008 when the domestic money and foreign exchange markets came under pressure. The overnight interest rates eased in mid-October 2008 in response to the successive monetary easing measures by the Reserve Bank which alleviated the liquidity pressures. The overnight interest rates have remained below the upper bound of the LAF corridor since November 3, 2008. Interest rates on various other segments of the money market and government securities market have also softened markedly (Table 10).

Table 10: Interest Rates (%)

Segment/Instrument	October 2008	January 23, 2009
Call Money	9.90	4.21
CBLO	7.73	3.85
Market Repo	8.40	4.24
Commercial Paper	14.17	10.98*
Certificates of Deposit	10.00	8.85*
91-day Treasury Bills	7.44	4.67
10-year Government Securities	7.45	5.87

* Pertains to December 2008.

35. The rupee had appreciated against major currencies in 2007-08 due to large capital inflows. It depreciated during 2008-09 so far reflecting extraordinary developments in international financial markets and portfolio outflows by foreign institutional investors (FIIs). It has remained range-bound since November 2008 (Table 11).

Table 11: Rupee Exchange Rate

Rupee per Unit of	Range	April 2008	November 2008	January* 2009
US Dollar	Maximum	40.46	50.52	49.19
	Minimum	39.89	47.18	48.37
Euro	Maximum	63.80	64.68	68.09
	Minimum	62.25	60.57	63.60
Pound Sterling	Maximum	79.94	80.26	74.42
	Minimum	78.66	72.14	67.61
100 Japanese Yen	Maximum	39.58	53.12	55.58
	Minimum	38.36	47.31	51.90

* Up to January 23, 2009.

36. Equity markets weakened sharply till end-October 2008 in tandem with global stock markets, particularly Asian markets, reflecting further deterioration in the global financial market sentiment, FII outflows, slowdown in industrial growth and lower corporate profits. The BSE Sensex declined from an all-time high of 20873 on January 8, 2008 to a low of 8451 on November 20, 2008. The equity market has since remained generally range-bound; the BSE Sensex was at 8674 on January 23, 2009.

37. The outlook for the domestic financial markets will be determined largely by the developments in global financial markets and domestic liquidity conditions. The banking system has been in surplus liquidity mode since mid-November 2008. The pressure on the exchange rate of the rupee has eased due to moderation in capital outflows. In addition, the decline in global commodity prices, particularly crude oil, is expected to further ease the pressure on foreign currency on account of oil imports.

External Sector

38. India's current account deficit (CAD) of the balance of payments (BoP) widened in the first half of 2008-09 in comparison with the corresponding period of the previous year due to a large trade deficit, reflecting high oil prices even as private transfers and software export earnings were sustained. As net capital flows declined sharply, the overall balance of payments position turned marginally negative during the first half of 2008-09 as against a large surplus in the corresponding period of the previous year (Table 12). Import growth had moderated during October-November 2008 reflecting the fall in international oil prices and slowing domestic demand. During the same period, export growth turned negative reflecting slowing global demand. Going forward, it is expected that imports may slow down faster than exports.

Table 12: India's Balance of Payments

(US $ billion)

	April-September	
	2007-08	2008-09
Exports	72.6	96.7
Imports	115.9	165.9
Trade Balance	- 43.2	- 69.2
Invisibles, net	32.3	46.8
Current Account Balance	- 11.0	- 22.3
Capital Account*	51.4	19.8
Change in Reserves#	(-) 40.4	(+) 2.5

* Including errors and omissions.

On a BoP basis (excluding valuation): (-) indicates increase; (+) indicates decrease.

39. The reversal of capital flows has raised concerns about management of the BoP, particularly with reference to outstanding external debt with residual maturity of less than one year. These concerns are somewhat misplaced as the following analysis will show.

40. India's external debt with residual maturity of less than one year as at end-March 2008 was estimated at around US $ 85 billion (as per revised data), which would mature during the financial year 2008-09. Sovereign debt and commercial borrowings are most likely to be rolled over during 2008-09. Indeed, the BoP data for the first half of the year (April-September 2008) indicate net positive accretions beyond roll-over under both these heads. Current trends indicate that under NRI deposits, not only will the maturing debt be rolled over but there will be net accretions as a result of the upward adjustment in interest rate ceilings on such deposits. Here again, available data up to December 2008 show net accretions. That leaves trade credit of the order of US $ 43.2 billion to be repaid during 2008-09. Of this, as much as US $ 28.1 billion has already been disbursed during April-November 2008 leaving a balance of US $ 15.1 billion. There are reports that large inflows are in the pipeline on account of commitments of buyers' credit by the importers and oil companies. Even conservatively projecting that only a small portion of this balance would be rolled over, India's external payment situation remains stable.

41. The overall approach to the management of India's foreign exchange reserves takes into account the changing composition of the balance of payments and endeavours to reflect the 'liquidity risks' associated with different types of flows and other requirements. As capital inflows during 2007-08 were far in excess of the normal absorptive capacity of the economy, there was substantial accretion to foreign exchange reserves by US $ 110.5 billion. The foreign exchange reserves declined by US $ 23.4 billion from US $ 309.7 billion as at end-March 2008 to US $ 286.3 billion by end-September 2008 largely reflecting valuation effects. Excluding valuation effects, the decline was US $ 2.5 billion. Between October 2008

and January 16, 2009 foreign exchange reserves declined by US $ 34.1 billion to US $ 252.2 billion, including valuation effects. India's current level of foreign exchange reserves remains comfortable.

Overall Outlook

42. At the heart of the global financial crisis lie the non-functional and frozen financial markets. In sharp contrast to their international counterparts, the financial system in India has been resilient and stable. Barring some tightness in liquidity during mid-September to early October, the money, foreign exchange and government securities markets have been orderly as reflected in market rates, spreads and transaction volumes relative to those observed during normal times. India's banking system remains healthy, well-capitalised, resilient and profitable. Credit markets have been functioning well and banks have been expanding credit, notwithstanding the perceptions in some quarters of lack of adequate credit from the banks to the commercial sector.

43. Over the last five years, India clocked 8.8 per cent average annual growth, driven largely by domestic consumption and investment even as the share of net exports rose. While the benign global environment, easy liquidity and low interest rates helped, at the heart of India's growth have been its growing entrepreneurial spirit and rise in productivity. These fundamental strengths continue to be in place. Nevertheless, the global crisis will dent India's growth trajectory as investments and exports slow. Clearly, there is a period of painful adjustment ahead of us. However, once the global economy begins to recover, India's turnaround will be sharper and swifter, backed by our strong fundamentals and the untapped growth potential. Meanwhile, the challenge for the Government and the Reserve Bank is to manage the adjustment with as little pain as possible.

II. Stance of Monetary Policy

44. Since September 2008, international developments have largely circumscribed domestic policy responses. There have been severe disruptions in the international money and

foreign exchange markets since September 2008. Policymakers in governments, central banks and in other regulating agencies of financial institutions around the world responded to the crisis with aggressive, radical and unconventional measures to restore calm and confidence in financial markets and bring them back to normalcy. The immediate challenge was to maintain financial stability, which moved up in the hierarchy of objectives.

Earlier Policy Measures

September 2008

45. Global financial crisis also had spillover effects on financial markets in India causing an unusual tightening of liquidity in mid-September, which was compounded by transient local factors such as advance tax payments. The domestic equity market was severely affected by the global meltdown of asset prices. The foreign exchange market also came under pressure. Access to external financing was constrained following re-pricing of risks and higher credit spreads. Responding to the evolving situation, the Reserve Bank announced the following measures on September 16, 2008:

- A firm assurance to meet any demand-supply gaps of foreign exchange in the domestic foreign exchange market.
- A second LAF was re-introduced on a daily basis.
- Interest rate ceilings on FCNR(B) and NR(E)RA deposits were increased by 50 basis points each to LIBOR/swap rates minus 25 basis points and LIBOR/swap rates plus 50 basis points respectively.
- As a temporary measure, scheduled banks were allowed to avail of additional liquidity support under the LAF to the extent of up to one per cent of their net demand and time liabilities from their SLR portfolio and seek waiver of penal interest.

October 2008

46. Liquidity conditions tightened further in October 2008 as contagion from the US financial crisis spread to Europe and Asia. Many central banks took co-ordinated actions to infuse liquidity in their jurisdictions. In addition, in order to enhance dollar liquidity, the US Fed provided currency swap lines to select central banks. Financial markets in Asia and Australia were also severely affected. The call money rate in the domestic market touched a peak of 19.8 per cent on October 10, 2008 with LAF repo volume crossing Rs. 90,000 crore during the early part of October 2008. In view of persisting uncertainty in global financial markets and its impact on India and continuing shortage of liquidity reflected in repo volume, the following measures were taken by the Reserve Bank in October 2008:

- The CRR was reduced by 250 basis points from 9.0 per cent to 6.5 per cent effective from the fortnight beginning October 11, 2008.
- A 14-day special repo facility for a notified amount of Rs. 20,000 crore was instituted to alleviate liquidity stress faced by mutual funds, and banks were allowed temporary use of SLR securities for collateral purposes by an additional 0.5 per cent of NDTL exclusively for this purpose.
- Commercial banks and all-India term lending and refinancing institutions were allowed to lend against and buy back certificates of deposit (CDs) held by mutual funds.
- The Reserve Bank temporarily provided a sum of Rs. 25,000 crore as the first instalment under the Agricultural Debt Waiver and Debt Relief Scheme to scheduled banks and NABARD immediately, pending Parliamentary sanction and consequent release of funds by the Central Government.
- Interest rate ceilings on FCNR(B) and NR(E)RA deposits were increased further by 50 basis points

each to LIBOR/swap rates *plus* 25 basis points and LIBOR/swap rates *plus* 100 basis points respectively.

- Banks were permitted to borrow funds from their overseas branches and correspondent banks to the extent of 50 per cent of their unimpaired Tier-I capital or US $ 10 million, whichever is higher.
- The Reserve Bank announced that it would institute special market operations to meet the foreign exchange requirements of public sector oil marketing companies against oil bonds when they become available.
- On October 20, 2008 the repo rate under the LAF was reduced by 100 basis points to 8.0 per cent.
- The systemically important non-deposit taking non-banking financial companies (NBFCs-ND-SI) were permitted to raise short-term foreign currency borrowings.

47. On the eve of announcement of the Mid-Term Review, external commercial borrowings (ECBs) up to US $ 500 million per borrower per financial year were permitted for rupee expenditure and/or foreign currency expenditure for permissible end-uses under the automatic route. Further, the all-in-cost ceiling for ECBs of average maturity period of three years and up to five years was raised to 300 basis points, and over five years, to 500 basis points above 6-month LIBOR.

November 2008

48. Global financial conditions continued to remain uncertain and unsettled. Early signs of a global recession were evident by late October. Globally, commodity prices, including crude, began to abate which reduced domestic inflationary pressures. On the growth front, it was important to ensure that credit requirements for productive purposes were adequately met so as to support the growth momentum of the economy. Accordingly, the following measures were taken on November 1, 2008:

- The repo rate under the LAF was reduced by 50 basis points to 7.5 per cent with effect from November 3, 2008.

- The CRR was reduced by 100 basis points from 6.5 per cent to 5.5 per cent of NDTL.
- The statutory liquidity ratio (SLR), which was relaxed on a temporary basis earlier, was made permanent and reduced to 24 per cent of NDTL effective November 8, 2008.
- In order to provide further liquidity comfort, a special refinance facility for scheduled commercial banks (excluding RRBs) up to 1.0 per cent of each bank's NDTL as on October 24, 2008 was introduced under Section 17(3B) of the Reserve Bank of India Act, 1934 up to a maximum period of 90 days.
- On October 15, 2008 the Reserve Bank introduced a 14-day special repo facility allowing banks to avail additional liquidity support exclusively for the purpose of meeting the liquidity requirements of mutual funds to the extent of 0.5 per cent of their NDTL. Subsequently, this facility was extended for NBFCs and the relaxation in the maintenance of the SLR was enhanced to the extent of up to 1.5 per cent of their NDTL.
- Buy-back of MSS dated securities was announced to provide another avenue for injecting liquidity to be calibrated with the market borrowing programme of the Government of India.

49. On November 7, 2008 Indian public and private sector banks that have foreign branches or subsidiaries were provided a forex swap facility of tenor up to three months with the Reserve Bank. Further, for funding the swap, banks were allowed to borrow under the LAF for the corresponding tenor at the prevailing repo rate.

50. There were indications that the global slowdown was deepening with a larger than expected impact on the domestic economy, particularly for the medium and small industry sector and export-oriented units. In the context of these developments, further augmenting rupee and forex liquidity, and strengthening and improving credit delivery mechanisms

were needed for sustaining the growth momentum. Accordingly, the following measures were taken on November 15, 2008:

- The special term repo facility introduced for the purpose of meeting the liquidity requirements of MFs and NBFCs, was extended till end-March 2009. Banks can avail of this facility either on an incremental basis or on a rollover basis within the entitlement of up to 1.5 per cent of their NDTL.
- Interest rate ceilings on FCNR(B) and NR(E)RA deposits were further raised by 75 basis points each to LIBOR/swap rates plus 100 basis points and LIBOR/swap rates plus 175 basis points respectively.
- Housing finance companies (HFCs) registered with the National Housing Bank (NHB) were permitted to raise short-term foreign currency borrowings under the approval route.
- The Reserve Bank permitted Indian corporates to prematurely buy back their FCCBs at prevailing discounted rates.
- The period of entitlement of the first slab of pre-shipment rupee export credit was extended from 180 days to 270 days.
- The aggregate limit of export credit refinance (ECR) facility for scheduled banks (excluding RRBs) was enhanced from 15 per cent to 50 per cent of the outstanding export credit eligible for refinance.
- SIDBI and the NHB were allocated Rs. 2000 crore and Rs. 1000 crore respectively against banks' estimated shortfall in priority sector lending in March 2009.
- Banks were encouraged to use the special refinance facility under Section 17(3B) of the Reserve Bank of India Act, 1934 for the purpose of lending to micro and small enterprises.
- The provisioning requirements for all types of standard assets were reduced to a uniform level of 0.40 per cent, except in the case of direct advances to

the agricultural and SME sectors which continue to attract provisioning of 0.25 per cent, as hitherto.

- Risk weights on banks' exposures to all unrated claims on corporates, claims secured by commercial real estate and claims on NBFCs-ND-SI were reduced to 100 per cent from 150 per cent.

51. On November 28, 2008 the Reserve Bank announced the following measures for liquidity management and improving credit flows:

- The special refinance facility under Section 17(3B) of the Reserve Bank of India Act, 1934 introduced on November 1, 2008 was extended up to June 30, 2009.
- The special term repo facility was expanded to enable banks to accommodate the funding needs of HFCs. The facility was extended up to June 30, 2009.
- The forex swap facility of tenor up to three months was extended up to June 30, 2009.
- The period of entitlement of the first slab of post-shipment rupee export credit was extended from 90 days to 180 days.

December 2008

52. The global outlook deteriorated further during December 2008. There were indications that the recession would be deeper and the recovery longer than anticipated earlier. There was also increasing evidence of slackening of domestic economic activity. The available data indicated that the demand for bank credit started moderating despite comfortable liquidity. The reduction in prices of petrol and diesel announced on December 5, 2008 further eased inflationary pressures. To improve the credit flow to productive sectors at viable costs so as to sustain the growth momentum, the Reserve Bank took the following measures on December 6 and 11, 2008:

- The repo rate was reduced under the LAF by 100 basis points from 7.5 per cent to 6.5 per cent and the reverse repo rate by 100 basis points from 6.0 per cent to 5.0 per cent, effective December 8, 2008.

- A refinance facility was introduced for SIDBI, NHB and EXIM Bank for Rs. 7,000 crore, Rs. 4,000 crore and Rs. 5,000 crore respectively. This facility will be available up to March 31,2010.
- Authorised Dealers Category-I banks were permitted to consider applications for premature buy-back of FCCBs from their customers.
- Loans granted by banks to HFCs for on-lending for housing up to Rs. 20 lakh per dwelling unit were classified under priority sector.
- Commercial real estate exposures restructured up to June 30, 2009 were allowed to be treated as standard assets. As a one-time measure, the second restructuring done by banks of exposures (other than exposures to commercial real estate, capital market exposures and personal/consumer loans) up to June 30, 2009 was also made eligible for concessional regulatory treatment.
- The prescribed interest rate as applicable to post-shipment rupee export credit (not exceeding BPLR minus 2.5 percentage points) was extended to overdue bills up to 180 days.

January 2009

53. While domestic financial markets continued to function in an orderly manner, India's growth trajectory was impacted both by the global financial crisis and the follow-on global economic downturn. This impact turned out to be deeper and wider than earlier anticipated. Concurrently, because of fall in global commodity prices coupled with supply and demand management measures at home, headline inflation was on the decline. Even as some public sector and private sector banks had cut lending rates in response to the Reserve Bank's monetary policy stance, concerns over rising credit risk together with the slowing of economic activity appeared to have moderated credit growth. Accordingly, in order to stimulate growth, the Reserve Bank took the following further measures on January 2, 2009:

- The repo rate under the LAF was reduced by 100 basis points from 6.5 per cent to 5.5 per cent with effect from January 5, 2009.
- The reverse repo rate under the LAF was reduced by 100 basis points from 5.0 per cent to 4.0 per cent with effect from January 5, 2009.
- The CRR was reduced from 5.5 per cent to 5.0 per cent of NDTL effective from the fortnight beginning January 17, 2009.

54. The Government has announced the setting up of a special purpose vehicle (SPV) for addressing the temporary liquidity constraints of systemically important non-deposit taking non-banking financial companies (NBFCs-ND-SI). The mechanism would be as follows: The SPV would issue government guaranteed securities to the Reserve Bank. The SPV will, in turn, use the funds to acquire only investment grade commercial papers and non-convertible debentures of the NBFCs. During its appraisal, the SPV will ensure that the NBFCs use the money only for addressing liquidity constraints and not for business expansion. The total support from the Reserve Bank will be limited to Rs. 20,000 crore with an option to raise it by a further Rs. 5,000 crore. The facility will be available for a limited period to address current liquidity concerns of NBFCs.

Liquidity Impact

55. The cumulative reduction in the CRR by 400 basis points since mid-September 2008 released additional Rs. 1,60,000 crore of primary liquidity. Unwinding of MSS has released primary liquidity of a little over Rs. 63,000 crore. Further, potential liquidity has been made available through various refinance facilities for banks and financial institutions to the tune of Rs. 80,000 crore. The term repo facility gives an additional potential liquidity of Rs. 60,000 crore. The SPV for NBFC will augment potential liquidity by another Rs. 25,000 crore. In sum, the actions of the Reserve Bank since mid-September 2008 have resulted in augmentation of actual/potential liquidity of over Rs. 3,88,000 crore. In

addition, the permanent reduction in SLR by 1.0 per cent of NDTL has made available liquid funds of the order of Rs. 40,000 crore for the purpose of credit expansion (Table 13).

Table 13: Actual/Potential Release of Primary Liquidity since mid-September 2008

	Measure/Facility	Amount (Rs. crore)
1.	Cash Reserve Ratio (CRR) Reduction	1,60,000
2.	MSS Unwinding	63,045
3.	Term Repo Facility	60,000
4.	Increase in Export Credit Refinance	25,500
5.	Special Refinance Facility for SCBs (Non-RRB)	38,500
6.	Refinance Facility for SIDBI/NHB/EXIM Bank	16,000
7.	Liquidity Facility for NBFCs through SPV	25,000
Total (1 to 7)		3,88,045
Memo: Statutory Liquidity Ratio (SLR) Reduction 40,000		

56. The liquidity situation has improved significantly following several measures taken by the Reserve Bank. The overnight call money rate, which generally hovered above the repo rate during September-October 2008, has softened considerably and has moved towards the lower bound of the LAF corridor since early November 2008. Other money market rates such as discount rate of CDs, CPs and CBLO rate softened in tandem with the overnight call money rate. The yield on 10-year government securities has remained below 6 per cent since mid-December 2008. The LAF window has been generally in an absorption mode since mid-November 2008. The liquidity problem faced by mutual funds appears to have eased considerably. Many commercial banks have reduced their benchmark prime lending rates since mid-November 2008.

Growth Projection

57. The Reserve Bank's Mid-Term Review of October 2008 had estimated real GDP growth for 2008-09 in the range of 7.5–8.0 per cent. Since then the outlook on real GDP growth has been affected further and the downside risks to growth have amplified because of slowdown of industrial

activity and weakening of external demand as reflected in decline in exports. Services sector activities are likely to further decelerate in the second half of 2008-09. Keeping in view the slowdown in industry and services and with the assumption of normal agricultural production, the projection of overall real GDP growth for 2008-09 is revised downwards to 7.0 per cent with a downward bias.

Inflation Projection

58. Pressures on commodity prices have abated markedly around the world, reflecting slump in global demand. The sharp decline in crude oil prices together with the slide in prices of metals, foodgrains and cement has influenced inflation expectations in most parts of the world. In the domestic market, inflation in terms of the wholesale price index is already below 7.0 per cent, which was projected earlier for end-March 2009. While prices of manufactured products and of the fuel group have declined in line with international trends, inflation on account of primary articles still remains at the double digit level, reflecting sustained price pressures, particularly on food articles. As per current assessment, the inflation rate is expected to moderate further in the last quarter of 2008-09. Keeping in view the global trend in commodity prices and the domestic demand-supply balance, WPI inflation is now projected to decelerate to below 3.0 per cent by end-March 2009.

59. Notwithstanding the projected decline in headline WPI inflation, it needs to be noted that consumer price inflation is yet to moderate and the decline in inflation expectations has not been commensurate with the sharp fall in WPI inflation. Even within aggregate WPI inflation, the primary articles inflation is still in double digits. Similarly, WPI inflation excluding food and fuel remains higher this year as compared with the previous year. In view of the divergent movement of various price indices and their components, and overall increase in global economic uncertainties, an assessment of underlying inflation for policy purposes becomes inherently complex. With WPI inflation having moderated significantly, consumer price inflation would also decline, though with a lag.

Towards its policy endeavour of ensuring price stability with well-anchored inflation expectations, the Reserve Bank will take into account the behaviour of all the price indices and their components.

60. The conduct of monetary policy would continue to condition and contain perception of inflation in the range of 4.0-4.5 per cent so that an inflation rate of around 3.0 per cent becomes the medium-term objective, consistent with India's broader integration into the global economy and with the goal of maintaining self-accelerating growth over the medium-term. However, it is recognised that the headline WPI inflation could fall well below 3.0 per cent in the short-run partly because of the statistical reason of high base, and the global trends caused by exceptionally high oil and commodity prices in early 2008.

Monetary Projection

61. Monetary and credit aggregates continue to expand at a higher rate than projected in the Annual Policy Statement of April 2008. The liquidity overhang built-up in recent years due to unprecedented surge in capital inflows, however, is gradually diminishing. The Reserve Bank is committed to provide adequate liquidity for all productive activities on a continuous basis. As the upside risks to inflation have declined, monetary policy has been responding to slackening economic growth in the context of significant global stress. Accordingly, the projection of money supply (M3) growth for 2008-09 is raised to 19.0 per cent from 16.5-17.0 per cent earlier. Consistent with this, the aggregate deposit growth for 2008-09 is revised to 19.0 per cent from 17.0 per cent earlier. The projection of growth of adjusted non-food credit, including investment in bonds/debentures/shares of public sector undertakings and private corporate sector and CP, for 2008-09 is revised to 24.0 per cent from 20.0 per cent earlier. As always, these numbers are provided as indicative projections and not as targets.

Overall Assessment

62. As indicated earlier, India has been affected by the global financial crisis through the financial and real channels.

There is considerable dismay about why this should be the case when, in fact, India's financial system is sound and healthy, and its merchandise exports constitute only 13.5 per cent of GDP. The answer clearly is that India has rapidly integrated into the global system and has linkages with the rest of the world not just through trade channels, but also through two-way movements of capital and finance. As an integral part of a globalising world, India cannot be expected to remain immune to a global crisis of this nature and magnitude; and in responding to the crisis, India has to share the uncertainty on the way forward just like the rest of the world.

63. Both the Government and the Reserve Bank have acted to protect the economy from the adverse impact of the crisis. While the Government has announced two major fiscal stimulus packages, the endeavour of the Reserve Bank has been to provide ample rupee liquidity, ensure comfortable dollar liquidity and maintain a monetary policy environment conducive for the continued flow of credit to productive sectors. Towards this endeavour, the Reserve Bank has adopted both conventional measures such as, for example, reduction of the CRR, as well as unconventional measures such as, for example, the dollar swap facility for banks.

64. Measures aimed at expanding rupee liquidity included significant reduction in the CRR, a special repo window under the LAF for banks for on-lending to non-banking financial companies, housing finance companies and mutual funds, and a special refinance facility that banks can access without any collateral. The Reserve Bank is also unwinding the MSS securities roughly synchronised with the government borrowing programme in order to manage liquidity. In addition, an SPV is being set up to provide liquidity support to NBFCs.

65. Measures aimed at managing forex liquidity include upward adjustment of the interest rate ceilings on the FCNR(B) and NR(E)RA deposits, substantial relaxation of the ECB regime, allowing NBFCs/HFCs access to foreign borrowing and allowing corporates to buy back FCCBs to take advantage of the discount in the prevailing depressed global markets. The

Reserve Bank has also instituted a rupee-dollar swap facility for banks with overseas branches to give them comfort in managing their short-term funding requirements.

66. Measures to encourage flow of credit to sectors that are coming under pressure include extension of the period of pre-shipment and post-shipment credit for exports, expansion of the refinance facility for exports, counter-cyclical adjustment of provisioning norms for all types of standard assets barring some exceptions, reduction of risk weights on banks' exposure to certain sectors which had been increased earlier counter-cyclically, and expansion of the lendable resources available to the Small Industries Development Bank of India, the National Housing Bank and the Export-Import Bank of India.

67. To improve the flow of credit to productive sectors at viable costs so as to sustain the growth momentum, the Reserve Bank signalled a lowering of the interest rate structure by significantly reducing both its key policy rates—the repo rate and the reverse repo rate. The SLR has also been reduced by one percentage point releasing funds to banks for credit deployment.

68. In the context of tightening liquidity in the recent period, the major challenge for the Reserve Bank has been to infuse liquidity in the system and assure the markets that it will continue to maintain a comfortable liquidity position. Accordingly, the policy actions of the Reserve Bank since mid-September 2008 have resulted in the augmentation of active/potential liquidity in the system of over Rs. 3,88,000 crore. The Reserve Bank has also assured market participants that it will endeavour to maintain the overnight money market rates within the LAF corridor. The Reserve Bank will continue to pursue this stance of ensuring ample liquidity in the market and maintaining the overnight money market rates within the LAF corridor. In order to do so, the Reserve Bank will, as in the past, employ both conventional and unconventional measures.

69. The Reserve Bank has acted aggressively and pre-emptively on monetary policy accommodation, particularly through interest rate cuts in terms of both magnitude and pace.

In the space of just one quarter, the repo rate has been reduced from 9.0 per cent to 5.5 per cent and the reverse repo rate from 6.0 per cent to 4.0 per cent, thereby bringing down both of them to historically lowest levels. The transmission of the policy interest rate signal has been effective in the money and government securities markets; however, the transmission in the credit market has so far been subdued. Most banks have reduced lending and deposit rates to some extent, but a few have yet to do so. In the Reserve Bank's view, the policy easing done by it in the last few months allows for considerable room for banks to respond more actively to the policy cues.

70. As indicated earlier, the demand for credit from the banking sector has increased as other sources of funds to the commercial sector have shrunk. Available information (as on January 23, 2009) suggests that the total flow of resources to the commercial sector from all sources, estimated at about Rs. 4,85,000 crore during the fiscal year 2008-09 so far, has been lower than about Rs. 4,99,000 crore in the corresponding period of the previous year. While bank credit has substituted for the shortfall in other sources of funds to some extent, a complete substitution has so far not taken place.

71. Given the uncertain outlook of resource availability from both external and non-bank domestic sources, the Reserve Bank has raised its indicative projection of total flow of credit from the banking sector to the commercial sector to 24.0 per cent for 2008-09 from 20.0 per cent envisaged in the Annual Policy Statement. With a view to enabling banks to sustain the current level of credit flow alongside an enhanced government market borrowing programme, the Reserve Bank's monetary operations will be conducted so as to be consistent with the revised indicative money supply projection of 19.0 per cent for 2008-09, higher than the 16.5-17.0 per cent envisaged in the Annual Policy Statement.

72. To arrest the moderation in economic growth, it is critical that banks expand the flow of credit to productive sectors of the economy and do so at viable rates. At the same time, banks should monitor their loan portfolios and take early action to prevent delinquencies down the road, and safeguard

the gains of the last several years in improving asset quality. The Reserve Bank appreciates that risk management is a difficult task in normal circumstances; it is even more challenging in an environment of uncertainty and downturn. Towards this shared endeavour of maintaining the flow of credit to productive sectors, the Reserve Bank will take calibrated monetary policy actions as necessary and at the appropriate time.

73. Although the origins of the crisis are common around the world, the crisis has impacted different economies differently. Importantly, in advanced economies where it originated, the crisis spread from the financial sector to the real sector. In emerging economies, the transmission of external shocks to domestic vulnerabilities has typically been from the real sector to the financial sector. Countries have responded to the crisis depending on their specific country circumstances. In particular, while policy responses in advanced economies have had to contend with both the financial crisis and recession, in India, the policy response has been predominantly driven by the need to arrest moderation in economic growth. Our ability to respond has been facilitated by the continued smooth functioning of our financial markets and the well-capitalised and healthy banking system. Thus, even as policy responses across countries are broadly similar, their precise design, quantum, sequencing and timing have varied. This has been the case with India too. While we have certainly studied and evaluated measures taken by other central banks around the world, we have calibrated and designed our responses keeping in view India's specific economic context.

Policy Stance

74. Keeping in view the above assessment of the global scenario and domestic economy, particularly the outlook on growth and inflation, the stance of monetary policy for the rest of 2008-09 will be as follows:

- Provision of comfortable liquidity to meet the required credit growth consistent with the overall projection of economic growth.

- Respond swiftly and effectively with all possible measures as warranted by the evolving global and domestic situation impinging on growth and financial stability.
- Ensure a monetary and interest rate environment consistent with price stability, well-anchored inflation expectations and orderly conditions in financial markets.

75. Given the uncertain outlook on the global crisis, it is difficult to precisely anticipate every development. The Reserve Bank will continue to maintain vigil, monitor domestic and global developments, and take swift and effective action to minimise the impact of the crisis and restore the economy to its potential growth path with price stability. The response to the Reserve Bank's policy actions over the last several months is still unfolding. As demonstrated in the recent past, the Reserve Bank will act swiftly and decisively as and when evolving external and domestic conditions so warrant.

III. Monetary Measures

Bank Rate

76. The Bank Rate has been kept unchanged at 6.0 per cent.

Repo Rate/Reverse Repo Rate

77. The repo rate under the LAF has been kept unchanged at 5.5 per cent.

78. The reverse repo rate under the LAF has been kept unchanged at 4.0 per cent.

79. The Reserve Bank has the flexibility to conduct repo/reverse repo auctions at a fixed rate or at variable rates as circumstances warrant.

80. The Reserve Bank retains the option to conduct overnight or longer term repo/reverse repo under the LAF depending on market conditions and other relevant factors. The Reserve Bank will continue to use this flexibly including the right to accept or reject tender(s) under the LAF, wholly or

partially, if deemed fit, so as to make efficient use of the LAF in daily liquidity management.

Cash Reserve Ratio

81. The cash reserve ratio (CRR) of scheduled banks has been kept unchanged at 5.0 per cent of NDTL.

Liquidity Facilities

82. The Reserve Bank has allowed banks to avail liquidity support under the LAF for the purpose of meeting the funding requirements of mutual funds (MFs), non-banking financial companies (NBFCs) and housing finance companies (HFCs) through relaxation in the maintenance of SLR up to 1.5 per cent of their NDTL. Second, a special refinance facility for scheduled commercial banks (excluding RRBs) was provided by the Reserve Bank on November 1, 2008 under Section 17 (3B) of the RBI Act, 1934 up to 1.0 per cent of each bank's NDTL as on October 24, 2008. Both these facilities are currently available up to June 30, 2009. In order to ensure that banks continue to have flexibility in their liquidity management operations in the current market conditions, it has been decided:

- To extend both the refinance facilities up to September 30, 2009.

Annual Policy Statement 2009-10

83. The Annual Policy Statement for 2009-10 will be announced on April 21, 2009.

17

Some Reflections on the Recent Global Financial Turmoil—An Indian Perspective*

10 January 2009

Every year, this forum provides an opportunity to collectively review and analyse the developments of the past year in the forex market. But the past year has been like never before and now the focus is on the impact of the financial crisis on the real economy. The financial meltdown has resulted in effective nationalisation of major financial institutions in the US, UK and Eurozone. So far global banks, mortgage lenders and insurance firms have announced write downs of over US$ 800 billion. There has been a massive increase in central bank lending to the banking system and rescue packages totalling almost US$ 3 trillion have been announced by governments around the world. Monetary policy has been eased aggressively but given the lagged impact attention has shifted to fiscal policy. From this side, I can say that the past year has indeed been a challenging one which has reinforced the futility of finding clean corner solutions to evolving situations and each decision necessarily involves managing

---

* Keynote address by Ms Shyamala Gopinath, Deputy Governor of the Reserve Bank of India, at the Annual Conference of the Foreign Exchange Dealers' Association of India (FEDAI), Kolkata. Assistance of Mr. Vaibhav Chaturvedi in preparation of the remarks is gratefully acknowledged.

different objectives while finding the immediate focus points without dissipating the gains of reforms undertaken.

Forex Markets in India—Recent Developments

2. As far as the Indian foreign exchange market is concerned, during the last five years the sources of supply and demand have changed significantly with large transactions emanating from capital account unlike in the past when current account transactions dominated the foreign exchange market. The behaviour as well as the incentive structure of the participants who use the forex market for undertaking current account transactions differ significantly from those who use the market for capital account transactions. Therefore managing the capital account, particularly debt flows, even while we are getting more integrated is an important instrument in our overall macro-economic management. In the last few years we had to address the challenge of large capital inflows and had therefore in consultation with Government taken certain measures to calibrate these flows by requiring external commercial borrowings (ECB) to be used for foreign currency expenditure. Measures to liberalise outflows for resident individuals, mutual funds, and corporates were also pursued. The global financial crisis and deleveraging have now led to reversal and/or modulation of capital flows particularly foreign institutional investor flows, ECBs and trade credit.

3. In response to the emerging global developments, the RBI has taken a series of measures to augment forex and domestic liquidity. Some of the measures taken to augment forex liquidity are:

- US dollar swap lines of up to US$ 10 billion for Indian banks with overseas branches and subsidiaries. The actual utilisation, as of January 7, 2009 is only US$ 247 million.
- Increasing interest rate ceilings for FCNR(B) and NRE deposits to LIBOR/SWAP rates plus 100 basis points and LIBOR/SWAP rates plus 175 basis points respectively.

- ECB policy, which is an instrument of capital account management, has been liberalised to revert to the pre-May 2007 period. It may be recalled that due to large capital flows, the end use of ECB proceeds was limited to foreign currency expenditures. Further liberalisation in terms of expanding eligible borrowers and end-use has also been undertaken viz.:
    - Housing Finance Companies, registered with National Housing Bank (NHB) have been permitted to raise short-term foreign currency borrowings.
    - NBFCs, which are exclusively involved in financing of the infrastructure sector, may avail of ECBs from multilateral/regional financial institutions and Government owned development financial institutions for on-lending to the borrowers in the infrastructure sector under the Approval route.
    - Payment for obtaining license/permit for 3G Spectrum will be considered an eligible end-use for the purpose of ECB.
    - The corporates in the Hotels, Hospitals and Software sectors to avail of ECB up to US$ 100 million per financial year, under the Automatic Route, for foreign currency and/or Rupee capital expenditure for permissible end-use.
    - Spreads on ECBs and trade credits were increased and the all-in-cost ceilings on ECBs were dispensed with under the Approval route.
- Limit on overseas borrowings by banks was enhanced from 25 per cent to 50 per cent of unimpaired Tier I capital. Overseas borrowings for on-lending to exporters continue to remain outside the ceiling.
- In order to enable EXIM bank to continue to offer buyers credit against lines of credit as well as pre-shipment and post-shipment finance, RBI has extended a line of credit of Rs. 5000 crore.
- EXIM is also eligible to avail of swap facility up to US$ 1 billion under the facility permitted for banks.

- The FII limit for investment in corporate bonds has been hiked to US$ 15 billion from US$ 6 billion.

4. The Indian foreign exchange market has grown significantly in the last several years. The daily average turnover has gone up from about US$ 5 billion per day in 1998 to more than US$ 50 billion per day in 2008. There is also evidence of growing merchant turnover reflecting the huge increase in external transactions. The bid offer spreads are also narrow.

Table 1: Forex Market Activity

	April '05-Mar '06	April '06-Mar '07	April '07-Mar '08	April '08-Dec '08
Total turnover (US$ billion)	4,404	6,571	12,304	9,621
Inter-bank to Merchant ratio	2.6:1	2.7:1	2.37:1	2.66:1
Spot/Total Turnover (%)	50.5	51.9	49.7	45.9
Forward/Total Turnover (%)	19.0	17.9	19.3	21.5
Swap/Total Turnover (%)	30.5	30.1	31.1	32.7

Source: RBI.

5. The spot foreign exchange market remains the most important segment but the derivative segment has also grown. In the derivative market foreign exchange swaps account for the largest share of the total turnover of derivatives in India followed by forwards and options. Significant milestones in the development of derivatives market have been (i) permission to banks to undertake cross currency derivative transactions subject to certain conditions (1996), (ii) allowing corporates to undertake long-term foreign currency swaps that contributed to the development of the term currency swap market (1997), (iii) allowing dollar rupee options (2003) and (iv) introduction of currency futures (2008). I would like to emphasise that currency swaps allowed companies with ECBs to swap their foreign currency liabilities into rupees. However, since banks could not carry open positions the risk was allowed to be transferred to any other resident corporate. Normally such risks should be taken by corporates who have natural hedge or have potential foreign exchange earnings. But often corporate assume these risks due to interest rate differentials and views on currencies. This period has also witnessed several

relaxations in regulations relating to forex markets and also greater liberalisation in capital account regulations leading to greater integration with the global economy.

6. Cash settled exchange traded currency futures have made foreign currency a separate asset class that can be traded without any underlying need or exposure and on a leveraged basis on the recognized stock exchanges with credit risks being assumed by the central counterparty. Since the commencement of trading of currency futures in all the three exchanges, the value of the trades has gone up steadily from Rs. 17,429 crores in October 2008 to Rs. 45,803 crores in December 2008. The average daily turnover in all the exchanges has also increased from Rs. 871 crores to Rs. 2,181 crores during the same period. The turnover in the currency futures market is in line with the international scenario, where I understand the share of futures market ranges between 2-3 per cent.

The Broader Theme

7. In my remarks today I thought it would be appropriate and relevant to touch upon the big picture and underline some lessons that we can draw from the crisis relevant to regulation, financial markets and the market infrastructure and reflect on these. We will continue to learn from the lessons as the crisis is still evolving but these are certain topical issues.

(i) As was to be expected, the financial sector turmoil has triggered a reassessment internationally of the existing theoretics and metrics about the financial sector developments of the past two decades and the simultaneous evolution of the global regulatory framework enshrined in the Basel framework. Questions are being asked and answers being sought to some of the key issues regarding leverage, transparency, and liquidity underlying at the heart of the crisis.

(ii) What the current crisis has done is to question the very fundamentals of the entire financial framework. What is the role of the financial system in an economy *vis-à-vis* the real sector? If the financial sector exists, as traditionally conceived to intermediate financial resources for optimal channelisation to productive sectors, then over the last few years the script has gone terribly bad. The world of finance, as had come to be epitomized in the market volumes and turnovers and derivative outstandings got disconnected by far from the real sector.

(iii) The importance of containing systemic leverage has been underlined. While obviously there can't be market stops and starts for this purpose but the whole incentive structure built in the public policy framework needs to be aligned with the objective of disincentivising leverage beyond a point. Any future financial market reform measure and introduction of new innovations/products must be preceded by an assessment of the resultant leverage for the system in quantifiable terms.

(iv) Financial sector entities need to be seen and regulated as risk repositories in the system—any notion of their risks being dissipated into or outside the system is inherently flawed. There is therefore need for limits, prudential safeguards and adequate capital to support the risks. It is also necessary to understand the 4 BIS Review 4/2009 substance of a product and not merely the nomenclature.[1] Once this understanding is there the income recognition and accounting treatment becomes clear. Receipt of premia/fees for assuming a contingent liability will then not be treated as income but as funds for meeting potential future liabilities.

---

1. For instance, in the context of CDS, the Superintendent of the New York State Insurance Department Mr. Eric Dinallo recently mentioned in his deposition before the Hearing of a US Senate Committee on "The Role of Financial Derivatives in Current Financial Crisis" that "The Insurance Department has determined that covered credit default swaps are insurance and therefore, potentially subject to state regulation.... Our goal is to ensure the terms of credit default swaps are written as a mechanism for protecting buyers against actual losses and not for betting on the credit quality of a third party."

(v) It is now recognised that the current micro-economic-driven prudential regulatory framework, including Basel II is procyclical which further worsens the impact of crises on institutions. In 2000, the Bank of Spain introduced a dynamic, rules-based loan-loss provisioning system in which provisions increase in periods of higher credit growth and economic expansion, and decrease in times of low or negative growth, thereby contributing to smooth income and capital over time. RBI also did something similar when we increased the risk weight as also the general provisioning requirement on exposures to sectors which showed high credit growth. This was reduced recently when growth moderated.

(vi) The increasing focus on holistic approach towards regulation of financial entities is a welcome change from the view that allowed a growing proportion of products and participants to go unregulated on the grounds that they had no systematic impact. This approach resulted in the shadow banking system made up of unregulated SIVs and conduits distributing opaque structured products containing risky assets with the active marketing of rating agencies.

In India also, one view used to be that only deposit taking NBFCs need regulation to protect the interest of depositors and that the non-deposit taking NBFCs do not pose any such risk and therefore need not be regulated. It was, however, realised that the inter-linkages of these NBFCs with the other components of the financial system have grown over the years and their growing presence in various financial markets could, in the absence of regulatory steps lead to risk transfers which could have systemic implications. You are well aware how in the recent past, through a gradual non-disruptive process, an attempt has been made to bring systemically important non-deposit taking NBFCs under a more harmonised regulatory framework, including the capital adequacy norms and exposure norms. These measures have reduced the unlimited leverage possibilities available to NBFCs.

(vii) Another important aspect has been the treatment of off-balance sheet exposures and consolidation of off-balance sheet vehicles and conduits. While applying prudential norms, there is need to treat off-balance sheet transactions similar to on balance sheet transactions for the purpose of capital adequacy norms and risk management. In the case of off-balance sheet vehicles a broader view needs to be taken from a prudential point of view on consolidation. The critical issue should be not merely the ownership but where the risk resides. In this context, a review of the current conversion factors and risk weights for off-balance sheet items is necessary. Similarly it is recognized that the potential liquidity risks also need to be captured.

Pursuant to the announcement in the Annual Policy Statement of April 2008, the RBI over a period and after consultations with market participants has announced the following measures:

- Strengthening of the capital adequacy norms for off-balance sheet transactions covering foreign exchange and interest rate exposures. It mandated use of current exposure method for measuring the credit equivalent amount i.e. the exposures had to be marked to market, and prescribed provisioning requirement for the exposure amount as applicable to standard assets of the concerned counterparty. Credit conversion factors were also increased across maturities.
- In regard to asset classification it was clarified that the amount due on a derivative contract will be treated as NPA if not received within 90 days. In that case all other funded facilities granted to the client will also be classified as non-performing asset following the principle of borrower-wise

classification as per the existing asset classification norms. However, in the case of complex derivative contracts that were entered into between April 2007 and June 2008, the RBI suggested that the unpaid amounts may be parked in a separate account and borrower-wise classification will not apply.

- In cases where a derivative contract is restructured, the MTM value of the contract on the date of the restructuring should be cash settled.

(viii) While the factors responsible for the crisis are many, one that is being debated widely is the contribution of fair value accounting framework for complex and conventional financial instruments in amplifying the crisis. The problem lies in the procyclical nature of the standard and the difficulty in valuing financial instruments when markets are illiquid or in distressed conditions.

Although fair value may increase transparency of the company accounts, it may not always reflect the true intrinsic value in both upswings and under excessively stressed market conditions.

There is a need to distinguish the basic financial and prudential analysis from a purely "financial" accounting framework. There is also need to clearly appreciate that the accounting reporting has a role as a source of information and as such will indicate the value of the company at the moment of the statement of accounts. Fair value for prudential purposes is more forward looking in its approach as it includes not only incurred losses but also expected losses. This tension can be addressed by the regulators addressing the regulatory and prudential aspects in the case of banks. Keeping in view the systemic implications of the standards, regulators will have to carry out an in-depth assessment of the concepts and tools relating to valuation.

(ix) Great emphasis is now being laid on implementing a central counterparty for OTC derivatives particularly for credit default swaps. Well regulated counterparties reduce potential for disruption in financial markets and promote operational efficiencies and transparency.

In India as early as in 2001, the Clearing Corporation of India was set up to settle interbank spot forex transactions and all outright and repo transactions in government securities whether negotiated or order driven systems. CCII has also introduced a collateralised money market instrument called CBLO which is also settled through the CCP. CCIL has also commenced non-guaranteed settlement of OTC trades in interest rate swaps on 27 November 2008. Guaranteed settlement of these trades will commence later once we clarify the exposure requirements. In the near future it will also act as central counterparty for forward contracts which will mitigate risks releasing counterparty exposure limits. The margins are in the form of cash and government bonds ensuring the quality and liquidity of the settlement guarantee fund.

(x) Recent developments will also pave the way for more effective regulation rather than reliance on self-regulation, credit rating agencies assessments or setting of standards by industry participants.

(xi) Lastly, on the issue of selling of complex products, we have to collectively work towards a viable framework. What is the solution? In this context I would like to recount the application of a surprisingly simple idea to the realm of public policy that has received tremendous attention after being advocated by Richard Thaler and Cass Sunstein in their international bestseller "Nudge". The authors advocate the use of "choice architecture" by businesses or governments to influence choices in ways that encourage choosers to make decisions in their best interest. They call it "libertarian paternalism". This involves utilizing "nudges" such as the wording of choices in ways that influence individual actions, designing default choices (in the absence of action) that do not penalize individuals, limiting choices to those that are more comprehensible, taxing detrimental choices, and providing full disclosure to better inform decision-makers. Can we take a cue? I will urge FEDAI to take it up as a special assignment and suggest a framework that is both practical and implementable while ensuring the best interests of all stakeholders.

8. The experience and lessons of the present crisis will be extremely useful for us in going forward with the process of financial market liberalisation. While there is not and should not be any stifling of innovations in the financial sector, it is important to distinguish financial innovation from conventional product, service or process innovation in terms of the systemic costs these entail. Socially useful as it is, financial innovation should not be allowed to outpace its understanding by the multitude of market participants and stakeholders—a process facilitated by appropriate reporting, accounting and governance standards and enforced by regulatory and supervisory regime.

9. FEDAI plays a special role in the foreign exchange market for ensuring smooth and speedy growth of the market in all its aspects. All authorised dealers are required to become members of the FEDAI and execute an undertaking to the effect that they would abide by the terms and conditions stipulated by the FEDAI for transacting foreign exchange business. As the forex market grows in the spot and derivative segments including currency futures, the FEDAI as a self-regulatory organisation needs to focus on supporting orderly growth, promoting market integrity and sound practices with the ultimate objective of supporting the real economy. I wish the conference all success.

18

Text of Address of US President Barack Obama to Both Houses of Congress Outlining his Plans for America

24 February 2009

...I know that for many Americans watching right now, the state of our economy is a concern that rises above all others. And rightly so....

But while our economy may be weakened and our confidence shaken; though we are living through difficult and uncertain times, tonight I want every American to know this:

> We will rebuild, we will recover, and the United States of America will emerge stronger than before.

Progress and Prosperity

The weight of this crisis will not determine the destiny of this nation. The answers to our problems don't lie beyond our reach. They exist in our laboratories and universities; in our fields and our factories; in the imaginations of our entrepreneurs and the pride of the hardest-working people on Earth. Those qualities that have made America the greatest force of progress and prosperity in human history we still possess in ample measure. What is required now is for this country to pull together, confront boldly the challenges we face, and take responsibility for our future once more.

Now, if we're honest with ourselves, we'll admit that for too long, we have not always met these responsibilities—as a government or as a people. I say this not to lay blame or look backwards, but because it is only by understanding how we arrived at this moment that we'll be able to lift ourselves out of this predicament.

The fact is, our economy did not fall into decline overnight. Nor did all of our problems begin when the housing market collapsed or the stock market sank. We have known for decades that our survival depends on finding new sources of energy. Yet we import more oil today than ever before. The cost of health care eats up more and more of our savings each year, yet we keep delaying reform. Our children will compete for jobs in a global economy that too many of our schools do not prepare them for. And though all these challenges went unsolved, we still managed to spend more money and pile up more debt, both as individuals and through our government, than ever before.

In other words, we have lived through an era where too often, short-term gains were prized over long-term prosperity; where we failed to look beyond the next payment, the next quarter, or the next election. A surplus became an excuse to transfer wealth to the wealthy instead of an opportunity to invest in our future. Regulations were gutted for the sake of a quick profit at the expense of a healthy market. People bought homes they knew they couldn't afford from banks and lenders who pushed those bad loans anyway. And all the while, critical debates and difficult decisions were put off for some other time on some other day.

Well that day of reckoning has arrived, and the time to take charge of our future is here.

Now is the time to act boldly and wisely—to not only revive this economy, but to build a new foundation for lasting prosperity. Now is the time to jumpstart job creation, re-start lending, and invest in areas like energy, health care, and education that will grow our economy, even as we make hard choices to bring our deficit down. That is what my economic agenda is designed to do, and that's what I'd like to talk to you about tonight.

Recovery Plan

It's an agenda that begins with jobs.

As soon as I took office, I asked this Congress to send me a recovery plan by President's Day that would put people back to work and put money in their pockets. Not because I believe in bigger government—I don't. Not because I'm not mindful of the massive debt we've inherited—I am. I called for action because the failure to do so would have cost more jobs and caused more hardships. In fact, a failure to act would have worsened our long-term deficit by assuring weak economic growth for years. That's why I pushed for quick action. And tonight, I am grateful that this Congress delivered, and pleased to say that the American Recovery and Reinvestment Act is now law.

Over the next two years, this plan will save or create 3.5 million jobs. More than 90 per cent of these jobs will be in the private sector—jobs rebuilding our roads and bridges; constructing wind turbines and solar panels; laying broadband and expanding mass transit.

Because of this plan, there are teachers who can now keep their jobs and educate our kids. Health care professionals can continue caring for our sick. There are 57 police officers who are still on the streets of Minneapolis tonight because this plan prevented the layoffs their department was about to make.

Because of this plan, 95 per cent of the working households in America will receive a tax cut—a tax cut that you will see in your paychecks beginning on April 1st.

Because of this plan, families who are struggling to pay tuition costs will receive a $2,500 tax credit for all four years of college. And Americans who have lost their jobs in this recession will be able to receive extended unemployment benefits and continued health care coverage to help them weather this storm.

I know there are some in this chamber and watching at home who are skeptical of whether this plan will work. I understand that skepticism. Here in Washington, we've all seen how quickly good intentions can turn into broken promises and wasteful spending. And with a plan of this scale comes enormous responsibility to get it right.

That is why I have asked Vice President Biden to lead a tough, unprecedented oversight effort—because nobody messes with Joe. I have told each member of my Cabinet as well as mayors and governors across the country that they will be held accountable by me and the American people for every dollar they spend. I have appointed a proven and aggressive Inspector General to ferret out any and all cases of waste and fraud. And we have created a new website called recovery.gov so that every American can find out how and where their money is being spent.

Choked off

So the recovery plan we passed is the first step in getting our economy back on track. But it is just the first step. Because even if we manage this plan flawlessly, there will be no real recovery unless we clean up the credit crisis that has severely weakened our financial system.

I want to speak plainly and candidly about this issue tonight, because every American should know that it directly affects you and your family's well-being. You should also know that the money you've deposited in banks across the country is safe; your insurance is secure; and you can rely on the continued operation of our financial system. That is not the source of concern.

The concern is that if we do not re-start lending in this country, our recovery will be choked off before it even begins.

You see, the flow of credit is the lifeblood of our economy. The ability to get a loan is how you finance the purchase of everything from a home to a car to a college education; how stores stock their shelves, farms buy equipment, and businesses make payroll.

But credit has stopped flowing the way it should. Too many bad loans from the housing crisis have made their way onto the books of too many banks. With so much debt and so little confidence, these banks are now fearful of lending out any more money to households, to businesses, or to each other.

When there is no lending, families can't afford to buy homes or cars. So businesses are forced to make layoffs. Our economy suffers even more, and credit dries up even further.

That is why this administration is moving swiftly and aggressively to break this destructive cycle, restore confidence, and re-start lending.

We will do so in several ways. First, we are creating a new lending fund that represents the largest effort ever to help provide auto loans, college loans, and small business loans to the consumers and entrepreneurs who keep this economy running.

Second, we have launched a housing plan that will help responsible families facing the threat of foreclosure lower their monthly payments and re-finance their mortgages. It's a plan that won't help speculators or that neighbor down the street who bought a house he could never hope to afford, but it will help millions of Americans who are struggling with declining home values—Americans who will now be able to take advantage of the lower interest rates that this plan has already helped bring about. In fact, the average family who re-finances today can save nearly $2000 per year on their mortgage.

Third, we will act with the full force of the federal government to ensure that the major banks that Americans depend on have enough confidence and enough money to lend even in more difficult times. And when we learn that a major bank has serious problems, we will hold accountable those responsible, force the necessary adjustments, provide the support to clean up their balance sheets, and assure the continuity of a strong, viable institution that can serve our people and our economy.

Accountable

I understand that on any given day, Wall Street may be more comforted by an approach that gives banks bailouts with no strings attached, and that holds nobody accountable for their reckless decisions. But such an approach won't solve the problem. And our goal is to quicken the day when we re-start lending to the American people and American business and end this crisis once and for all.

I intend to hold these banks fully accountable for the assistance they receive, and this time, they will have to clearly demonstrate how taxpayer dollars result in more lending for the American taxpayer. This time, CEOs won't be able to use taxpayer money to pad their paychecks or buy fancy drapes or disappear on a private jet. Those days are over.

Still, this plan will require significant resources from the federal government—and yes, probably more than we've already set aside. But while the cost of action will be great, I can assure you that the cost of inaction will be far greater, for it could result in an economy that sputters along for not months or years, but perhaps a decade. That would be worse for our deficit, worse for business, worse for you, and worse for the next generation. And I refuse to let that happen.

I understand that when the last administration asked this Congress to provide assistance for struggling banks, Democrats and Republicans alike were infuriated by the mismanagement and results that followed. So were the American taxpayers. So was I.

So I know how unpopular it is to be seen as helping banks right now, especially when everyone is suffering in part from their bad decisions. I promise you—I get it.

But I also know that in a time of crisis, we cannot afford to govern out of anger, or yield to the politics of the moment. My job—our job—is to solve the problem. Our job is to govern with a sense of responsibility. I will not spend a single penny for the purpose of rewarding a single Wall Street executive, but I will do whatever it takes to help the small business that can't pay its workers or the family that has saved and still can't get a mortgage.

That's what this is about. It's not about helping banks—it's about helping people. Because when credit is available again, that young family can finally buy a new home. And then some company will hire workers to build it. And then those workers will have money to spend, and if they can get a loan too, maybe they'll finally buy that car, or open their own business. Investors will return to the market, and American families will see their retirement secured once more. Slowly, but surely, confidence will return, and our economy will recover.

Crisis

So I ask this Congress to join me in doing whatever proves necessary. Because we cannot consign our nation to an open-ended recession. And to ensure that a crisis of this magnitude never happens again, I ask Congress to move quickly on legislation that will finally reform our outdated regulatory system. It is time to put in place tough, new common-sense rules of the road so that our financial market rewards drive and innovation, and punishes short-cuts and abuse.

The recovery plan and the financial stability plan are the immediate steps we're taking to revive our economy in the short-term. But the only way to fully restore America's economic strength is to make the long-term investments that will lead to new jobs, new industries, and a renewed ability to compete with the rest of the world. The only way this century will be another American century is if we confront at last the price of our dependence on oil and the high cost of health care; the schools that aren't preparing our children and the mountain of debt they stand to inherit. That is our responsibility.

In the next few days, I will submit a budget to Congress. So often, we have come to view these documents as simply numbers on a page or laundry lists of programs. I see this document differently. I see it as a vision for America—as a blueprint for our future.

My budget does not attempt to solve every problem or address every issue. It reflects the stark reality of what we've inherited—a trillion dollar deficit, a financial crisis, and a costly recession.

Given these realities, everyone in this chamber—Democrats and Republicans—will have to sacrifice some worthy priorities for which there are no dollars. And that includes me.

But that does not mean we can afford to ignore our long-term challenges. I reject the view that says our problems will simply take care of themselves; that says government has no role in laying the foundation for our common prosperity.

Big Ideas

For history tells a different story. History reminds us that at every moment of economic upheaval and transformation, this nation has responded with bold action and big ideas. In the midst of civil war, we laid railroad tracks from one coast to another that spurred commerce and industry. From the turmoil of the Industrial Revolution came a system of public high schools that prepared our citizens for a new age. In the wake of war and depression, the GI Bill sent a generation to college and created the largest middle-class in history. And a twilight struggle for freedom led to a nation of highways, an American on the moon, and an explosion of technology that still shapes our world.

In each case, government didn't supplant private enterprise; it catalyzed private enterprise. It created the conditions for thousands of entrepreneurs and new businesses to adapt and to thrive.

We are a nation that has seen promise amid peril, and claimed opportunity from ordeal. Now we must be that nation again. That is why, even as it cuts back on the programs we don't need, the budget I submit will invest in the three areas that are absolutely critical to our economic future: energy, health care, and education.

It begins with energy.

We know the country that harnesses the power of clean, renewable energy will lead the 21st century. And yet, it is China that has launched the largest effort in history to make their economy energy efficient. We invented solar technology, but we've fallen behind countries like Germany and Japan in producing it. New plug-in hybrids roll off our assembly lines, but they will run on batteries made in Korea.

Well I do not accept a future where the jobs and industries of tomorrow take root beyond our borders—and I know you don't either. It is time for America to lead again.

Thanks to our recovery plan, we will double this nation's supply of renewable energy in the next three years. We have also made the largest investment in basic research funding in American history—an investment that will spur not only new discoveries in energy, but breakthroughs in medicine, science, and technology.

We will soon lay down thousands of miles of power lines that can carry new energy to cities and towns across this country. And we will put Americans to work making our homes and buildings more efficient so that we can save billions of dollars on our energy bills.

Innovation

But to truly transform our economy, protect our security, and save our planet from the ravages of climate change, we need to ultimately make clean, renewable energy the profitable kind of energy. So I ask this Congress to send me legislation that places a market-based cap on carbon pollution and drives the production of more renewable energy in America. And to support that innovation, we will invest fifteen billion dollars a year to develop technologies like wind power and solar power; advanced biofuels, clean coal, and more fuel-efficient cars and trucks built right here in America.

As for our auto industry, everyone recognizes that years of bad decision-making and a global recession have pushed our automakers to the brink. We should not, and will not, protect them from their own bad practices. But we are committed to the goal of a re-tooled, re-imagined auto industry that can compete and win. Millions of jobs depend on it. Scores of communities depend on it. And I believe the nation that invented the automobile cannot walk away from it.

None of this will come without cost, nor will it be easy. But this is America. We don't do what's easy. We do what is necessary to move this country forward.

For that same reason, we must also address the crushing cost of health care.

This is a cost that now causes a bankruptcy in America every thirty seconds. By the end of the year, it could cause 1.5 million Americans to lose their homes. In the last eight years, premiums have grown four times faster than wages. And in each of these years, one million more Americans have lost their health insurance. It is one of the major reasons why small businesses close their doors and corporations ship jobs overseas. And it's one of the largest and fastest-growing parts of our budget.

Given these facts, we can no longer afford to put health care reform on hold.

Already, we have done more to advance the cause of health care reform in the last thirty days than we have in the last decade. When it was days old, this Congress passed a law to provide and protect health insurance for eleven million American children whose parents work full-time. Our recovery plan will invest in electronic health records and new technology that will reduce errors, bring down costs, ensure privacy, and save lives. It will launch a new effort to conquer a disease that has touched the life of nearly every American by seeking a cure for cancer in our time. And it makes the largest investment ever in preventive care, because that is one of the best ways to keep our people healthy and our costs under control.

Not Easy

This budget builds on these reforms. It includes an historic commitment to comprehensive health care reform—a down-payment on the principle that we must have quality, affordable health care for every American. It's a commitment that's paid for in part by efficiencies in our system that are long overdue. And it's a step we must take if we hope to bring down our deficit in the years to come.

Now, there will be many different opinions and ideas about how to achieve reform, and that is why I'm bringing together businesses and workers, doctors and health care providers, Democrats and Republicans to begin work on this issue....

I suffer no illusions that this will be an easy process. It will be hard. But I also know that nearly a century after Teddy Roosevelt first called for reform, the cost of our health care has weighed down our economy and the conscience of our nation long enough. So let there be no doubt: health care reform cannot wait, it must not wait, and it will not wait another year.

The third challenge we must address is the urgent need to expand the promise of education in America.

In a global economy where the most valuable skill you can sell is your knowledge, a good education is no longer just a pathway to opportunity—it is a pre-requisite.

Right now, three-quarters of the fastest-growing occupations require more than a high school diploma. And yet, just over half of our citizens have that level of education. We have one of the highest high school dropout rates of any industrialized nation. And half of the students who begin college never finish.

This is a prescription for economic decline, because we know the countries that out-teach us today will out-compete us tomorrow. That is why it will be the goal of this administration to ensure that every child has access to a complete and competitive education—from the day they are born to the day they begin a career.

Already, we have made an historic investment in education through the economic recovery plan. We have dramatically expanded early childhood education and will continue to improve its quality, because we know that the most formative learning comes in those first years of life. We have made college affordable for nearly seven million more students. And we have provided the resources necessary to prevent painful cuts and teacher layoffs that would set back our children's progress.

But we know that our schools don't just need more resources. They need more reform. That is why this budget creates new incentives for teacher performance; pathways for advancement, and rewards for success. We'll invest in innovative programs that are already helping schools meet high standards and close achievement gaps. And we will expand our commitment to charter schools.

Doors of Opportunity

It is our responsibility as lawmakers and educators to make this system work. But it is the responsibility of every citizen to participate in it. And so tonight, I ask every American to commit to at least one year or more of higher education or career training. This can be community college or a four-year school; vocational training or an apprenticeship. But whatever the training may be, every American will need to get more than a high school diploma. And dropping out of high school is no longer an option. It's not just quitting on yourself, it's quitting on your country—and this country needs and values the talents of every American. That is why we will provide the support necessary for you to complete college and meet a new goal: by 2020, America will once again have the highest proportion of college graduates in the world.

I know that the price of tuition is higher than ever, which is why if you are willing to volunteer in your neighborhood or give back to your community or serve your country, we will make sure that you can afford a higher education. And to encourage a renewed spirit of national service for this and future generations, I ask this Congress to send me the bipartisan legislation that bears the name of Senator Orrin Hatch as well as an American who has never stopped asking what he can do for his country—Senator Edward Kennedy.

These education policies will open the doors of opportunity for our children. But it is up to us to ensure they walk through them. In the end, there is no program or policy that can substitute for a mother or father who will attend those parent/teacher conferences, or help with homework after dinner, or turn off the TV, put away the video games, and read to their child. I speak to you not just as a President, but as a father when I say that responsibility for our children's education must begin at home.

There is, of course, another responsibility we have to our children. And that is the responsibility to ensure that we do not pass on to them a debt they cannot pay. With the deficit we inherited, the cost of the crisis we face, and the long-term challenges we must meet, it has never been more important to ensure that as our economy recovers, we do what it takes to bring this deficit down.

I'm proud that we passed the recovery plan free of earmarks, and I want to pass a budget next year that ensures that each dollar we spend reflects only our most important national priorities.

Yesterday, I held a fiscal summit where I pledged to cut the deficit in half by the end of my first term in office. My administration has also begun to go line by line through the federal budget in order to eliminate wasteful and ineffective programs. As you can imagine, this is a process that will take some time. But we're starting with the biggest lines. We have already identified two trillion dollars in savings over the next decade.

Health Reform

In this budget, we will end education programs that don't work and end direct payments to large agribusinesses that don't need them. We'll eliminate the no-bid contracts that have wasted billions in Iraq, and reform our defense budget so that we're not paying for Cold War-era weapons systems we don't use. We will root out the waste, fraud, and abuse in our Medicare program that doesn't make our seniors any healthier, and we will restore a sense of fairness and balance to our tax code by finally ending the tax breaks for corporations that ship our jobs overseas.

In order to save our children from a future of debt, we will also end the tax breaks for the wealthiest 2 per cent of Americans. But let me perfectly clear, because I know you'll hear the same old claims that rolling back these tax breaks means a massive tax increase on the American people: if your family earns less than $250,000 a year, you will not see your taxes increased a single dime. I repeat: not one single dime. In fact, the recovery plan provides a tax cut—that's right, a tax cut—for 95 per cent of working families. And these checks are on the way.

To preserve our long-term fiscal health, we must also address the growing costs in Medicare and Social Security. Comprehensive health care reform is the best way to strengthen Medicare for years to come. And we must also begin a conversation on how to do the same for Social Security, while creating tax-free universal savings accounts for all Americans.

Finally, because we're also suffering from a deficit of trust, I am committed to restoring a sense of honesty and accountability to our budget. That is why this budget looks ahead ten years and accounts for spending that was left out under the old rules—and for the first time, that includes the full cost of fighting in Iraq and Afghanistan. For seven years, we have been a nation at war. No longer will we hide its price.

We are now carefully reviewing our policies in both wars, and I will soon announce a way forward in Iraq that leaves Iraq to its people and responsibly ends this war.

And with our friends and allies, we will forge a new and comprehensive strategy for Afghanistan and Pakistan to defeat al Qaeda and combat extremism. Because I will not allow terrorists to plot against the American people from safe havens half a world away.

Sacred Trust

As we meet here tonight, our men and women in uniform stand watch abroad and more are readying to deploy. To each and every one of them, and to the families who bear the quiet burden of their absence, Americans are united in sending one message: we honor your service, we are inspired by your sacrifice, and you have our unyielding support. To relieve the strain on our forces, my budget increases the number of our soldiers and Marines. And to keep our sacred trust with those who serve, we will raise their pay, and give our veterans the expanded health care and benefits that they have earned.

To overcome extremism, we must also be vigilant in upholding the values our troops defend—because there is no force in the world more powerful than the example of America. That is why I have ordered the closing of the detention center at Guantanamo Bay, and will seek swift and certain justice for captured terrorists—because living our values doesn't make us weaker, it makes us safer and it makes us stronger. And that is why I can stand here tonight and say without exception or equivocation that the United States of America does not torture.

In words and deeds, we are showing the world that a new era of engagement has begun. For we know that America cannot meet the threats of this century alone, but the world cannot meet them without America. We cannot shun the negotiating table, nor ignore the foes or forces that could do us harm. We are instead called to move forward with the sense of confidence and candor that serious times demand.

To seek progress toward a secure and lasting peace between Israel and her neighbors, we have appointed an envoy to sustain our effort. To meet the challenges of the 21st century —from terrorism to nuclear proliferation; from pandemic disease to cyber threats to crushing poverty—we will strengthen old alliances, forge new ones, and use all elements of our national power.

And to respond to an economic crisis that is global in scope, we are working with the nations of the G-20 to restore confidence in our financial system, avoid the possibility of escalating protectionism, and spur demand for American goods in markets across the globe. For the world depends on us to have a strong economy, just as our economy depends on the strength of the world's.

As we stand at this crossroads of history, the eyes of all people in all nations are once again upon us—watching to see what we do with this moment; waiting for us to lead.

Great Privilege

Those of us gathered here tonight have been called to govern in extraordinary times. It is a tremendous burden, but also a great privilege—one that has been entrusted to few generations of Americans. For in our hands lies the ability to shape our world for good or for ill.

I know that it is easy to lose sight of this truth—to become cynical and doubtful; consumed with the petty and the trivial.

But in my life, I have also learned that hope is found in unlikely places; that inspiration often comes not from those with the most power or celebrity, but from the dreams and aspirations of Americans who are anything but ordinary.

I think about Leonard Abess, the bank president from Miami who reportedly cashed out of his company, took a $60 million bonus, and gave it out to all 399 people who worked for him, plus another 72 who used to work for him. He didn't tell anyone, but when the local newspaper found out, he simply said, "I knew some of these people since I was 7 years old. I didn't feel right getting the money myself."

I think about Greensburg, Kansas, a town that was completely destroyed by a tornado, but is being rebuilt by its residents as a global example of how clean energy can power an entire community—how it can bring jobs and businesses to a place where piles of bricks and rubble once lay. "The tragedy was terrible," said one of the men who helped them rebuild. "But the folks here know that it also provided an incredible opportunity."

And I think about Ty'Sheoma Bethea, the young girl from that school I visited in Dillon, South Carolina—a place where the ceilings leak, the paint peels off the walls, and they have to stop teaching six times a day because the train barrels by their classroom. She has been told that her school is hopeless, but the other day after class she went to the public library and typed up a letter to the people sitting in this room. She even asked her principal for the money to buy a stamp. The letter asks us for help, and says, "We are just students trying to become lawyers, doctors, congressmen like yourself and one day president, so we can make a change to not just the state of South Carolina but also the world. We are not quitters."

These words and these stories tell us something about the spirit of the people who sent us here. They tell us that even in the most trying times, amid the most difficult circumstances, there is a generosity, a resilience, a decency, and a determination that perseveres; a willingness to take responsibility for our future and for posterity.

Their resolve must be our inspiration. Their concerns must be our cause. And we must show them and all our people that we are equal to the task before us.

I know that we haven't agreed on every issue thus far, and there are surely times in the future when we will part ways. But I also know that every American who is sitting here tonight loves this country and wants it to succeed. That must be the starting point for every debate we have in the coming months, and where we return after those debates are done. That is the foundation on which the American people expect us to build common ground.

And if we do—if we come together and lift this nation from the depths of this crisis; if we put our people back to work and restart the engine of our prosperity; if we confront without fear the challenges of our time and summon that enduring spirit of an America that does not quit, then someday years from now our children can tell their children that this was the time when we performed, in the words that are carved into this very chamber, "something worthy to be remembered."

19

Obama's Speech on Executive Compensation

....

The economic crisis we face is unlike any we've seen in our lifetime. It's a crisis of falling confidence and rising debt. Of widely distributed risk and narrowly concentrated reward. A crisis written in the fine print of subprime mortgages, on the ledger lines of once-mighty financial institutions, and on the pink slips that have upended lives and cost the economy 2.6 million jobs last year alone.

We know that even if we do everything we should, this crisis was years in the making, and it will take more than weeks or months to turn things around.

But make no mistake:

A failure to act, and act now, will turn crisis into a catastrophe and guarantee a longer recession, a less robust recovery, and a more uncertain future. Millions more jobs will be lost. More businesses will be shuttered. More dreams will be deferred.

That's why I feel such a sense of urgency about the Economic Recovery and Reinvestment Plan that is before Congress today. With it, we can save or create more than three million jobs, doing things that will strengthen our country for generations to come. It is not merely a prescription for short-term spending—it's a strategy for long-term economic growth in areas like renewable energy, health care, and education.

Now, in the past few days I've heard criticisms of this plan that echo the very same failed theories that helped lead us into this crisis—the notion that tax cuts alone will solve all our problems; that we can ignore fundamental challenges like energy independence and the high cost of health care and still expect our economy and our country to thrive.

I reject that theory, and so did the American people when they went to the polls in November and voted resoundingly for change. So I urge members of Congress to act without delay. No plan is perfect, and we should work to make it stronger. But let's not make the perfect the enemy of the essential. Let's show people all over our country who are looking for leadership in this difficult time that we are equal to the task.

At the same time, we know that this Recovery and Reinvestment plan is only the first part of what we need to do to restore prosperity and secure our future. We also need a strong and viable financial system to keep credit flowing to businesses and families alike. My administration will do what it takes to restore our financial system; our recovery depends upon it. And so...Secretary Geithner will release a new strategy to get credit moving again—a strategy that will reflect the lessons of past mistakes while laying a foundation for the future.

But in order to restore our financial system, we've got to restore trust. And in order to restore trust, we've got to make certain that taxpayer funds are not subsidizing excessive compensation packages on Wall Street.

We all need to take responsibility. And this includes executives at major financial firms who turned to the American people, hat in hand, when they were in trouble, even as they paid themselves their customary lavish bonuses. ...that's the height of irresponsibility. That's shameful. And that's exactly the kind of disregard for the costs and consequences of their actions that brought about this crisis: a culture of narrow self-interest and short-term gain at the expense of everything else.

This is America. We don't disparage wealth. We don't begrudge anybody for achieving success. And we believe that success should be rewarded. But what gets people upset—

and rightfully so—are executives being rewarded for failure. Especially when those rewards are subsidized by US taxpayers.

For top executives to award themselves these kinds of compensation packages in the midst of this economic crisis is not only in bad taste—it's a bad strategy—and I will not tolerate it as President. We're going to be demanding some restraint in exchange for federal aid—so that when firms seek new federal dollars, we won't find them up to the same old tricks.

As part of the reforms we are announcing..., top executives at firms receiving extraordinary help from US taxpayers will have their compensation capped at $500,000—a fraction of the salaries that have been reported recently. And if these executives receive any additional compensation, it will come in the form of stock that can't be paid up until taxpayers are paid back for their assistance.

Companies receiving federal aid are going to have to disclose publicly all the perks and luxuries bestowed upon senior executives and provide an explanation to the taxpayers and to shareholders as to why these expenses are justified. And we're putting a stop to these kinds of massive severance packages we've all read about with disgust; we're taking the air out of the golden parachute.

We're asking these firms to take responsibility, to recognize the nature of this crisis and their role in it. We believe that what we've laid out should be viewed as fair and embraced as basic common sense.

Finally, these guidelines we're putting in place are only the beginning of a long-term effort. We're going to examine the ways in which the means and manner of executive compensation have contributed to a reckless culture and quarter-by-quarter mentality that in turn have wrought havoc in our financial system. We're going to be taking a look at broader reforms so that executives are compensated for sound risk management and rewarded for growth measured over years, not just days or weeks.

We've all got to pull together and take our share of responsibility. That's true here in Washington. That's true on Wall Street. The American people are carrying a huge burden as a result of this economic crisis: bearing the brunt of its effects as well as the costs of extraordinary measures we're taking to address it. The American people expect and demand that we pursue policies that reflect the reality of this crisis—and that will prevent these kinds of crises in the future.

20

Congress Trumps Obama by Cuffing Bonuses for CEOs

13 February 2009

The stimulus package Congress passed...imposes new limits on executive compensation that could significantly curb multimillion dollar pay packages on Wall Street and goes much further than restrictions proposed by the Obama administration....

The bill, which President Obama is expected to sign..., limits bonuses for executives at all financial institutions receiving government funds to no more than a third of their annual compensation. The bonuses must be paid in company stock that can be redeemed only when the government investment has been repaid. With the measure, lawmakers seek to address public outrage over extravagant Wall Street paydays even as taxpayers bail out the industry.

Unlike the rules issued by the White House, the limits in the stimulus bill would apply to top executives and the highest-paid employees at all 359 banks that have already received government aid. "This is a big deal. This is a problem," said Scott Talbott, chief lobbyist for the nation's largest financial services firms. "It undermines the current incentive structure." Talbott said banking executives expected certain restrictions would be applied to them but are concerned that some of the most highly paid employees, such as top traders, who bring in hefty sums for the company, would flee to hedge funds or foreign banks that have not accepted US government funds.

The White House restrictions capped executive pay at $500,000 and allowed companies to award unlimited stock. Those rules applied only to institutions that receive government funds in the future and under limited circumstances. Bonuses make up much of financial executives' take-home pay, so the new rules could significantly diminish their compensation. For example, Goldman Sachs chief executive Lloyd Blankfein made $68.5 million in 2007—a Wall Street record—but $67.9 million of that was in bonus and other incentive pay that analysts said would be subject to the new rules.

Citigroup's top executive, Vikram Pandit, has voluntarily agreed to a $1 salary until his company returns to profitability. In theory, this means that Pandit would be allowed an annual bonus of pennies. Critics of excessive executive pay assert that companies have always found ways around compensation rules. ..., they noted that more stringent measures—such as a $400,000 cap on all forms of compensation—did not survive last-minute wrangling by House and Senate leaders on the final compromise stimulus bill. To offset the new rules, inserted by Sen. Christopher J. Dodd (D-Conn.), compensation boards could just significantly raise the base salary of executives, the critics said. "Congress missed a huge opportunity to set a strict and measurable limit on executive pay," said Sarah Anderson, a director at the Institute for Policy Studies in Washington. "I'm afraid companies will find ways to shift compensation to other pots and continue to make massive payouts that have so outraged the American people." But several compensation experts said that is unlikely, given the glaring spotlight on an issue that is not expected to go away anytime soon. Excessive compensation has received increasing scrutiny as the pay gap between executives and average workers widened in recent years. Public furor reached a boiling point with news that billions of dollars in bonuses were paid to Wall Street employees last year even as the banks took billions in taxpayer bailout money. The bonus restrictions would apply to a varying number of employees at each firm, depending on how much money the firm has taken in government assistance. At banks receiving less than $25 million, the limits would apply to only the highest-paid employee. For those receiving $25 million to $250 million, the restriction would apply to the five highest-paid employees. The top five executives and ten highest-paid employees would be affected at firms receiving $250 million to $500 million. At firms getting more than half a billion dollars, which would include all of the Wall Street giants, the rules would apply to the top five executives and the 20 highest-paid employees. Taxpayers have injected $45 billion each into Citigroup and Bank of America.

Other measures in the bill include a ban on golden parachutes to departing executives. This would apply to the top 10 most highly-paid employees at all financial institutions currently receiving government aid. The measure allows companies to continue to pay out deferred compensation and benefits such as pensions. There are billions of dollars in such awards on the books of financial institutions.

The restrictions imposed by the Obama administration ...prohibited golden parachutes to the top ten executives of companies requiring massive injections. It also allowed companies to pay up to a year's compensation in severance to the next 25 highest-paid employees.

The stimulus bill also would require the 359 financial institutions to hold a "say on pay" vote at their shareholder meetings until the government funds were returned. The provision, which activist shareholder groups have sought in recent years, is essentially an annual up-or-down vote on executive pay packages and would be nonbinding.

..., bank compensation lawyers, pay consultants and accountants were combing through the executive compensation rules, which make up 11 pages in the 1,073-page stimulus bill. While there was disagreement over the interpretation of finer points, which would need to be clarified by the Treasury Department, there was broad agreement that the new rules would do more to affect executive pay than years of shareholder efforts combined.

A common argument from executives against reining in huge Wall Street bonuses is that it would cause the most talented to flee to hedge funds and private equity groups. The free market, they say, should dictate pay levels.

Even some who have long pushed for executive pay reform are concerned that the new rules do not provide enough incentive to executives. Because executives payouts would not be significant, they say, the executives might not be inclined to work hard to return the government money. "The people who work on Wall Street are motivated by money," said Nell Minow of the Corporate Library. "And we should make sure we hold that carrot in front of them until we get the last dime."

21

Remarks of President-Elect Barack Obama as Prepared for Delivery of American Recovery and Reinvestment

8 January 2009

Throughout America's history, there have been some years that simply rolled into the next without much notice or fanfare. Then there are the years that come along once in a generation—the kind that mark a clean break from a troubled past, and set a new course for our nation.

This is one of those years.

We start 2009 in the midst of a crisis unlike any we have seen in our lifetime—a crisis that has only deepened over the last few weeks. Nearly two million jobs have now been lost, and on Friday we are likely to learn that we lost more jobs last year than at any time since World War II. Just in the past year, another 2.8 million Americans who want and need full-time work have had to settle for part-time jobs. Manufacturing has hit a twenty-eight-year low. Many businesses cannot borrow or make payroll. Many families cannot pay their bills or their mortgage. Many workers are watching their life savings disappear. And many, many Americans are both anxious and uncertain of what the future will hold.

I don't believe it's too late to change course, but it will be if we don't take dramatic action as soon as possible. If nothing is done, this recession could linger for years. The unemployment rate could reach double digits. Our economy could fall $1 trillion short of its full capacity, which translates into more than $12,000 in lost income for a family of four. We could lose a generation of potential and promise, as more young Americans are forced to forgo dreams of college or the chance to train for the jobs of the future. And our nation could lose the competitive edge that has served as a foundation for our strength and standing in the world.

In short, a bad situation could become dramatically worse.

This crisis did not happen solely by some accident of history or normal turn of the business cycle, and we won't get out of it by simply waiting for a better day to come, or relying on the worn-out dogmas of the past. We arrived at this point due to an era of profound irresponsibility that stretched from corporate boardrooms to the halls of power in Washington, DC. For years, too many Wall Street executives made imprudent and dangerous decisions, seeking profits with too little regard for risk, too little regulatory scrutiny, and too little accountability. Banks made loans without concern for whether borrowers could repay them, and some borrowers took advantage of cheap credit to take on debt they couldn't afford. Politicians spent taxpayer money without wisdom or discipline, and too often focused on scoring political points instead of the problems they were sent here to solve. The result has been a devastating loss of trust and confidence in our economy, our financial markets, and our government.

Now, the very fact that this crisis is largely of our own making means that it is not beyond our ability to solve. Our problems are rooted in past mistakes, not our capacity for future greatness. It will take time, perhaps many years, but we can rebuild that lost trust and confidence. We can restore opportunity and prosperity. We should never forget that our workers are still more productive than any on Earth. Our universities are still the envy of the world. We are still home to the most brilliant minds, the most creative entrepreneurs, and the most advanced technology and innovation that history has ever known. And we are still the nation that has overcome great fears and improbable odds. If we act with the urgency and seriousness that this moment requires, I know that we can do it again.

That is why I have moved quickly to work with my economic team and leaders of both parties on an American Recovery and Reinvestment Plan that will immediately jumpstart job creation and long-term growth.

It's a plan that represents not just new policy, but a whole new approach to meeting our most urgent challenges. For if we hope to end this crisis, we must end the culture of anything goes that helped create it—and this change must begin in Washington. It is time to trade old habits for a new spirit of responsibility. It is time to finally change the ways of Washington so that we can set a new and better course for America.

There is no doubt that the cost of this plan will be considerable. It will certainly add to the budget deficit in the short-term. But equally certain are the consequences of doing too little or nothing at all, for that will lead to an even greater deficit of jobs, incomes, and confidence in our economy. It is true that we cannot depend on government alone to create jobs or long-term growth, but at this particular moment, only government can provide the short-term boost necessary to lift us from a recession this deep and severe. Only government can break the vicious cycles that are crippling our economy—where a lack of spending leads to lost jobs which leads to even less spending; where an inability to lend and borrow stops growth and leads to even less credit.

That is why we need to act boldly and act now to reverse these cycles. That's why we need to put money in the pockets of the American people, create new jobs, and invest in our future. That's why we need to re-start the flow of credit and restore the rules of the road that will ensure a crisis like this never happens again.

That work begins with this plan—a plan I am confident will save or create at least three million jobs over the next few years. It is not just another public works program. It's a plan that recognizes both the paradox and the promise of this moment—the fact that there are millions of Americans trying to find work, even as, all around the country, there is so much work to be done. That's why we'll invest in priorities like energy and education; health care and a new infrastructure that are necessary to keep us strong and competitive in the 21st century. That's why the overwhelming majority of the jobs created will be in the private sector, while our plan will save the public sector jobs of teachers, cops, firefighters and others who provide vital services.

To finally spark the creation of a clean energy economy, we will double the production of alternative energy in the next three years. We will modernize more than 75 per cent of federal buildings and improve the energy efficiency of two million American homes, saving consumers and taxpayers billions on our energy bills. In the process, we will put Americans to work in new jobs that pay well and can't be outsourced—jobs building solar panels and wind turbines; constructing fuel-efficient cars and buildings; and developing the new energy technologies that will lead to even more jobs, more savings, and a cleaner, safer planet in the bargain.

To improve the quality of our health care while lowering its cost, we will make the immediate investments necessary to ensure that within five years, all of America's medical records are computerized. This will cut waste, eliminate red tape, and reduce the need to repeat expensive medical tests. But it just won't save billions of dollars and thousands of jobs—it will save lives by reducing the deadly but preventable medical errors that pervade our health care system.

To give our children the chance to live out their dreams in a world that's never been more competitive, we will equip tens of thousands of schools, community colleges, and public universities with 21st century classrooms, labs, and libraries. We'll provide new computers, new technology, and new training for teachers so that students in Chicago and Boston can compete with kids in Beijing for the high-tech, high-wage jobs of the future.

To build an economy that can lead this future, we will begin to rebuild America. Yes, we'll put people to work repairing crumbling roads, bridges, and schools by eliminating the backlog of well-planned, worthy and needed infrastructure projects. But we'll also do more to retrofit America for a global economy. That means updating the way we get our electricity by starting to build a new smart grid that will save us money, protect our power sources from blackout or attack, and deliver clean, alternative forms of energy to every corner of our nation. It means expanding broadband lines across America, so that a small business in a rural town can connect and compete with their counterparts anywhere in the world. And it means investing in the science, research, and technology that will lead to new medical breakthroughs, new discoveries, and entire new industries.

Finally, this recovery and reinvestment plan will provide immediate relief to states, workers, and families who are bearing the brunt of this recession. To get people spending again, 95 per cent of working families will receive a $1,000 tax cut—the first stage of a middle-class tax cut that I promised during the campaign and will include in our next budget. To help Americans who have lost their jobs and can't find new ones, we'll continue the bipartisan extensions of unemployment insurance and health care coverage to help them through this crisis. Government at every level will have to tighten its belt, but we'll help struggling states avoid harmful budget cuts, as long as they take responsibility and use the money to maintain essential services like police, fire, education, and health care.

I understand that some might be skeptical of this plan. Our government has already spent a good deal of money, but we haven't yet seen that translate into more jobs or higher incomes or renewed confidence in our economy. That's why the American Recovery and Reinvestment Plan won't just throw money at our problems—we'll invest in what works. The true test of the policies we'll pursue won't be whether they're Democratic or Republican ideas, but whether they create jobs, grow our economy, and put the American Dream within reach of the American people.

Instead of politicians doling out money behind a veil of secrecy, decisions about where we invest will be made transparently, and informed by independent experts wherever possible. Every American will be able to hold Washington accountable for these decisions by going online to see how and where their tax dollars are being spent. And as I announced..., we will launch an unprecedented effort to eliminate unwise and unnecessary spending that has never been more unaffordable for our nation and our children's future than it is right now.

We have to make tough choices and smart investments today so that as the economy recovers, the deficit starts to come down. We cannot have a solid recovery if our people and our businesses don't have confidence that we're getting our fiscal house in order. That's why our goal is not to create a slew of new government programs, but a foundation for long-term economic growth.

That also means an economic recovery plan that is free from earmarks and pet projects. I understand that every member of Congress has ideas on how to spend money. Many of these projects are worthy, and benefit local communities. But this emergency legislation must not be the vehicle for those aspirations. This must be a time when leaders in both parties put the urgent needs of our nation above our own narrow interests.

Now, this recovery plan alone will not solve all the problems that led us into this crisis. We must also work with the same sense of urgency to stabilize and repair the financial system we all depend on. That means using our full arsenal of tools to get credit flowing again to families and business, while restoring confidence in our markets. It means launching a sweeping effort to address the foreclosure crisis so that we can keep responsible families in their homes. It means preventing the catastrophic failure of financial institutions whose collapse could endanger the entire economy, but only with maximum protections for taxpayers and a clear understanding that government support for any company is an extraordinary action that must come with significant restrictions on the firms that receive support. And it means reforming a weak and outdated regulatory system so that we can better withstand financial shocks and better protect consumers, investors, and businesses from the reckless greed and risk-taking that must never endanger our prosperity again.

No longer can we allow Wall Street wrongdoers to slip through regulatory cracks. No longer can we allow special interests to put their thumbs on the economic scales. No longer can we allow the unscrupulous lending and borrowing that leads only to destructive cycles of bubble and bust.

It is time to set a new course for this economy, and that change must begin now. We should have an open and honest discussion about this recovery plan in the days ahead, but I urge Congress to move as quickly as possible on behalf of the American people. For every day we wait or point fingers or drag our feet, more Americans will lose their jobs. More families will lose their savings. More dreams will be deferred and denied. And our nation will sink deeper into a crisis that, at some point, we may not be able to reverse.

That is not the country I know, and it is not a future I will accept as President of the United States. A world that depends on the strength of our economy is now watching and waiting for America to lead once more. And that is what we will do.

It will not come easy or happen overnight, and it is altogether likely that things may get worse before they get better. But that is all the more reason for Congress to act without delay. I know the scale of this plan is unprecedented, but so is the severity of our situation. We have already tried the wait-and-see approach to our problems, and it is the same approach that helped lead us to this day of reckoning.

That is why the time has come to build a 21st century economy in which hard work and responsibility are once again rewarded. That's why I'm asking Congress to work with me and my team day and night, on weekends if necessary, to get the plan passed in the next few weeks. That's why I'm calling on all Americans—Democrats and Republicans—to put good ideas ahead of the old ideological battles; a sense of common purpose above the same narrow partisanship; and insist that the first question each of us asks isn't "What's good for me?" but "What's good for the country my children will inherit?"

More than any program or policy, it is this spirit that will enable us to confront this challenge with the same spirit that has led previous generations to face down war, depression, and fear itself. And if we do—if we are able to summon that spirit again; if are able to look out for one another, and listen to one another, and do our part for our nation and for posterity, then I have no doubt that years from now, we will look back on 2009 as one of those years that marked another new and hopeful beginning for the United States of America.

22

Bush's Speech on the Economic Crisis

13 November 2008

....

We live in a world in which our economies are interconnected. Prosperity and progress have reached farther than any time in our history. Unfortunately, as we have seen in recent months, financial turmoil anywhere in the world affects economies everywhere in the world. And so this weekend I'm going to host a Summit on Financial Markets and the World Economy with leaders from developed and developing nations that account for nearly 90 per cent of the world economy. Leaders of the World Bank, the International Monetary Fund, the United Nations, and the Financial Stability Forum are going to be there, as well. We'll have dinner at the White House tomorrow night, and we'll meet most of the day on Saturday.

The leaders attending this weekend's meeting agree on a clear purpose—to address the current crisis, and to lay the foundation for reforms that will help prevent a similar crisis in the future. We also agree that this undertaking is too large to be accomplished in a single session. The issues are too complex, the problem is too significant to try to solve, or to come up with reasonable recommendations in just one meeting. So this summit will be the first of a series of meetings.

It will focus on five key objectives: understanding the causes of the global crisis, reviewing the effectiveness of our responses thus far, developing principles for reforming our financial and regulatory systems, launching a specific action plan to implement those principles, and reaffirming our conviction that free market principles offer the surest path to lasting prosperity. (Applause.)

First, we're working toward a common understanding of the causes behind the global crisis. Different countries will naturally bring different perspectives, but there are some points on which we can all agree:

Over the past decade, the world experienced a period of strong economic growth. Nations accumulated huge amounts of savings, and looked for safe places to invest them. Because of our attractive political, legal, and entrepreneurial climates, the United States and other developed nations received a large share of that money.

The massive inflow of foreign capital, combined with low interest rates, produced a period of easy credit. And that easy credit especially affected the housing market. Flush with cash, many lenders issued mortgages and many borrowers could not afford them. Financial institutions then purchased these loans, packaged them together, and converted them into complex securities designed to yield large returns. These securities were then purchased by investors and financial institutions in the United States and Europe and elsewhere—often with little analysis of their true underlying value.

The financial crisis was ignited when booming housing markets began to decline. As home values dropped, many borrowers defaulted on their mortgages, and institutions holding securities backed by those mortgages suffered serious losses. Because of outdated regulatory structures and poor risk management practices, many financial institutions in America and Europe were too highly leveraged. When capital ran short, many faced severe financial jeopardy. This led to high-profile failures of financial institutions in America and Europe, led to contractions and widespread anxiety—all of which contributed to sharp declines in the equity markets.

These developments have placed a heavy burden on hardworking people around the world. Stock market drops have eroded the value of retirement accounts and pension funds. The tightening of credit has made it harder for families to borrow money for cars or home improvements or education of the children. Businesses have found it harder to get loans to expand their operations and create jobs. Many nations have suffered job losses, and have serious concerns about the worsening economy. Developing nations have been hit hard as nervous investors have withdrawn their capital.

We are faced with the prospect of a global meltdown. And so we've responded with bold measures. I'm a market-oriented guy, but not when I'm faced with the prospect of a global meltdown. At Saturday's summit, we're going to review the effectiveness of our actions.

Here in the United States, we have taken unprecedented steps to boost liquidity, recapitalize financial institutions, guarantee most new debt issued by insured banks, and prevent the disorderly collapse of large, interconnected enterprises. These were historic actions taken necessary to make—necessary so that the economy would not meltdown and affect millions of our fellow citizens.

In Europe, governments are also purchasing equity in banks and providing government guarantees for loans. In Asia, nations like China and Japan and South Korea have lowered interest rates and have launched significant economic stimulus plans. In the Middle East, nations like Kuwait and the UAE have guaranteed deposits and opened up new government lending to banks.

In addition, nations around the world have taken unprecedented joint measures. Last month, a number of central banks carried out a coordinated interest rate cut. The Federal Reserve is extending needed liquidity to central banks around the world. The IMF and World Bank are working to ensure that developing nations can weather this crisis.

This crisis did not develop overnight, and it's not going to be solved overnight. But our actions are having an impact. Credit markets are beginning to thaw. Businesses are gaining access to essential short-term financing. A measure of stability is returning to financial systems here at home and around the world. It's going to require more time for these improvements to fully take hold, and there's going to be difficult days ahead. But the United States and our partner are taking the right steps to get through this crisis.

In addition to addressing the current crisis, we will also need to make broader reforms to strengthen the global economy over the long-term. This weekend, leaders will establish principles for adapting our financial systems to the realities of the 21st century marketplace. We will discuss specific actions we can take to implement these principles. We will direct our finance ministers to work with other experts and report back to us with detailed recommendations on further reasonable actions.

One vital principle of reform is that our nations must make our financial markets more transparent. For example, we should consider improving accounting rules for securities, so that investors around the world can understand the true value of the assets they purchase.

Secondly, we must ensure that markets, firms, and financial products are properly regulated. For example, credit default swaps—financial products that insure against potential losses—should be processed through centralized clearinghouses instead of through unregulated, "over the counter" markets. By bringing greater stability to this large and important financial sector, we reduce the risk to our overall financial systems.

Third, we must enhance the integrity of our financial markets. For example, authorities in every nation should take a fresh look at the rules governing market manipulation and fraud—and ensure that investors are properly protected.

Fourth, we must strengthen cooperation among the world's financial authorities. For example, leading nations should better coordinate national laws and regulations. We should also reform international financial institutions such as the IMF and the World Bank, which are based largely on the economic order of 1944. To better reflect the realities of today's global economy, both the IMF and World Bank should modernize their governance structures. They should consider extending greater voter—voting power to dynamic developing nations, especially as they increase their contributions to these institutions. They should consider ways to streamline their executive boards, and make them more representative.

In addition to these important—to these management changes, we should move forward with other reforms to make the IMF and World Bank more transparent, accountable, and effective. For example, the IMF should agree to work more closely with member countries to ensure that their exchange rate policies are market-oriented and fair. And the World Bank should ensure its development programs reflect the priorities of the people they are designed to serve—and focus on measurable results.

All these steps require decisive actions from governments around the world. At the same time, we must recognize that government intervention is not a cure-all. For example, some blame the crisis on insufficient regulation of the American mortgage market. But many European countries had much more extensive regulations, and still experienced problems almost identical to our own.

History has shown that the greater threat to economic prosperity is not too little government involvement in the market, it is too much government involvement in the market. (Applause). We saw this in the case of Fannie Mae and Freddie Mac. Because these firms were chartered by the United States Congress, many believed they were backed by the full faith and credit of the United States government. Investors put huge amounts of money into Fannie and Freddie, which they used to build up irresponsibly large portfolios of mortgage-backed securities. And when the housing market declined, these securities, of course, plummeted in value. It took a taxpayer-funded rescue to keep Fannie and Freddie from collapsing in a way that would have devastated the global financial system. And there is a clear lesson: Our aim should not be more government—it should be smarter government.

All this leads to the most important principle that should guide our work: While reforms in the financial sector are essential, the long-term solution to today's problems is sustained economic growth. And the surest path to that growth is free markets and free people. (Applause)

This is a decisive moment for the global economy. In the wake of the financial crisis, voices from the left and right are equating the free enterprise system with greed and exploitation and failure. It's true this crisis included failures—by lenders and borrowers and by financial firms and by governments and independent regulators. But the crisis was not a failure of the free market system. And the answer is not to try to reinvent that system. It is to fix the problems we face, make the reforms we need, and move forward with the free market principles that have delivered prosperity and hope to people all across the globe.

Like any other system designed by man, capitalism is not perfect. It can be subject to excesses and abuse. But it is by far the most efficient and just way of structuring an economy. At its most basic level, capitalism offers people the freedom to choose where they work and what they do, the opportunity to buy or sell products they want, and the dignity that comes with profiting from their talent and hard work. The free market system provides the incentives that lead to prosperity—the incentive to work, to innovate, to save, to invest wisely, and to create jobs for others. And as millions of people pursue these incentives together, whole societies benefit.

Free market capitalism is far more than economic theory. It is the engine of social mobility—the highway to the American Dream. It's what makes it possible for a husband and wife to start their own business, or a new immigrant to open a restaurant, or a single mom to go back to college and to build a better career. It is what allowed entrepreneurs in Silicon Valley to change the way the world sells products and searches for information. It's what transformed America from a rugged frontier to the greatest economic power in history—a nation that gave the world the steamboat and the airplane, the computer and the CAT scan, the Internet and the iPod.

Ultimately, the best evidence for free market capitalism is its performance compared to other economic systems. Free markets allowed Japan, an island with few natural resources, to recover from war and grow into the world's second-largest economy. Free markets allowed South Korea to make itself into one of the most technologically advanced societies in the world. Free markets turned small areas like Singapore and Hong Kong and Taiwan into global economic players. Today, the success of the world's largest economies comes from their embrace of free markets.

Meanwhile, nations that have pursued other models have experienced devastating results. Soviet communism starved millions, bankrupted an empire, and collapsed as decisively as the Berlin Wall. Cuba, once known for its vast fields of cane, is now forced to ration sugar. And while Iran sits atop giant oil reserves, its people cannot put enough gasoline in its—in their cars.

The record is unmistakable: If you seek economic growth, if you seek opportunity, if you seek social justice and human dignity, the free market system is the way to go. (Applause.) And it would be a terrible mistake to allow a few months of crisis to undermine 60 years of success.

Just as important as maintaining free markets within countries is maintaining the free movement of goods and services between countries. When nations open their markets to trade and investment, their businesses and farmers and workers find new buyers for their products. Consumers benefit from more choices and better prices. Entrepreneurs can get their ideas off the ground with funding from anywhere in the world. Thanks in large part to open markets, the volume of global trade today is nearly 30 times greater than it was six decades ago—and some of the most dramatic gains have come in the developing world.

As President, I have seen the transformative power of trade up close. I've been to a Caterpillar factory in East Peoria, Illinois, where thousands of good-paying American jobs are supported by exports. I've walked the grounds of a trade fair in Ghana, where I met women who support their families by exporting handmade dresses and jewelry. I've spoken with a farmer in Guatemala who decided to grow high-value crops he could sell overseas—and helped create more than 1,000 jobs.

Stories like these show why it is so important to keep markets open to trade and investment. This openness is especially urgent during times of economic strain. Shortly after the stock market crash in 1929, Congress passed the Smoot-Hawley tariff—a protectionist measure designed to wall off America's economy from global competition. The result was not economic security. It was economic ruin. And leaders around the world must keep this example in mind, and reject the temptation of protectionism. (Applause.)

There are clear-cut ways for nations to demonstrate the commitment to open markets. The United States Congress has an immediate opportunity by approving free trade agreements with Colombia, Peru, and South Korea. America and other wealthy nations must also ensure this crisis does not become an excuse to reverse our engagement with the developing world. And developing nations should continue policies that foster enterprise and investment. As well, all nations should pledge to conclude a framework this year that leads to a successful Doha agreement.

We're facing this challenge together and we're going to get through it together. The United States is determined to show the way back to economic growth and prosperity. I know some may question whether America's leadership in the global economy will continue. The world can be confident that it will, because our markets are flexible and we can rebound from setbacks. We saw that resilience in the 1940s, when America pulled itself out of Depression, marshaled a powerful army, and helped save the world from tyranny. We saw that resilience in the 1980s, when Americans overcame gas lines, turned stagflation into strong economic growth, and won the Cold War. We saw that resilience after September the 11th, 2001, when our nation recovered from a brutal attack, revitalized our shaken economy, and rallied the forces of freedom in the great ideological struggle of the 21st century.

The world will see the resilience of America once again. We will work with our partners to correct the problems in the global financial system. We will rebuild our economic strength. And we will continue to lead the world toward prosperity and peace....

23

Text of President Bush's Speech on Financial Crisis

24 September 2008

.... This is an extraordinary period for America's economy.

Over the past few weeks, many Americans have felt anxiety about their finances and their future. I understand their worry and their frustration.

We've seen triple-digit swings in the stock market. Major financial institutions have teetered on the edge of collapse, and some have failed. As uncertainty has grown, many banks have restricted lending, credit markets have frozen, and families and businesses have found it harder to borrow money.

We're in the midst of a serious financial crisis, and the federal government is responding with decisive action.

We boosted confidence in money market mutual funds and acted to prevent major investors from intentionally driving down stocks for their own personal gain.

Most importantly, my administration is working with Congress to address the root cause behind much of the instability in our markets.

Financial assets related to home mortgages have lost value during the house decline, and the banks holding these assets have restricted credit. As a result, our entire economy is in danger.

So I propose that the federal government reduce the risk posed by these troubled assets and supply urgently needed money so banks and other financial institutions can avoid collapse and resume lending.

This rescue effort is not aimed at preserving any individual company or industry. It is aimed at preserving America's overall economy.

It will help American consumers and businesses get credit to meet their daily needs and create jobs. And it will help send a signal to markets around the world that America's financial system is back on track.

I know many Americans have questions tonight: How did we reach this point in our economy? How will the solution I propose work? And what does this mean for your financial future?

These are good questions, and they deserve clear answers.

First, how did our economy reach this point? Well, most economists agree that the problems we're witnessing today developed over a long period of time. For more than a decade, a massive amount of money flowed into the United States from investors abroad because our country is an attractive and secure place to do business.

This large influx of money to U.S. banks and financial institutions, along with low interest rates, made it easier for Americans to get credit. These developments allowed more families to borrow money for cars, and homes, and college tuition, some for the first time. They allowed more entrepreneurs to get loans to start new businesses and create jobs.

Unfortunately, there were also some serious negative consequences, particularly in the housing market. Easy credit, combined with the faulty assumption that home values would continue to rise, led to excesses and bad decisions.

Many mortgage-lenders approved loans for borrowers without carefully examining their ability to pay. Many borrowers took out loans larger than they could afford, assuming that they could sell or refinance their homes at a higher price later on.

Optimism about housing values also led to a boom in home construction. Eventually, the number of new houses exceeded the number of people willing to buy them. And with supply exceeding demand, housing prices fell, and this created a problem.

Borrowers with adjustable-rate mortgages, who had been planning to sell or refinance their homes at a higher price, were stuck with homes worth less than expected, along with mortgage payments they could not afford.

As a result, many mortgage-holders began to default. These widespread defaults had effects far beyond the housing market.

See, in today's mortgage industry, home loans are often packaged together and converted into financial products called mortgage-backed securities. These securities were sold to investors around the world.

Many investors assumed these securities were trustworthy and asked few questions about their actual value. Two of the leading purchasers of mortgage-backed securities were Fannie Mae and Freddie Mac.

Because these companies were chartered by Congress, many believed they were guaranteed by the federal government. This allowed them to borrow enormous sums of money, fuel the market for questionable investments, and put our financial system at risk.

The decline in the housing market set off a domino effect across our economy. When home values declined, borrowers defaulted on their mortgages, and investors holding mortgage-backed securities began to incur serious losses.

Before long, these securities became so unreliable that they were not being bought or sold. Investment banks, such as Bear Stearns and Lehman Brothers, found themselves saddled with large amounts of assets they could not sell. They ran out of money needed to meet their immediate obligations, and they faced imminent collapse.

Other banks found themselves in severe financial trouble. These banks began holding on to their money, and lending dried up, and the gears of the American financial system began grinding to a halt.

With the situation becoming more precarious by the day, I faced a choice, to step in with dramatic government action or to stand back and allow the irresponsible actions of some to undermine the financial security of all.

I'm a strong believer in free enterprise, so my natural instinct is to oppose government intervention. I believe companies that make bad decisions should be allowed to go out of business.

Under normal circumstances, I would have followed this course. But these are not normal circumstances. The market is not functioning properly. There has been a widespread loss of confidence, and major sectors of America's financial system are at risk of shutting down.

The government's top economic experts warn that, without immediate action by Congress, America could slip into a financial panic and a distressing scenario would unfold.

More banks could fail, including some in your community. The stock market would drop even more, which would reduce the value of your retirement account. The value of your home could plummet. Foreclosures would rise dramatically.

And if you own a business or a farm, you would find it harder and more expensive to get credit. More businesses would close their doors, and millions of Americans could lose their jobs.

Even if you have good credit history, it would be more difficult for you to get the loans you need to buy a car or send your children to college. And, ultimately, our country could experience a long and painful recession.

Fellow citizens, we must not let this happen. I appreciate the work of leaders from both parties in both houses of Congress to address this problem and to make improvements to the proposal my administration sent to them.

There is a spirit of cooperation between Democrats and Republicans and between Congress and this administration. In that spirit, I've invited Senators McCain and Obama to join congressional leaders of both parties at the White House tomorrow to help speed our discussions toward a bipartisan bill.

I know that an economic rescue package will present a tough vote for many members of Congress. It is difficult to pass a bill that commits so much of the taxpayers' hard-earned money.

I also understand the frustration of responsible Americans who pay their mortgages on time, file their tax returns every April 15th, and are reluctant to pay the cost of excesses on Wall Street.

But given the situation we are facing, not passing a bill now would cost these Americans much more later.

Many Americans are asking, how would a rescue plan work? After much discussion, there's now widespread agreement on the principles such a plan would include.

It would remove the risk posed by the troubled assets, including mortgage-backed securities, now clogging the financial system. This would free banks to resume the flow of credit to American families and businesses.

Any rescue plan should also be designed to ensure that taxpayers are protected. It should welcome the participation of financial institutions, large and small. It should make certain that failed executives do not receive a windfall from your tax dollars.

It should establish a bipartisan board to oversee the plan's implementation, and it should be enacted as soon as possible.

In close consultation with Treasury Secretary Hank Paulson, Federal Reserve Chairman Ben Bernanke, and SEC Chairman Chris Cox, I announced a plan on Friday.

First, the plan is big enough to solve a serious problem. Under our proposal, the federal government would put up to $700 billion taxpayer dollars on the line to purchase troubled assets that are clogging the financial system.

In the short-term, this will free up banks to resume the flow of credit to American families and businesses, and this will help our economy grow.

Second, as markets have lost confidence in mortgage-backed securities, their prices have dropped sharply, yet the value of many of these assets will likely be higher than their current price, because the vast majority of Americans will ultimately pay off their mortgages.

The government is the one institution with the patience and resources to buy these assets at their current low prices and hold them until markets return to normal.

And when that happens, money will flow back to the Treasury as these assets are sold, and we expect that much, if not all, of the tax dollars we invest will be paid back.

The final question is, what does this mean for your economic future? Well, the primary steps—purpose of the steps I've outlined tonight is to safeguard the financial security of American workers, and families, and small businesses. The federal government also continues to enforce laws and regulations protecting your money.

The Treasury Department recently offered government insurance for money market mutual funds. And through the FDIC, every savings account, checking account, and certificate of deposit is insured by the federal government for up to $100,000.

The FDIC has been in existence for 75 years, and no one has ever lost a penny on an insured deposit, and this will not change.

Once this crisis is resolved, there will be time to update our financial regulatory structures. Our 21st-century global economy remains regulated largely by outdated 20th-century laws.

Recently, we've seen how one company can grow so large that its failure jeopardizes the entire financial system.

Earlier this year, Secretary Paulson proposed a blueprint that would modernize our financial regulations. For example, the Federal Reserve would be authorized to take a closer look at the operations of companies across the financial spectrum and ensure that their practices do not threaten overall financial stability.

There are other good ideas, and members of Congress should consider them. As they do, they must ensure that efforts to regulate Wall Street do not end up hampering our economy's ability to grow.

In the long run, Americans have good reason to be confident in our economic strength. Despite corrections in the marketplace and instances of abuse, democratic capitalism is the best system ever devised.

It has unleashed the talents and the productivity and entrepreneurial spirit of our citizens. It has made this country the best place in the world to invest and do business. And it gives our economy the flexibility and resilience to absorb shocks, adjust, and bounce back.

Our economy is facing a moment of great challenge, but we've overcome tough challenges before, and we will overcome this one.

I know that Americans sometimes get discouraged by the tone in Washington and the seemingly endless partisan struggles, yet history has shown that, in times of real trial, elected officials rise to the occasion.

And together we will show the world once again what kind of country America is: a nation that tackles problems head on, where leaders come together to meet great tests, and where people of every background can work hard, develop their talents, and realize their dreams.

24

Senator Murray's Speech on Financial Crisis, Trade Policy, and Meeting the Challenges of the Global Economy

24 October 2008

....

Since it was formed in 1973, WCIT has proven to be an incredible forum for Washington state businesses, and I want to thank Kathleen Connors and her staff for their work advocating for Washington state trade.

...We know that there's a direct connection between your ability to sell everything from apples to operating systems overseas and how Washington state families put food on the table.

Normally, I would use this time to give you a picture of the political landscape in Washington, D.C., and how this is affecting our trade agenda. About whether Congress is trending more or less protectionist, and how we can work together to support trade. But as I speak to you today, the question of what's ahead for international trade has been overshadowed by more urgent questions about the future of our global economy.

In just a few months, we have seen a downturn in the U.S. housing market ignite a credit crisis that has spread throughout the financial systems of the world. Banks from England to Iceland to China are struggling. Fear and uncertainty have fueled dramatic swings in the stock markets. And restoring confidence in the world's financial system is now part of a coordinated, international effort.

There are plenty of reasons to be worried about what the long-term effect of this crisis will be on our economy.

We are paying for the years in which "anything goes" was the governing policy—in which this Administration turned its back while borrowers and lenders made irresponsible choices, and Wall Street investors took outrageous risks.

And hanging over it all are questions about our future: What will our economy look like when this crisis is finally resolved? Has our economic position fundamentally shifted in relation to the rest of the world? And how do we maintain our leadership?

I do believe we will resolve this crisis. So that's what I want to talk about with you today.

I want to talk about the steps we've already taken, what I believe we need to do in the short-term, and how we can ensure our nation maintains its political and economic leadership in the world.

Financial Rescue

The night that Treasury Secretary Hank Paulson, Fed Chairman Ben Bernanke, and SEC Chairman Chris Cox came up to Capitol Hill to meet with House and Senate Leadership is a night I will never forget.

As a member of Leadership, I had been in the previous meetings with Secretary Paulson talk about Bear Stearns, AIG and the takeover of Fannie and Freddie.

But walking into that room that night it felt totally different. They had come to ask for something they never believed they would be asking from Congress. All the efforts by the Fed, the Central Banks and by Treasury to try to prevent the economic collapse weren't working fast enough. We were facing a need for unprecedented actions.

And they came up to Capitol Hill to make it clear something bigger had to be done. Many of us were shocked, and frustrated to learn that the condition of our financial market had deteriorated to this point. My first reaction—and the reaction of many people across the country—was anger. People are furious because this crisis was preventable.

The hard truth is that greed got us to this point. Greed by bankers and brokers who took huge risks to turn short-term profits, greed by lenders who preyed on less-savvy buyers, and greed by individuals across this country who bought homes with loans they didn't understand and couldn't repay.

But Congressional leaders stood unified. And we worked hand-in-hand—across the aisle—on a rescue package to prevent the collapse of Wall Street from leading to the collapse of Main Street.

The first proposal from the Administration was laughable. It was a three-page document that gave the Treasury a blank check to do what they wanted with $700 billion of the taxpayer money. Obviously it was DOA once I and other leaders saw it.

So we went to work on a proposal that would provide oversight, transparency and accountability, make sure taxpayers get their money back, and provide strict limits on CEO pay.

Calls from constituents poured into my office while Congress and the Administration worked out a rescue plan. Virtually all of them were opposed to the plan. But I also heard from many of you—telling me how urgent it was that Congress take action. As one letter put it: Families across the state "will be hurt severely through no fault of their own if action is not taken soon".

I voted for the financial rescue, and I believe Congress did the right thing for our country by approving it. And I'm pleased that there is now a coordinated global response to the crisis—which has touched every corner of the world.

The $700 billion financial rescue approved by Congress earlier this month is being used to inject capital into the markets, buy the troubled assets banks now hold on their books, and get money flowing again.

Because we took steps to free up credit banks will be able to make loans, businesses will be able to continue to finance their day-to-day operations—like buying inventory and making payroll, and families will be able to get credit to refinance their mortgages or take out college loans for their kids.

What to Expect from Congress

But it's going to take time for the markets to stabilize. It's going to take even longer to see a broader economic recovery.

And now we're all asking questions about what this means for the future. What's going to happen in six months—two years—a decade down the line? Is the United States going to maintain its superpower status? And how does the answer to that question affect you as business leaders in the most trade dependent state in the nation?

I wish I had a crystal ball so that I could tell you. But I think a few things are certain. First, Congress will continue to hold hearings and investigations into the root causes of the economic crisis. We must move to re-evaluate and modernize regulations on our financial markets so that we don't get into this situation again.

Second, lawmakers in Washington, D.C., are already working on plans to help families who were hurting long before the credit crisis hit the financial markets. And I believe that's one of the first things Congress will take up after the election. We need something to help get the economy going in communities across the country—especially those that have been hardest hit by foreclosures.

The idea in these plans is to boost the economy by helping local businesses, and by putting people to work building roads, bridges, and schools that are desperately in need of repair.

So I think you can expect to see Congress continue to take action to address the economic crisis. And I believe both of those moves are the right thing to do to help get our economy back on track. But I also have one concern that everyone in this room should be aware of. And that is the outlook for international trade in the next year.

Trade

Even before this current financial crisis hit, the number of people in this country worried about trade and its impact on American jobs was growing.

And I am deeply worried that if Americans see our position in the world falling, if they fear their jobs are moving overseas with nothing to replace them this insecurity will begin to affect our trade policies. And we may see more people talk about walling off our country to protect us from competition.

This would be disastrous to the U.S. economy—and to the global economy—and I will fight any efforts to close our doors to trade.

Protectionism helped turn the 1929 stock market crash into the Great Depression. We increased tariffs that essentially pulled the plug on international trade. And that ultimately prevented the U.S. from helping absorb the impact of bank failures and inflation around the world.

By contrast, our ability to buy and sell goods internationally helped avert a global crisis when markets in Asia and Latin America crashed in 1998. And during this current crisis, trade has helped prevent our economy from spiraling even further out of control.

Trade has generated an estimated 2 million new jobs—primarily because we're actually selling more manufactured goods overseas. And these are good jobs, which pay 15 to 20 per cent more than the national average. But many people don't see it that way. They see only a downside.

A survey this month by the Chicago Council on Global Affairs found that 65 per cent of Americans believe that globalization is bad for their job security. Even more worrisome—64 per cent of Americans believe that the distribution of income in this country has become less fair—and 82 per cent of those people blame globalization and international trade.

When Americans think of trade, they picture a T-shirt factory that relocated to El Salvador—or the call center that has been outsourced to India. But they don't see the jobs that are created because trade has—exponentially—expanded the market for our products.

Let me share one more finding from that survey with you—only 24 per cent named supporting open trade as one of the things that will help us remain competitive in the world. That's the mindset we have to fight now.

I've talked about this before. Last year, I laid out a roadmap to help us move forward in the new trade landscape. I urged you to meet this challenge head-on, and make the case for the benefits of trade. I'll continue to fight for you every step of the way. But we all have to work together to make the case for how our state—and our entire country—benefit from trade. It's more important than ever before that we get the real story out there—and we need to do it before there's a significant movement to close our doors.

Our Future as a Global Leader

Now—given everything I've said so far—it may sound like the outlook for our country is bleak. But I'm optimistic about the future. We've learned from mistakes in the past. We've faced economic turmoil before. And we've always turned things around. We can do it this time too.

But in order to make that happen, we need to develop a strategy for the longer-term.

We need to think seriously about where this nation is going in the future, what our role in the new global economy will be, and—most importantly—what we want it to be.

I believe that if we are going to maintain our leadership in the world, we must overcome some of the biggest challenges we face in this country—and be willing to make investments that will pay dividends in the future.

I think we can do it. So before I close, I want to give you an idea of what I think that entails.

First, we must return to a culture of fiscal discipline and reduce the national debt.

George Bush will leave office having racked up the largest national debt in history. You may have heard that the number has become too big for the National Debt Clock they have in New York City. They'll have to make the clock bigger to fit the number on it.

Economists say our debt is the biggest challenge we face as we attempt to recover from this current crisis. And we've never been in this situation before.

We haven't been borrowing to pay for investments that will benefit us in the future. We've been spending money we don't have, in order to sustain a way of life we can't afford, while leaving the bill for our children and grandchildren to pay. We have to go back to living within our means and figure out a way to pay our bills. And we have to do it now.

Second, we've got to fix our broken health care system. If our debt is the biggest challenge we face, health care is next. Health care costs are devastating our families, and crippling our businesses and state budgets. Congress will be taking up health care reform when we return next year. And as a senior member of the Health, Education, Labor, and Pensions Committee, I'll be a key part of that discussion.

This is a difficult problem to solve, but doing nothing is not an option.

Third, we must develop a smart, realistic, and innovative energy policy that will end our addiction to foreign oil, provide a reliable source of energy, and help us protect the environment for future generations.

Fourth, we must start planning now for how we will pay for infrastructure repairs. Everything from roads and bridges, to sewage treatment plants and schools across this country will all require significant investment in the next several years. A sound infrastructure is critical if we are going to remain competitive in the global marketplace. Yet as I speak, we have less money to spend than we did just a decade ago. We must have a strategy to make these investments.

And finally, we absolutely must ensure that American workers are prepared to compete in the global economy. I imagine a future in which we lead the world in new industries from health care to renewable energy. And our workers are the key to making that a reality.

But if they don't have the skills to take these jobs—if our high schools and colleges aren't producing graduates with cutting-edge computer, math, science, and reasoning abilities—we will be left behind. Many of you in this room have been talking about this challenge for several years now. Bill Gates has sounded alarm bells about how inadequate our high schools are. I've been focused in the Senate on ways to help our workers stay competitive—as well as on new ideas that will help improve our schools at every level—from preschool to college.

This fall, I introduced a bill that would provide incentives for leaders in industry, education, workforce, and economic development to work together in our communities and identify ways to help our students prepare to succeed in the 21st century economy. My bill was the result of discussions I had throughout the state with people from across the spectrum—including many of you. And we're already jumpstarting the conversation about new partnerships and innovative ideas that improve education and keep our economy strong.

Ultimately, the bill would help students get the experience and education they need to take jobs in emerging industries where there is a high demand for good workers. And it will help you stay competitive in the global economy.

Conclusion

So, in conclusion, this is an extraordinary time. We face serious challenges. And how we ultimately meet these challenges will determine our position in the world economy.

I've laid out my ideas for what we need to do to maintain our leadership. At the end of the day, we have to have a serious discussion about what we want our future to look like—and then what that will take. And I believe that you—as industry leaders in this state and in the nation—need to be a central part of that conversation.

Just as your voices were important as we moved toward an emergency response to the economic crisis, your opinions and ideas will continue to be important as we formulate a strategy for the future. And I look forward to working with you in the months and years to come.

25

Timothy Geithner's Speech at the Council on Foreign Relations Corporate Conference, 2008: The Current Financial Challenges: Policy and Regulatory Implications

6 March 2008

....

I am going to talk...about some of the challenges facing the US and financial system. These problems took a long time to build up, and, even with a forceful mix of public policy and action by the private sector, they will take time to resolve.

The central questions are: what caused the crisis and what explains its severity—What mix of policy measures will best contain the damage—And what changes to the financial system are likely to produce greater stability and resilience in the future?

Origins

The origins of this crisis lie in complex interaction of number of forces. Some were the product of market forces. Some were the product of market failures. Some were the result of incentives created by policy and regulation. Some of these were evident at the time, others are apparent only with the benefit of hindsight. Together they produced a substantial financial boom on a global scale.

In the five years leading up to the present stress, the world experienced an unusual mix of financial conditions.

Real short-term interest rates were reduced around the world, following a nearly decade long secular decline in inflation rates, a slowdown in growth at the turn of this decade and subsequent deflation. As central banks raised their policy rates when the outlook improved and deflation risks had dissipated, both real and nominal long-term interest rates remained anomalously low.

Global savings appeared to rise faster than did perceived real investment opportunities, and this development helped to push down real long-term interest rates around the world. At the same time, many emerging market economies built up very large levels of official reserves to reduce external vulnerability and to hold the value of their currencies stable against the dollar. The exchange rate policies in these economies—economies that together accounted for a increasing share of global GDP—made overall global financial conditions more accommodative, even as the United States and other countries tightened their monetary policies.

Expected and realized volatility in both debt and equity markets were remarkably low for most of the last half a decade. Term premiums declined and remained low over much of this period. Credit spreads across a wide range of asset classes fell to levels that assumed unusually low levels of future losses. In the United States, credit, and mortgage credit in particular, expanded relative to GDP. Many households—including those previously lacking access to credit or with access only to expensive credit—found they could borrow on a significant scale to finance the purchase of a home and other expenses. Prices rose across a range of real and financial assets, most notably the prices of homes.

This constellation of broad economic and financial conditions was accompanied by rapid innovation in financial instruments that made credit risk easier to trade and, in principle at least, to hedge. These instruments allowed investors to buy insurance or protection against a broader range of individual credit risks, such as the default by a home owner or a company. Issuance of asset-backed securities (ABS), collateralized debt obligations (CDOs) and collateralized loan obligations (CLOs), as well as credit default swaps (CDS), expanded on a dramatic scale, particularly from 2005 through to mid-2007. And over this same period, the composition of the assets in ABS, as well as in CDOs and CLOs, shifted to higher credit risk mortgages and loans issued by noninvestment grade companies.

Even though these instruments allow credit risk to be shared, their holders remain exposed to the less probable, but potentially very damaging effects of a significant increase in losses driven by macroeconomic factors. As underwriting standards deteriorated over this period, this exposure grew. And yet risk premia continued to fall, suggesting that investors did not fully appreciate the dynamic that was at work. As the boom persisted, investors grew more confident in the relative stability of macro and financial conditions and in the high levels of liquidity of the recent past, and projected that stability into the future. That confidence in a more stable future led to greater leverage and a larger exposure to the risk of a less benign world.

The interaction of these forces made the financial system as a whole more vulnerable to a range of different weaknesses. The models used by issuers to structure these products and by credit rating agencies to assess risk and assign ratings turned out to be much more sensitive to macroeconomic assumptions than was apparent to investors at the time. Assumptions about home price appreciation and the correlation of defaults within the underlying collateral pool were particularly critical in this context.

The proliferation of credit risk transfer instruments was driven in part by an assumption of frictionless, uninterrupted liquidity. This left credit and funding markets more vulnerable when liquidity receded. Banks and other financial institutions lent substantial amounts of money on the assumption that they would be able to distribute that risk easily into liquid markets. A sizable fraction of long-term assets—assets with exposure to different forms of credit risk—ended up in vehicles financed with very short-term liabilities and was placed with investors and funds that were also exposed to liquidity risk.

As is often the case during periods of rapid change, more significant concentrations of risk were present than was apparent at the time. Banks and investment banks sold insurance against what seemed like low probability events, but did so at what even at the time seemed like low prices. And on the assets they retained, these same institutions purchased insurance from financial guarantors and other firms that were exposed to the same risks.

The crisis exposed a range of weaknesses in risk management practices within financial institutions in the United States and throughout the world. Today, a group of the primary supervisors of the largest banks and investment banks in the world released a comprehensive assessment of risk management practices in these institutions. This assessment will help lay the foundation for consensus on changes to supervision going forward in the major financial centers. The report examines a range of practices that helped determine relative performance during this crisis. Banks and investment banks with stronger risk management practices and cultures did substantially better. The most common failures were in how firms dealt with uncertainty about the scale of losses they would face in a less benign economic and financial environment; the scale of the cushion they built up against that uncertainty; how well they managed the internal tension between risk and reward; and how quickly they moved to mitigate risk as conditions deteriorated.

The typical arsenal of risk management tools relies, by necessity, on history and experience, and as a result has only limited value in assessing the scale of potential future losses. These limitations were particularly damaging in a period in which significant innovation in financial instruments and market structure was coupled with relatively stable macroeconomic and financial conditions. Uncertainty about the future, and the greater complexity of leveraged structured products, created a dense fog around estimates of potential loss, making institutions and markets more vulnerable to an adverse surprise when conditions changed, and making it harder to manage the many principal agent problems inherent in the financial business.

In effect, some major banks and investments banks made the choice to follow the market down as underwriting practices eroded. They took on more exposure to low probability but extremely adverse events, despite the potential consequences of getting caught when the music stopped. And even though the largest firms were able to move quickly to protect themselves as conditions worsened, those actions had significant negative effects on market functioning and liquidity.

The current episode has a basic dynamic in common with all past crises. As market participants have moved to reduce exposure to further losses, to step on the brake, the brake became the accelerator, amplifying the shock. Measured risk has increased more quickly than many institutions have been able reduce it, and attempts to reduce it have added to volatility and downward pressure on prices, further increasing measured exposure to risk. Uncertainty about the market value of securities and about counterparty credit risk has increased, and many hedges have not performed as intended. The rational actions taken by even the strongest financial institutions to reduce exposure to future losses have caused significant collateral damage to market functioning. This, in turn, has intensified the liquidity problems for a wide range of bank and nonbank financial institutions.

In this environment, banks have faced several different types of liquidity and funding challenges. They have been called on to fund a range of different contingent liquidity and credit commitments, as is typically the case in crises. The substantial impairment of securitization and syndication markets has been an additional challenge because it has reduced banks' access to liquidity and their capacity to move assets off balance sheets. As the market value of many securities has declined, and investors have reduced their willingness to finance more risky assets, liquidity conditions have eroded further. In response, even the strongest institutions have become much more cautious, building up large cushions of liquidity, bringing down leverage and reducing financing for their leveraged counterparties.

Policy Measures

The self-reinforcing dynamic within financial markets has intensified the downside risks to growth for an economy that is already confronting a very substantial adjustment in housing and the possibility of a significant rise in household savings.

The intensity of the crisis is in part a function of the size of the preceding financial boom, but also of the speed of the deterioration in confidence about the prospects for growth and in some of the basic features of our financial markets. The damage to confidence—confidence in ratings, in valuation tools, in the capacity of investors to evaluate risk—will prolong the process of adjustment in markets. This process carries with it risks to the broader economy. Macroeconomic and supervisory policies have an important role to play in containing those risks.

Let me mention several critical areas of policy.

Monetary policy. The Federal Open Market Committee (FOMC) has reduced the nominal federal funds rate target substantially in a relatively short period of time, with much of this reduction occurring ahead of the deterioration in confidence and the broader slowdown in spending that is now apparent. But even with those reductions in short-term interest rates in place, financial conditions have tightened as risk spreads on a wide range of asset classes and institutions have increased considerably. The critical risk to the economic outlook remains the potential for the strains in financial markets to have an outsized adverse effect on real economic activity, particularly by exacerbating the already significant weakness in the housing sector. It is important for monetary policy and liquidity instruments to be used proactively in addressing this risk.

But this is not the only challenge we face. Headline and core inflation have come in higher than anticipated, and inflation expectations have also moved up. If the risk of significant damage to growth from these financial market pressures is attenuated and if global growth remains strong and drives a continuing rise in energy and commodity prices, then inflation may not moderate as much as we anticipate. If the medium term outlook for inflation deteriorates significantly, the FOMC will move with appropriate speed and force to address this risk.

This requires a fine balance. The principal challenge for policy is to provide an adequate degree of insurance against the downside risks that still confront the economy as a whole, without adding to concerns about inflation over the medium term. We cannot know with confidence today what level of the short-term real funds rate will be consistent with our objectives of sustainable growth and low inflation, but if turbulent financial conditions and the associated downside risks to growth persist, monetary policy may have to remain accommodative for some time.

Liquidity provision. Although concerns about credit quality are at the root of the current problems in financial markets, a substantial impairment in market liquidity conditions can exacerbate and prolong the adjustment in credit conditions. To mitigate this risk, we have taken a series of actions to help reduce the risk that market liquidity conditions exacerbate the adjustment process in credit markets.

By allowing institutions to finance with the central bank assets they could no longer finance as easily in the market, we have reduced the need for them to take other actions, such as selling other assets into distressed markets, or withdrawing credit lines extended to other financial institutions, that would have amplified pressures in markets. These measures—the Term Auction Facility and swap arrangements—have had some success in mitigating market pressures, in part by providing a form of insurance against future stress. We now have in place a cooperative framework for liquidity provision among the major central banks. And we have considerable flexibility to adjust the dimensions of these liquidity tools. We will keep them in place as long as necessary, and continue to adapt them where we see a compelling case to do so.

Encouraging financial repair. The Federal Reserve is working closely with other financial supervisors and regulators to facilitate the adjustment underway in markets. This approach has two important elements. The first is to encourage improvements in the quality of valuation methods and disclosure by the major regulated financial institutions and the necessary adjustment in valuations and reserves to reflect the deterioration in expected losses. Better disclosure can reduce some uncertainty about the incidence and magnitude of potential losses across the financial system, although it is important to note that these estimates of losses are a function of the outlook for the economy and will necessarily change as expectations of the future change.

The second element is to encourage new equity capital raising, so that the burden for preserving capital ratios does not fall principally on actions, such as asset sales or reduced lending, that might exacerbate the credit crunch. We have seen a very substantial flow of new capital into the financial system much more quickly than has been the case in past crises. More will come. Those institutions that move more quickly will obviously be in a stronger position to deal with the challenges, and take advantage of the opportunities, ahead.

Fiscal stimulus. Monetary policy can, of course, play a powerful role in reducing the downside risks to growth, but overall policy will be more effective, particularly given the strains to the financial sector, if the full burden does not fall on the tools available to the Federal Reserve. Fiscal policy can play an important role. The stimulus program signed into law by the President will provide a meaningful level of support to growth, somewhere in the range of three quarters to one and half of a percentage point of GDP growth over the next few quarters.

Targeted support for housing. Policy can also play an important role in helping cushion the effects of the fall in housing prices and the rise in foreclosures in the United States. The decline in house prices and the surge in foreclosures now underway will have significant spillovers to other homes in the same neighborhoods, effects that are not fully incorporated into decisions by private creditors and investors to workout mortgages on mutually beneficial terms. The degree to which mortgages are now held in securitized and complex leverage structures exacerbates the incentive and coordination problems inherent in this situation. Carefully designed, targeted programs in cooperation with the private sector can play an important role in resolving the various constraints that are now impeding economically viable mortgage restructurings. Given the breakdowns in the securitization process and its potential impact on the supply of new mortgage credit, it also makes sense to explore ways to expand the scope for existing government programs to support financing of new homes.

This policy framework—macroeconomic stimulus, liquidity support, new equity for the financial system, and targeted support for housing—will help reduce the risks to the outlook and bring about an earlier return to growth rates more in line with the economy's long-term potential.

Longer Term Reforms of the Financial System

The unwinding of this global financial boom has caused a substantial degree of stress to the financial system.

Was this preventable? I don't believe that asset price and credit booms are preventable. They cannot be effectively diffused preemptively. There is no reliable early warning system for financial shocks. And yet policy plays an important role in determining the dimensions of financial booms, and policy helps determine the ability of the financial system and the economy to adjust to its aftermath. We need to undertake a broad set of changes to address the vulnerabilities in our financial system revealed by this crisis. Just as a long list of factors contributed to the trauma, there is no single reform that offers the promise of sufficient change.

The Presidents Working Group on Financial Markets and the Financial Stability Forum, which bring together policymakers and regulators from the major financial centers around the world, are in the process of outlining a comprehensive framework of reforms. Many of these recommendations will focus on changes to the mortgage finance market, the ratings process for ABS and structured credit products more broadly, regulatory and accounting treatment of these instruments and special purpose financing vehicles, the disclosure requirements on instruments and institutions, and other dimensions of the securitization process.

I want to conclude with a few comments on some of the broader policy questions we face in designing these reforms.

Regulatory reform and simplification. The regulations that affect incentives in the U.S. financial system have evolved into a very complex and uneven framework, with substantial opportunities for arbitrage, large gaps in coverage, significant inefficiencies, and large differences in the degree of oversight and restraint upon institutions that engage in very similar economic activities. Some illustrations of this include the large shift in subprime mortgage originations to less regulated institutions; the incentives to shift risk to where accounting and capital treatment is more favorable; and the amount of risk built up in entities that operate in the grey areas of implied support from much larger affiliated institutions.

We need to move to a simpler framework, with a more uniform set of rules applied evenly across entities involved in similar functions, and a more effective balance of regulation and market discipline. And institutions that are banks, or are built around banks, with special access to the safety net, need to be subject to a stronger form of consolidated supervision than our current framework provides.

Capital. The U.S. banking system entered this financial shock with capital cushions significantly above the regulatory thresholds, and in a stronger position to withstand a downturn than was the case in the past. This has made it possible for bank balance sheets to expand rapidly, which in turn has helped offset the effects of the withdrawal of many nonbank financial institutions from credit markets.

Yet the shock absorbers in the financial system as a whole—the financial cushions that are critical to financial stability—have proved to be thinner, and behavior has been more pro-cyclical than desirable.

This is in part the consequence of changes in the structure of the financial system. Because banks are now a smaller share of the system, a given level of stress on nonbanks creates greater strain on the system as a whole. It is in part the consequence of the fact that the present system focuses on mitigating the risks of firm specific shocks, rather than a systematic market shock. And it is in part the consequence of the fact that the present system is not designed to induce institutions, particularly the largest ones, to internalize the negative consequences, the negative externalities, of their actions on markets as a whole in conditions of stress.

There is no simple solution to this problem. It requires a broad look at the design of the present capital regime, the incentives it creates for holding different forms of risk, and the scope of the application of these requirements. As we move to a more modern and risk-sensitive capital framework and reduce the perverse incentives in the current capital requirements, we need to make sure that reserves, capital, and liquidity provisions are more forward looking, and adjust appropriately through the peaks and valleys of the cycle. This will increase the scope for banks and other institutions that are subject to risk-based capital requirements to act more as a stabilizing force in response to future financial market shocks.

Market infrastructure. We are in the midst of a dramatic period of financial innovation and growth in derivative instruments, but the pace of change the growth in volume has brought a lot of challenges. Substantial progress has been made to strengthen this infrastructure over the past two and a half years, and the resilience of the broader financial infrastructure has been a source of strength for the financial system during this crisis. However, the systems and practices that support the over-the-counter (OTC) derivatives market significantly lags that of securities markets and other mature markets. We need to move quickly to put in place a more integrated operational infrastructure that supports all major OTC derivatives products, is highly automated, has robust operational resilience and risk management, and is capable of handling very substantial growth in volumes.

Conclusion

The US economic and financial system is undergoing a very challenging period of adjustment, and we are likely to be living with a high degree of uncertainty for some period of time about the ultimate magnitude and duration of the slowdown underway. But it is important to recognize that we have already seen a lot of adjustment. Prices and risk premia in many markets already reflect a much more sober and cautious view of the world than they did a year ago. And the degree of stress on markets that we have seen over the past six months is due in part to the sheer magnitude and speed of that adjustment to a more cautious view of the future.

The United States, the world economy, and the financial system as a whole, are more resilient, than they were on the eve of previous downturns. The improvements in productivity growth in the United States of the past decade have been followed by significant improvements in potential growth and wealth accumulation in many other countries. The scale of investable assets around the globe is very substantial, and this will be an important source of demand for risk assets. The improvements in monetary policy credibility and in financial strength developed over the past few decades mean that policy around the world has more room to adjust to deal with the challenge in the present environment.

Nevertheless, the challenges that remain are substantial. The speed and agility with which public policymakers and private financial institutions respond to the continuing pressures in a rapidly evolving environment will determine how quickly and how smoothly market conditions return to normal—and how rapidly the risks to the economic outlook are mitigated.

26

US Senate Approves Stimulus Plan

The US Senate has passed an economic stimulus plan expected to cost some $838 bn (£573 bn).

The Democratic-controlled Senate voted 61-37 to approve the measure, with few Republicans opting to back it.

Tough negotiations are now expected in order to reconcile the Senate bill with the House of Representatives' version.

President Barack Obama welcomed the vote as a good start. It came as the US Treasury Secretary unveiled a bank bail-out plan worth some $1.5 trillion.

'No Assurance'

The president, who says the stimulus measure is needed to create up to four million jobs and lift the economy, has said he wants the final package to reach his desk by 16 February.

Speaking at a public event in Fort Myers, Florida, Mr Obama said the passage of the Senate legislation was "good news" but warned there was still work to do.

"We've still got to get the House bill and the Senate bill to match up before it gets sent to my desk, so we have a little more work to do over the next couple of days," he said.

Democratic Senate Majority Leader Harry Reid said he would send a completed version of the legislation to Mr Obama "as soon as possible".

But Mitch McConnell, the Republican Senate Minority Leader, complained that the bill was "full of waste", adding:

"We have no assurance it will create jobs or revive the economy."

Democrats in the Senate secured support for the bill from three Republican senators, Susan Collins and Olympia Snowe from Maine and Arlen Specter from Pennsylvania.

The House and Senate measures are largely similar, but there are differences over how to expand the federal medical program, Medicaid, and on spending priorities.

While the House bill would give more money to schools, local governments and individual states, the Senate bill devotes more resources to tax cuts.

White House spokesman Robert Gibbs said Mr Obama would address a joint session of the House and the Senate on 24 February to outline his agenda.

Meanwhile, under Treasury Secretary Timothy Geithner's bank bail-out plan, the size of a key Federal Reserve lending program will be expanded to $1 trillion from $200 bn.

In addition, a public-private investment fund of $500 bn will be created to absorb banks' toxic assets and could be expanded to $1 trillion.

27

US Treasury Secretary Tim Geithner Outlines Comprehensive Financial Stability Plan

10 February 2009

..., our nation faces the most severe financial crisis since the Great Depression. It is a crisis of confidence, of capital, of credit, and of consumer and business demand. Rather than providing the credit that allows new ideas to flourish into new jobs, or families to afford homes and autos, we have seen banks and other sources of credit freeze up—contributing to and potentially accelerating what already threatens to be a serious recession. Restarting our economy and job creation requires both jumpstarting economic demand for goods and services through our American Recovery and Reinvestment Act and simultaneously ensuring through our new Financial Stability Plan that businesses with good ideas have the credit to grow and expand, and working families can get the affordable loans they need to meet their economic needs and power an economic recovery.

To address the financial crisis, the Financial Stability Plan is designed to attack our credit crisis on all fronts with our full arsenal of financial tools and the resources commensurate to the depth of the problem. To be successful, we must address the uncertainty, troubled assets and capital constraints of our financial institutions as well as the frozen secondary markets that have been the source of around half of our lending for everything from small business loans to auto loans.

To protect taxpayers and ensure that every dollar is directed toward lending and economic revitalization, the Financial Stability Plan will institute a new era of accountability, transparency and conditions on the financial institutions receiving funds. To ensure that we are responding to this crisis as one government, Secretary Timothy Geithner—working in collaboration and joined by Federal Reserve Chairman Ben Bernanke, FDIC Chair Sheila Bair, Office of Thrift Supervision Director John Reich and Comptroller of the Currency John Dugan—is bringing the full force and full range of financial tools available to cleaning up lingering problems in our banking system, opening up credit and beginning the process of financial recovery.